ARTHUR C. CLARKE

Other Titles in
Critical Companions to Popular Contemporary Writers
Kathleen Gregory Klein, Series Editor

ARTHUR C. CLARKE

A Critical Companion

Robin Anne Reid

CRITICAL COMPANIONS TO POPULAR CONTEMPORARY WRITERS
Kathleen Gregory Klein, Series Editor

Greenwood Press
Westport, Connecticut • London

PR 6005 .L36 Z57 1997

Reid, Robin Anne, 1955-

Arthur C. Clarke

Library of Congress Cataloging-in-Publication Data

Arthur C. Clarke : a critical companion / Robin Anne Reid.
     p.   cm. — (Critical companions to popular contemporary
writers, ISSN 1082–4979)
   Includes bibliographical references and index.
   ISBN 0–313–29529–8 (alk. paper)
   1. Clarke, Arthur Charles, 1917–   —Criticism and interpretation.
2. Science fiction, English—History and criticism.   I. Reid, Robin
Anne, 1955–   .   II. Series.
   PR6005.L36Z57   1997
   823'.914—dc21   96–37046

British Library Cataloguing in Publication Data is available.

Library of Congress Catalog Card Number: 96–37046
ISBN: 0–313–29529–8
ISSN: 1082–4979

First published in 1997

Greenwood Press, 88 Post Road West, Westport, CT 06881
An imprint of Greenwood Publishing Group, Inc.

Printed in the United States of America

∞

The paper used in this book complies with the
Permanent Paper Standard issued by the National
Information Standards Organization (Z39.48–1984).

10 9 8 7 6 5 4 3 2 1

To my mother,
who encourages and supports me in every way possible.

To my father,
who first introduced me to science fiction.

To my teachers who taught literature,
but encouraged me to read and write everything.

To my students,
who teach me every day.

Contents

viii   Contents

Series Foreword

The authors who appear in the series Critical Companions to Popular Contemporary Writers are all best-selling writers. They do not have only one successful novel, but a string of them. Fans, critics, and specialist readers eagerly anticipate their next book. For some, high cash advances and breakthrough sales figures are automatic; movie deals often follow. Some writers become household names, recognized by almost everyone.

But novels are read one by one. Each reader chooses to start and, more importantly, to finish a book because of what she or he finds there. The real test of a novel is in the satisfaction its readers experience. This series acknowledges the extraordinary involvement of readers and writers in creating a best-seller.

The authors included in this series were chosen by an Advisory Board composed of high school English teachers and high school and public librarians. They ranked a list of best-selling writers according to their popularity among different groups of readers. Writers in the top-ranked group who had not received book-length, academic literary analysis (or none in at least the past ten years) were chosen for the series. Because of this selection method, Critical Companions to Popular Contemporary Writers meets a need that is not addressed elsewhere.

The volumes in the series are written by scholars with particular expertise in analyzing popular fiction. These specialists add an academic focus to the popular success that these best-selling writers already enjoy.

The series is designed to appeal to a wide range of readers. The general reading public will find explanations for the appeal of these well-known writers. Fans will find biographical and fictional questions answered. Students will find literary analysis, discussions of fictional genres, carefully organized introductions to new ways of reading the novels, and bibliographies for additional research. Students will also be able to apply what they have learned from this book to their readings of future novels by these best-selling writers.

Each volume begins with a biographical chapter drawing on published information, autobiographies or memoirs, prior interviews, and, in some cases, interviews given especially for this series. A chapter on literary history and genres describes how the author's work fits into a larger literary context. The following chapters analyze the writer's most important, most popular, and most recent novels in detail. Each chapter focuses on a single novel. This approach, suggested by the Advisory Board as the most useful to student research, allows for an in-depth analysis of the writer's fiction. Close and careful readings with numerous examples show readers exactly how the novels work. These chapters are organized around three central elements: plot development (how the story line moves forward), character development (what the reader knows about the important figures), and theme (the significant ideas of the novel). Chapters may also include sections on generic conventions (how the novel is similar to or different from others in its same category of science fiction, fantasy, thriller, etc.), narrative point of view (who tells the story and how), symbols and literary language, and historical or social context. Each chapter ends with an "alternative reading" of the novel. The volume concludes with a primary and secondary bibliography, including reviews.

The Alternative Readings are a unique feature of this series. By demonstrating a particular way of reading each novel, they provide a clear example of how a specific perspective can reveal important aspects of the book. In each alternative reading section, one contemporary literary theory—such as feminist criticism, Marxism, new historicism, deconstruction, or Jungian psychological critique—is defined in brief, easily comprehensible language. That definition is then applied to the novel to highlight specific features that might go unnoticed or be understood differently in a more general reading of the novel. Each volume defines two or three specific theories, making them part of the reader's understanding of how diverse meanings may be constructed from a single novel.

Taken collectively, the volumes in the Critical Companions to Popular

Contemporary Writers series provide a wide-ranging investigation of the complexities of current best-selling fiction. By treating these novels seriously as both literary works and publishing successes, the series demonstrates the potential of popular literature in contemporary culture.

Kathleen Gregory Klein
Southern Connecticut State University

Acknowledgments

I would like to thank the Reading Group of the *East Texas Women's Association* of Texas A&M University–Commerce who workshopped a draft of Chapter 2: Donna Dunbar-Odom, Judy Ann Ford, Mee-Gaik Lim, and Melanie McCoy. Their comments proved helpful not only in revising that chapter but in working on other chapters. I would also like to thank my colleagues in the Department of Literature and Languages for their support and encouragement. For help on research and bibliographic material, I would like to thank Colin Charlon and Elias Nyamlell Wakoson for spending part of their time during the summer in the library. I would also like to thank Scott Downing for help with interlibrary loans, and the Reference Librarians in Gee Library. For special help regarding computers, programs, and materials, I would like to thank Mary Brunz, Penny Dooley, Shannon Ashbaugh, and Amanda Nodland. Funding for this research was provided in part through Organized Research of Texas A&M University–Commerce. Finally, I would like to thank Kathleen Gregory Klein and Barbara A. Rader for their patience and editorial advice.

1

The Life of Arthur C. Clarke

Born in 1917, Arthur C. Clarke began publishing his work in school magazines and fan magazines (fanzines) in the early 1930s. His first professional publication was a nonfiction piece published in 1942; his first professional sale of a short story was in 1946. He has published steadily ever since, with his most recent novel, *3001: The Final Odyssey* appearing in March, 1997. A 1984 bibliography (Samuelson xiii), which includes only material in print through December 1980, lists over nine hundred primary works by Clarke, both fiction and nonfiction, including novels, short stories, science articles, and anthologies. Besides his written work, Clarke has also worked on films (the most famous of which is *2001: A Space Odyssey*), documentaries, and radio and television series; has given hundreds of lectures; has founded a developing world communications center, which became the Arthur C. Clarke Centre for Modern Technologies in 1984; and was named Chancellor of the University of Moratuwa, in Sri Lanka. His professional writing career has spanned over fifty years, and he has been awarded major prizes for his scientific writing and his science fiction. In 1986 his peers in the Science Fiction Writers of America awarded him the Grand Master Award for life achievement.

And yet the same Arthur C. Clarke wrote the following letter to a friend in 1938:

> I don't want writing fame, and can see no reason to believe
> that I have any great literary ability. I can turn out an amusing
> story at times, and if I spent enough time in perfecting my
> style I believe that I could do better than most of the "pulp"
> writers. . . . As I haven't the time to devote to writing seri-
> ously, I shall just put pen to paper when the mood seizes me
> and no oftener. (McAleer 30)

Apparently, the mood seizes him often. Any short biography of Clarke
can give only the highlights of a long and productive life. Readers interested in Clarke's life will find several books worth reading. Clarke has
published two books with some autobiographical content. One is *The
View from Serendip*, a collection of essays describing his lifetime involvement with "Space, Serendip, and the Sea" (3). Serendip is an older name
for Ceylon, now Sri Lanka, where Clarke has lived since 1956. *Astounding
Days: A Science Fictional Autobiography* is Clarke's tribute to the science
fiction magazine that changed his life, *Astounding Stories* (now published
as *Analog*). Additionally, an authorized biography by Neil McAleer
draws on personal interviews with Clarke, his family and friends, and
Clarke's papers to present the first full-length biography of one of the
earliest "space cadets" (1).

Two aspects of Clarke's personality that come across strongly in his
autobiographical writings and in the biography are useful in considering
the events of his life in relation to his writing. The first is his enthusiasm
and optimism. His hope that humanity can transcend and evolve, moving into space without destruction and national conflicts, is clear in all
his works. He considers his writing and lecturing to be a way of helping
to achieve that goal. The second is his interest in education. From his
earliest years he has spent his life wondering about and learning about
the universe. His excitement over what he learns is so great that he has
to share it with as many people as possible, and he is always looking
for new and improved ways to further education, especially in the sciences.

This biographical chapter will present a brief overview of Clarke's
childhood, his involvement with groups promoting space travel and science fiction, his experiences during World War II, his interest in science
and the education of the general public, his marriage, his life in Sri
Lanka, his illness, and his writing career. Clarke, at the age of seventy-
nine, is still writing and publishing. As a writer and speaker, he has
lived a good deal of his life in the public eye, but as McAleer notes, there

are some aspects of a person's life that should be private and are not appropriate for biographies (xiii). Autobiographies are a different matter, of course. Clarke has chosen to share a good deal of his memories with his readers in various forms over the years, ranging from interviews to essays, but obviously there are parts of his life he has chosen not to share. Thirty of his early journals exist, but Clarke told a friend that "no one looks at them until fifty years after my death" (McAleer 366). Readers and fans of writers enjoy learning more about the life of a writer, but readers must also respect the right of a living writer to privacy.

Clarke was born on December 16, 1917, in Minehead, England. His father, Charles Wright Clarke, was fighting in France at the time. His mother, Mary Nora Clarke, was living at her mother's house and continued living there until the war ended. After the war, the Clarkes bought a farm but could not make a living and had to sell it. Three more children were born: Frederick, Mary, and Michael. The family moved to another farm in 1924, which is still in the family, run by Michael. Clarke visited his grandmother's house regularly and remembers spending a good deal of his youth on Morehead Beach (*Serendip* 3). Charles Clarke, who had been gassed in the trenches during the war, died in 1931 at the age of forty-three. Clarke became responsible for the household at age thirteen and remembers his mother teaching riding, breeding terriers, and taking in paying guests (*Astounding Days* 10). Clarke himself worked at the local post office.

Clarke became interested in both science and science fiction early in life. When he was seven, he became interested in fossils, dinosaurs, and flying. He built his own telescopes and rockets. His family was involved in various communication technologies as well. His father worked with telegraph and telephone systems before and after the war, his father's brother and his mother worked as telegraphists, and his father's sister was a postmistress. Clarke worked at the post office during his teens and can remember listening in to a radio call from New York City. He also built transmitters and crystal radio sets (McAleer 10–15).

His first introduction to science fiction magazines came from a neighbor, "an elderly gentlemen (he must have been at least thirty) named Larry Kille," who gave him a copy of *Amazing Stories* when Clarke was eleven (*Astounding Days* 4). Clarke describes the cover as showing Jupiter rising over one of its moons where a spaceship from Earth had landed. Larry Kille's grandmother had a great effect on the young Clarke because she ran a knitting machine, which was cutting-edge technology in the 1920s.

Several of Clarke's teachers were important influences on him. His education began at the Bishops Lydeard Elementary school. Maud Hanks, the schoolmistress, encouraged his storytelling, and Clarke thanks her for her encouragement in his autobiography *Astounding Days*. At the age of nine, Clarke began his secondary education at Huish's Grammar School, a preparatory school. McAleer interviewed Bobby Pleass, who taught the young Clarke physics and math. Apparently Clarke was perceived by the other teachers as lazy, but Pleass remembers speaking up for him because he felt that he was ahead of the teachers (16).

Clarke remembers finding his first *Astounding Stories of Super-Science* in "The Dungeon" at Huish (a study room in the basement). This science fiction magazine was the one that started Clarke collecting the "Yankee pulps," which he continued to do for years, maintaining his collection until he had to leave London during World War II. Years later, he was able to acquire the complete run of *Astounding* on microfiche, and he gleefully reports that "in six small plastic boxes, I have the virtually imperishable equivalent of several bookcases of disintegrating pulp; I can easily carry a ten-year run of the magazine in one hand" (*Astounding Days* 15).

Clarke was not able to attend a university because of the lack of money. Instead, he took the civil service exam, getting a perfect score in mathematics, and entered the Exchequer and Audit Department. At the age of eighteen, in 1936, he moved to London to begin work. His job involved auditing teacher pensions, which gave him a great deal of time to spend on his real interests. These involved meeting the people, some of whom he had been corresponding with, who shared his interest in space travel and science fiction.

Clarke had joined the British Interplanetary Society (BIS) when he was sixteen years old, and he began attending their meetings in London. In 1938 he moved from renting a one-room "bedsit" to a larger flat, which he shared with Bill Temple, a friend who was also a member of the BIS and an aspiring writer. This flat became the regular meeting place of the BIS, and Clarke served in different offices. Eventually, the editor of a science fiction fanzine called *Novae Terrae* was invited to move in as well, and the three began editing the magazine jointly (McAleer 25–34).

Although much of the general public in England and America viewed members in such groups as cranks and crackpots, a number of them went on to become engineers, rocket scientists, and science fiction writers. The BIS was dedicated to designing a spaceship that would take a man to the moon and return and to promoting space travel to the general public. Clarke wrote brochures and other material for the BIS and began publishing in fanzines. The BIS and the fan meetings gave him the opportunity to develop many of the ideas he would use during his later writing, both fiction and nonfiction. But the various groups had to disband temporarily when Britain declared war on Germany in 1939. Some members were conscripted (drafted), and others volunteered. Clarke's job was exempt from conscription, and he spent the first year of the war starting to develop the story idea that eventually became the novel *Against the Fall of Night*. Clarke spent 1940 and 1941 in London and North Wales (McAleer 35–42).

Although Clarke was at first deferred, he believed that he would soon be conscripted. Because he was interested in astronomy, he studied celestial navigation and secretly enlisted in the Royal Air Force (RAF). He was made an "aircrafthand and radio wireless mechanic/aircraftsman class II" in March 1941 (McAleer 43). At this time the policy was to put "Church of England" on the dog tags of anyone who had no formal religious affiliation. Clarke insisted that his dog tags be changed to "pantheist" because of his opposition to any organized religion based on faith. Pantheism equates God with natural forces of the universe, a philosophy Clarke could support (McAleer 43–44). Given the nature of this philosophy, Clarke has apparently never seen any contradiction between his long-held aversion to organized religions and the fact that many of his science fiction works have spiritual themes.

Clarke received electronics training and worked in radio direction finding, or RDF. Clarke excelled at electronics and became an instructor, earning the rank of corporal. During his off-duty time, Clarke continued reading technical literature, writing and publishing an article titled "More Television Waveforms" in *Electronic Engineering* in 1942. Publication of the article led to an assignment at a radar installation, where he began working for the first time with trained scientists. The project involved the newest technology in radar, a testing program for the first blind approach radar, a system in which a controller gives instructions to pilots for landing. An American team of scientists who had developed the radar brought the system to England for testing. Although the RAF had some doubts, the loss of planes due to the English weather convinced them to try the system (McAleer 45–50).

Clarke later based his one non–science fiction novel, *Glide Path*, on this project and has often written stories about the trials and tribulations of new and unproven technology. Additionally, Clarke attributes the time spent at the testing site, removed from bombings, with giving him the chance to develop the principles of communication satellites. During his five years in the RAF, he was also writing fiction and nonfiction. He sold his first short story to John W. Campbell, editor of *Astounding Science Fiction*, for $180 in 1945; it was published in 1946 (McAleer 52–53).

A great many things changed in the public and government perceptions about space travel after the war. Germany's rocket development changed people's minds about the possibility of using rockets for space travel, and scientists like Wernher von Braun moved to America and began working on developing rockets. But groups like the BIS still had to convince people that space travel was worth doing. Many ideas were advanced, but Clarke proposed what would become one of the more well-known ones.

During the war, he had published an article discussing how a system of satellites in geostationary orbits could provide worldwide communication. Geostationary satellites are those placed above the equator at certain locations. They travel at the same speed as the Earth rotates, which makes them appear to stay in the same place. At the time, little attention was paid to the article because the technology to place the satellites in orbit did not exist. After the war, the United States Navy started working on the idea because they wanted improved communications. The first geostationary satellite was launched in 1963. Clarke is credited with originating the idea of satellites to provide global communication (the knowledge of the orbital locations was not original), but because he published the article without patenting his idea, he has made no money on the concept—other than the $40.00 he was paid for the article (McAleer 57).

After the war, Clarke decided to get a college education in science rather than return to his civil service job. He began his undergraduate work at King's College, London, in 1946, studying math and physics. Clarke completed the three-year program in two years, achieving the highest honors possible. While completing his degree, he also served as chair of the BIS, began lecturing publicly (which he would continue to do for decades), and wrote and published short stories and articles. During his second year in college, he wrote his first science fiction novel, *Prelude to Space*, which was published first in serial form and then as a book. One of Clarke's major purposes in writing the book was to influence and educate the general public about the potential for space travel, and to emphasize the importance of international cooperation. Although advances in communication represented the possibility of world unification, the atomic bomb threatened another possibility. Clarke's concern about the potential for such destruction was mirrored in his fiction and has been expressed throughout his career (McAleer 58–65).

Although Clarke started graduate work in astronomy, he found it dull. When he was offered the chance of a job, he left school to become the assistant editor of *Physics Abstracts*, a journal that printed abstracts, or summaries, of scientific articles. The job of abstracting required reading, classifying, and indexing scientific articles in every language and was an incredible education in itself. After work, Clarke socialized with his group of friends at the White Horse Pub, which became the fictional location for his humorous stories about pseudoscience written during the fifties and published as *Tales from the "White Hart"* in 1957 (McAleer 64–68).

Clarke worked at this job for about a year before realizing that it interfered with his writing. When he received his first commission for a book, he left the editorial job to begin writing full-time. His first published book was a nonfiction book on space travel, *Interplanetary Flight: An Introduction to Astronautics*, written for a general audience. Clarke's first visit to America came after another of his popular science books, *The Exploration of Space*, was published in America by the Book-of-the-Month club. This publication, unusual for a popular science book, contributed to Clarke's status as a science writer. In 1952 he sailed to New York to appear on radio and television shows. During the fifties, his science fiction did not do as well as his nonfiction. *The Sands of Mars*, which was the first novel set on Mars that described Mars in terms of the scientific knowledge of the time, had only three printings and sold about eight thousand copies (McAleer 68–78). This situation would change dramatically with the publication of *2001: A Space Odyssey*, which has gone through fifty printings and sold three million copies (McAleer 181).

When Clarke returned to London, he shared a house with his brother Fred and Fred's wife Dorothy. He was working on several projects at the same time, a habit of his. One of the projects was revising an earlier story that was expanded and published as *Childhood's End* by Ballantine Books. This publishing company had been recently begun by Ian and Betty Ballantine, who were dedicated to publishing science fiction in book form, simultaneously in hardback and mass-market paperback. Previously, major publishers in America would not publish science fiction, leaving it to the small presses. The Ballantines bought *Childhood's End*, *Expedition to Earth*, and *Prelude to Space* as the beginning of their long partnership with Clarke (McAleer 89–91).

Visiting America again in 1953, Clarke entered into another new partnership when he met Marilyn Mayfield on a trip to Florida where he
was scuba diving, one of his favorite pastimes. Their courtship and marriage covered approximately six months. Marilyn had a young son from
her first marriage, but medical problems kept her from having any more
children. The couple soon began to experience tensions related to their
different interests and religious beliefs, the full-time writing Clarke was
engaged in, and the fact that they could not have children. They separated within six months, although their marriage was not legally dis-
solved for another ten years (McAleer 98–100).

In 1954 Clarke took a journey that would move him away from England and, as he says in *Serendip*, turn his attention from space to the
sea. He and his friend Mike Wilson planned to explore Australia's Great
Barrier Reef, a 1,250 mile long coral reef. Wilson met Clarke in London
and introduced him to scuba diving, which soon became a major interest.
Clarke enjoys diving for several reasons: "the new techniques of free-
diving . . . gave human beings a cheap and simple way of experiencing
the 'weightlessness' of space travel," and diving "could also supply adventure, beauty, strangeness, wonder" (*Serendip* 3). He wrote a good part
of *The City and the Stars* on the journey from London to Sydney, as well
as reading *The Lord of the Rings* by J.R.R. Tolkien, whom he had met in
the forties, along with C. S. Lewis (*Serendip* 4; McAleer 63). The story of
diving along the Great Barrier Reef was published as *The Coast of Coral*
complete with photographs, and Clarke would later use the location in
his later fiction, such as *The Deep Range, Dolphin Island*, and *Imperial Earth*.

But perhaps the most important event of the trip was the afternoon
the ship spent at Colombo, Ceylon. Clarke so enjoyed the stay that he
persuaded Wilson to schedule their next diving trip to the Indian Ocean.
By January 1956 they were on their way back to Ceylon. Clarke enjoyed
the intellectual, cultural, and historical challenges of Ceylon, although
he admits that he did not enjoy the spicy food. The partners began to
dive at the sites of sunken ships, described in *The Reefs of Taprobane*. By
May 1956 Clarke was planning to live in Ceylon and commute annually
to America (McAleer 115–123). He would later use a good deal of the
three thousand years of history and culture in Ceylon in his novel *The
Fountains of Paradise*.

Clarke's plan to live in Ceylon became a way of life that was to last
for approximately twenty years. Because of the different residency, citizenship, and tax laws in the United Kingdom, America, and Ceylon/Sri
Lanka, as well as the lack of reciprocal tax treaties, Clarke had to leave

Ceylon for six months every year. He spent these annual exiles lecturing, often in America on multistate tours. Many people assumed that Clarke lived outside Britain because Ceylon was a tax haven or because he was a recluse. Neither is true. He notes that the taxes in Ceylon were high, and that he sees a great many people, both at his home and while traveling.

The problems were caused by the different legal definitions existing in three different nations. Clarke maintained his British citizenship while owning a house in Ceylon from 1956 to the present. When he began working with filmmaker Stanley Kubrick in 1964 on the project that became the film *2001*, he had to stay in New York for so long that he obtained a Resident Alien card. He notes that the card always made him "feel like a certified extraterrestrial, which seemed highly appropriate under the circumstances" (*Serendip* 53). He would have to deal with the difficulties of being a citizen of one country while living in another and maintaining a resident status in a third until 1974 when Sri Lanka passed a law that became known as "The Clarke Act." This law allowed "foreigners of good will" to be exempted from paying local taxes on money brought into the country (184). Clarke was the first person given the "Resident Guest" visa and could then live in Sri Lanka full-time without any financial penalties.

When Clarke first moved to Ceylon, he entered into partnership with Mike Wilson. Over the years, they published books and made films together, began a salvage business, and finally worked together on an expedition for sunken treasure. These activities, as well as the heavy tax system, contributed to Clarke's financial problems. Clarke began writing and publishing short stories and articles for a time because of the better rate of return and because magazines such as *Playboy* reached a much larger audience than books. But a possible short story suddenly turned into a novel, and he produced *A Fall of Moondust* in a three-month writing marathon in September, October, and November of 1960. Harcourt Brace purchased the rights to *Moondust*, and he and Wilson decided to turn the underwater salvage business over to one of their associates (McAleer 144–149). Clarke has announced several times that he is stopping writing or that he has written his last novel. Fortunately for his fans, he has never followed through on those statements.

While living in Ceylon, Clarke enjoyed an experience that usually only happens in books: participating in a treasure hunt. One of the places Clarke and Wilson regularly dived at was the Great Basses Reef. Wilson planned to make a film there and recruited two American boys to work

on it in 1961. One day they were doing some pleasure diving and discovered a wreck, bringing up two cannons and several large lumps of
silver coins. In 1963, working with an archeologist, they returned to the
reef. The expedition was a great success. They retrieved over three hundred pounds of silver coins, a large cannon, and a variety of other artifacts. Clarke published two books about the adventure. One was a
juvenile, *Indian Ocean Treasure*, and the second was a longer account, *The
Treasure of the Great Reef* (*Serendip* 27–39; McAleer 151–156).

Events during the late 1950s and early 1960s encouraged Clarke to
maintain his interest in space, even while engaging in work related to
the sea. He identifies two events that are so important to him that he
will always remember where he was when they happened: the first
atomic bomb used against Japan, and Sputnik. He remembers being in
Barcelona on October 5, 1957, for the Eighth International Astronautical
Congress. A phone call from a London journalist who wanted his comments about the launch woke him with the news about Sputnik. He had
to revise a recently published book (*The Making of a Moon*) on the United
States Vanguard satellite program because the Russian satellite was
launched first (*Serendip* 9–10). Sputnik initiated the ''space race'' between
Russia and America, and the first manned spaceflights soon followed. A
Russian cosmonaut, Yuri Gagarin, first orbited the Earth in April 1961;
an American astronaut, Alan B. Shepard, Jr., made a successful suborbital
flight that same month. Then, in 1969, Neil Armstrong became the first
human to set foot on the Moon. Clarke has enjoyed meeting many of the
cosmonauts and astronauts over the years and enjoys using their names
in various ways in his novels (names for future spaceships, etc.) (McAleer
130, 158–160).

The successful development of the space programs, due partially to
the competition between Russia and America during the years of the
Cold War, changed Clarke's lectures. As he notes in an article published
in 1958, ''the opinionated little man in the front row who was quite sure
that space travel was impossible—because no one had ever done it before'' had disappeared from his life, thanks to the Russians (McAleer
133). Instead, he had to deal with people who believed in the existence
of flying saucers. He began trying to debunk what he saw as a religion,
rather than actual alien ships, by describing his own UFO experiences
that always turned out to have a rational explanation (weather balloons,
satellites, and so forth). Clarke also began making the point that the
move into space was the natural, next step of an evolutionary process
that began when life moved from the sea to the land (McAleer 133–136).

Because of his extensive work and fame as a science writer, lecturer, and science fiction writer, Clarke was asked to participate in covering the Apollo 11 mission with Walter Cronkite on television. He would also help cover the Apollo 12 and Apollo 15 missions. The experience of witnessing the liftoff and moon landing was thrilling for him. Cronkite and Clarke broadcast from on top of a special set created by the technicians to project multiple films and graphics simultaneously. This projection system was named HAL in honor of Clarke. Seeing Armstrong and Aldrin on the Moon was the fulfillment of Clarke's dreams, and he took the occasion of the broadcasts to talk about future possibilities for life in space (McAleer 227–230).

Unfortunately, an illness in 1962 would change Clarke's life. He hit his head on a door frame, and that same night he became ill. He was paralyzed for several months. Doctors in Sri Lanka diagnosed a spinal injury. He eventually recovered and was able to walk with crutches. He spent the time reading and thinking, and wrote *Dolphin Island* in several months. When Clarke visited London during the summer, doctors there diagnosed the cause of his paralysis as polio. While the specialists disagreed, Clarke set his own goal: to be able to dive again (*Serendip* 37; McAleer 162–169).

Clarke succeeded in achieving his goal. He was able to dive again and resumed his life much as before. But in 1986, experiencing the onset of difficulty walking, he visited a hospital in London. He was told by doctors there that he had only fifteen months to live because he had a degenerative disease known as amyotrophic lateral sclerosis, or Lou Gehrig's disease. Determined to try to finish all he wanted to do, he reacted by working furiously, as well as by following all the diet and exercise advice given by the doctors (McAleer 162–168, 342). When he was still alive and doing better a year and a half later, he visited Johns Hopkins to get an opinion from the specialists there. The tests took a week, and the diagnosis was postpolio syndrome, "old polio," from his episode of paralysis in 1962. As Clarke announced to his friends in a newsletter, "I have a good chance of seeing 2001, even if from a wheelchair (which, I have discovered, is the secret ingredient required for painless transit through today's over-crowded airports)" (357).

Since the diagnosis of postpolio syndrome in 1988, Clarke has published three new novels, *The Ghost from the Grand Banks*, *The Hammer of God*, and *3001: The Final Odyssey*; collaborated with Gentry Lee on *Rama II*, *The Garden of Rama*, and *Rama Revealed*; collaborated with Mike McQuay on *Richter 10*; and has overseen reprinting or expansion of earlier works. His illness may have slowed down his writing, but obviously it has not stopped it.

Trying to give any overview of Clarke's writing career in less than a book-length work is difficult, but a few general observations can be made. Although he was writing both nonfiction and fiction from the start, he first became known as a science writer, explaining the technical aspects of space travel for a general audience during the fifties and sixties. The release and publication of *2001: A Space Odyssey* (movie and novel) made Clarke famous as a science fiction writer. Starting in the seventies, he put most of his energy into his fiction, especially novels. His impact on the field of science fiction has been immense. For a number of years, he was known as one of the "Big Three," the most well known science fiction writers in English, the other two being Robert A. Heinlein and Isaac Asimov. Probably only Asimov published more books than Clarke did, and the two men had a long-lasting and friendly rivalry that both have written about. They also had a mutually agreed upon treaty for years: Each agreed to refer to the *other* one as the best science fiction writer. Clarke currently has over forty books in print, most of them fiction, and has continued to write and publish during the seventies, eighties, and into the ninties, even as many critics and readers assumed that traditional science fiction was a dying genre.

Clarke's influence is not limited only to the field of science fiction. He has spoken on hundreds of occasions, on university campuses and to political and scientific gatherings in various countries, promoting the ideas and causes that he is most associated with: global communication and unity, the free exchange of information, the need for more education, and various technological developments, including work with artificial intelligence. He has taken to the new developments in word processing and computers with great gusto; the first book written by Clarke on a word processor was *2010,* and his afterwords often note which computer and program he used in writing each book.

Since he became a permanent resident of Sri Lanka in 1975, Clarke has enjoyed living at home full time, except for carefully chosen trips. Often those trips are to receive awards. He has experienced losses in his life, such as the accidental death of Leslie Ekanayake, a member of his extended Sri Lankan family, in 1977, and the death of his mother, Nora, in 1980. Life has not always been easy on Sri Lanka because of ongoing political conflicts between the Sinhalese majority, who are primarily Buddhist, and the Tamil minority, who are Hindu. Armed conflicts and riots have occurred periodically since 1971. At one point the situation became so bad that Clarke and his extended family considered leaving Sri Lanka for Australia. But he manages to retain his optimism and enjoy life and writing. As he told his biographer: "If you are an optimist, you have a better chance of making a self-fulfilling prophecy. . . . If you say this is a wonderful world and we can make it better, then there is a chance that people will listen to you and do what you say" (McAleer 294). I am not sure there is any better way to sum up Arthur C. Clarke's life and writing than those words.

Science Fiction and Arthur C. Clarke

DEFINITION AND ORIGINS OF THE GENRE OF SCIENCE FICTION

Defining "science fiction" as a literary genre has not been a concern for academic critics until very recently. The word "genre" refers to a specific category of literature (or art or music) characterized by particular similarities of style, form, or content. Traditional definitions of science fiction conventions are usually based on the Golden Age of science fiction published in America, and to some extent, England, during the forties and into the fifties. The conventions concerning content include future settings, a reliance upon the principles of science, a sense of optimism about the future, and attempts at extrapolation or speculation about the development of humanity. The form of science fiction narratives varies, although one device commonly used is the third person omniscient narrator for the narrative point of view. (For a discussion of narrative point of view, see Chapter 3.) Many critics agree that there have been changes, both in conventions of content and form, since the sixties, and attempts to define science fiction as a genre have not resulted in any widely accepted definition.

The major problem seems to be trying to use and define the term as an umbrella one, an inclusive category containing a variety of subgenres, including fantasy and horror, especially when the content of the fiction

is selected as the defining characteristic. Using content as a defining characteristic is difficult when the books that have won awards for best science fiction include stories set in space and stories set on Earth; stories
about the future as well as stories about the past; stories that rely on the
principles of physics as well as stories that make up the principles of
magic. In recent years, the acronym "SF" (which can stand for "science
fiction," "science fantasy," or "speculative fiction") has come into use as
an inclusive category, or genre name, for some writers, editors, and critics. "Science fiction" can then mean a subgenre of SF, referring to what
used to be called "hard science fiction," which is the genre Arthur C.
Clarke has been most associated with during his career.

I use SF to stand for "speculative fiction," meaning a broad, or umbrella term, which includes the subgenres of science fiction, fantasy, horror, and even magical realism. All these subgenres share the attribute of
speculation, or extrapolation, basing plots and themes on the question
"What if?" The subgenres differ from each other in the nature of their
speculation, ranging from Celtic mythology to genetic engineering or
vampires, but all differ from realistic or naturalistic (what is often called
"mainstream") literature. The boundaries between SF and "realism" are
becoming increasingly blurred. Some mainstream writers have begun
using more fantastic elements, and some science fiction writers have begun using more realistic elements. Additionally, nobody agrees on the
definition of "realism." Clarke has been quoted as saying he chooses to
write science fiction because it is the only literature that "concerns itself
with reality" (McAleer 383).

The origin and the specific characteristics of science fiction have also
been the subject of debate. Science fiction has been a continually changing genre, able to incorporate a number of different ideas and subjects
and able to borrow formal elements from other genres as well. Four
elements are commonly identified as important aspects in the development of contemporary science fiction: the fantastic elements of myths
and epics, the literature of the eighteenth and nineteenth centuries, the
American pulp magazines of the 1920s, and the popularization of scientific knowledge in this century.

Myths and Epics

Some critics place the origins of science fiction at the beginning of
written literature, claiming that a wide variety of literary texts from dif-

ferent cultures, ranging over several millennia, are science fiction. This theory gives science fiction a respectably long and impressive heritage, and its appeal is probably partially due to the common assumption during much of the twentieth century that science fiction was not a "real" literature. Lester Del Rey argues that epics like *Gilgamesh*, a three thousand year old story about the king of Ur and his quest for immortality, are science fiction. These epics contain science fiction conventions, including: "the use of the superman hero, the trip beyond the world of reality and the possibility of immortality through drugs . . . [and] a long search for knowledge and understanding" (13). Although many will debate the claim that epics are science fiction, a strong argument can certainly be made that fantastic literature has a much longer history than the contemporary literary forms called "realistic" or "naturalistic," which began in the late nineteenth century and have continued into the twentieth. Del Rey focusses on the extent to which science fiction has retained the sense of wonderful events that were important in these early texts as an important element. This "sense of wonder" is a well-known phrase among writers and readers of science fiction, often fondly shortened to "sensawunda" in fan jargon. Clarke's work is often considered to have an epic scope, because his science fiction often covers millennia in the development of humanity and contains long and wondrous journeys of exploration.

Eighteenth and Nineteenth Century Literature

Acknowledging the extent to which both literary and popular writers respond to their social and cultural contexts, science fiction critics include the literature of earlier centuries in discussions of its origins. In *Trillion Year Spree: The History of Science Fiction*, Brian W. Aldiss looks at the intellectual and social changes of these earlier centuries, which included the theory of evolution, the development of other contemporary scientific disciplines, and the beginning of the Industrial Revolution. Aldiss argues that the development of the Gothic mode, Mary Shelley's *Frankenstein*, and literature by other writers of the period are important precursors of science fiction.

Science fiction shares the growing social perception that humanity is increasingly separate from the natural world, a perception that began with the Industrial Revolution and theories of evolution (Aldiss 16–17). This theme was originally expressed in the Gothic novels. Mary Shelley's

Frankenstein: Or, The Modern Prometheus shows the debate over the ethics of science, which became an important aspect of science fiction. Showing the close associations of the subgenres of SF, Shelley's work is also considered an important forerunner of contemporary horror fiction as well. Literary figures such as Edgar Allen Poe and Nathaniel Hawthorne also used the new ideas about science and the world in their literature.

Finally, born at the end of the nineteenth century and living into the twentieth, came two writers who are most often associated with the birth of science fiction: the French writer Jules Verne (1828–1905) and the British writer Herbert George (H. G.) Wells (1866–1946). Verne and Wells wrote popular books whose conventions came to be associated with science fiction. Verne's most famous works are probably *Journey to the Center of the Earth*, which describes an expedition into the hollow Earth, and *Twenty Thousand Leagues under the Sea*, which describes a fantastic trip in Captain Nemo's submarine. Verne is credited with making fantastic voyages and technological gadgets popular. He is probably appreciated more for his optimism than for his style, although the *Encyclopedia of Science Fiction* notes in the entry on Verne that bad translations from the original French may have been the cause of this critical view.

Wells, born nearly forty years after Verne, wrote such well-known books as *The Time Machine*, which takes the protagonist millions of years into the future to see the death of the Sun; *The Island of Dr. Moreau*, which explores issues of vivisection, genetics, and the boundaries between human and animal; and *The War of the Worlds*, which is about a Martian invasion halted by germs. Wells, a socialist, did not always see society and technology as positive, and his work has a somewhat grimmer tone than the earlier works of Verne and some of the later science fiction. Wells is generally credited with giving a literary stature to those ideas that became associated with science fiction. Both writers have had work popularized by radio and film versions, which is appropriate for important figures in a genre that is increasingly becoming known for its films as well as its books. Clarke's science fiction draws both on the sense of optimism associated with Verne's work and on the themes and traditions established by Wells.

American Pulp Magazines

Many science fiction writers stress the importance of the American pulp magazines that were published from the 1920s to the 1940s. The term "pulp magazine" describes magazines printed on cheap paper made from wood pulp, produced for popular consumption and mass distribution. As *The Encyclopedia of Science Fiction* notes, the shift to mass distribution and increased advertising made the magazines cheaper to buy, and that factor as well as the increasing literacy rate in the United States resulted in an entertainment revolution. Pulp magazines were available to a wider, more general audience instead of a limited more educated audience (979).

Pulps soon began specializing in a single genre; detective stories, westerns, horror, and adventure stories flourished. Important science fiction writers first published in pulps before American publishers took a chance with publishing science fiction in hardback or paperback formats. Some of the writers who published in the pulps were Edgar Rice Burroughs, A. Merritt, and Murray Leinster (Del Rey 24–29). Paper shortages after World War II and the growth of film as a popular entertainment medium ended the dominance of the pulp magazines. Clarke describes his own reading and collecting of pulp magazines and their importance to him as a writer in *Astounding Days*, his science fictional autobiography.

Popular Scientific Knowledge

The pulp fiction magazines were not the only important magazines published in the 1920s and 1930s. Another kind of magazine played a part in the development of science fiction. These magazines were published for what Lester Del Rey calls "hobbyists," people interested in the new and growing fields of science and technology. Del Rey makes it clear that these people (mostly men) were amateurs in the purest sense of the word—doing what they did because they loved it, not for money. The rapidly increasing growth of knowledge and the professional training programs in such fields as aviation, engineering, electronics, physics, etc., soon made it impossible for the popular science magazines to flourish in the same way as they did in the early 1900s. But the early hobbyists, and their magazines, were responsible for popularization of scientific knowledge. It is possible to speculate that science fiction itself has taken over the function of transmitting scientific knowledge to a general audience. Clarke was a hobbyist for years before studying math and physics at college, and some of his nonfiction writing seems closely related to the purpose of the earlier popular magazines: instructing people how to engage in scientific experimentation and thinking.

The editor credited with blending popular science and pulp fiction is Hugo Gernsback. Gernsback, a European immigrant, came to the United States in 1904 and began publishing *Modern Electrics* in 1908. The magazine was devoted to radio hobbyists and published primarily nonfiction. But when he published his own novel in serial form (titled *Ralph 124C41+*), he was encouraged by his readers to publish more fiction. Gernsback later solicited fiction for a magazine devoted to "scientific fiction," or *scientifiction*, his term for the literature based on the use of contemporary science and technology. He would publish a number of magazines devoted to this literature and is acknowledged by many as the father of science fiction, or at least, of the science fiction magazine (Clute and Nicholls 490). Del Rey also credits him with starting the first letter column, a favorite feature of the science fiction magazines, which led to increased communication between readers, editors, and writers. The major science fiction award voted by fans is called a Hugo in his honor, although his term for the literary genre was not accepted.

CLARKE AND THE GENRE OF SCIENCE FICTION

Certain aspects of content, style, characterization, and tone have come to define the genre of science fiction. The content relies heavily on the principles and use of science, often physics, engineering, and astronomy. Because of this reliance, a style of writing that depends on a scientific vocabulary and a lecturing tone is commonly used. Gregory Benford notes that science fiction "highly prizes faithfulness to the physical facts of the universe, while building upon them to realize new fictional worlds" (15). The style best suited to achieving this goal values accuracy and coherence. Traditional literary criticism tends to value literature written in ornate styles dedicated to exploring individual consciousness. When the style of science fiction is evaluated by such critics, it is often dismissed as flat or wooden. Benford argues that stylistic choices that involve the use of scientific vocabularies and a narrative voice that often sounds like and has the authority of a lecture must be understood as important stylistic choices, not a failure to meet another genre's standards.

Science fiction tends to depict certain kinds of characters, often considered flat when compared to realistic literature's rounded characters. Underlying the method of characterization in science fiction is a focus on humanity as a species rather than as unique individuals. David Hartwell discusses the tendency of science fiction to rely on certain conventional characters as heros or protagonists. The major characters are often presented as survivors and competent "Everymen" rather than unique individuals. These characters are the result of different conventions rather than of other literary genres used. Science fiction tends to rely more on action than on internal monologues to show an individual's character. Hartwell notes that the universe is often the primary antagonist, which means that there are few outright villains in science fiction (34).

John W. Campbell is the editor who is credited by many with establishing many of the conventions of the Golden Age of science fiction, especially its reliance on the principles of science. Campbell (1910–1971) trained in physics at MIT and Duke University and wrote and published science fiction under his name and his pseudonym, Don A. Stuart. He was editor of *Astounding Stories* (later retitled *Astounding Science Fiction* and *Analog*) from 1937 until he died (Clute and Nicholls 187). Campbell is credited with discovering and promoting most of the major science fiction writers of the forties and fifties, including Clarke. Campbell tended to value the sciences that were considered the most important at the time, specifically physics, chemistry, and astronomy, which all rely on math. The biological sciences were less important, the social sciences were almost ignored, and the humanities were completely dismissed (Hartwell 37).

Critiques of science fiction have pointed out the extent to which its conventions reflect the belief system and political philosophies of the 1950s. The belief in technology as a solution for all problems and belief in an ever-expanding universe are connected to the post-war boom experienced by America in the fifties. Kathryn Cramer discusses what she calls "technophilic" science fiction, science fiction that she argues oversimplifies the relationship between science and science fiction. The extent to which this science fiction presents technology as always the solution and never the cause of problems leads her to argue that science fiction is "the religious art of science" (25). Questioning how much science can be taught by stories and novels, she argues against the idea that science will always replace what we use. This idea has become a "cosmic belief in an ever-improving standard of living," which resembles an article of faith rather than a scientific idea or hypothesis (Cramer 28).

However science fiction is defined or debated, Clarke is considered by many to be one of its primary figures. Benford, Hartwell, and Cramer all use Clarke's work as an example of science fiction. He is one of the

"Big Three" (the other two being Robert A. Heinlein and Isaac Asimov) who dominated and defined the genre during the 1940s, 1950s, and into the 1960s when New Wave science fiction began to challenge the writing of the earlier period, reflecting some of the social changes that the decade has become known for. Clarke first published in *Astounding Stories* in 1946 and became one of the magazine's regular contributors, as were Heinlein and Asimov. All three published in the magazines first and then in books when the publishing demands changed. Clarke has won every science fiction award, some several times, as well as numerous awards for his nonfiction work. He was awarded the Science Fiction Writers of America Grand Master Award for life achievement in 1986. Numerous science and science fiction writers credit Clarke with inspiring them to go into the field, and *2001*, the movie he collaborated on with Stanley Kubrick, is defined by many as the most important science fiction movie ever made.

Clarke's science fiction not only exemplifies the major characteristics of the genre but transcends them. Because Clarke has done university work in math and physics and has published a good deal of nonfiction writing about science, the "lecturer" mode of writing often appears in his work as a necessary part of the story. Clarke, both in his fiction and nonfiction writing, considers education as one of his main goals. The desire to explain the science, both the actual and the extrapolated aspects of it, results in Clarke's narrative choices being consistent with the generic conventions. For example, there are chapters that explain background information on the science of each novel. (geology, math, physics, astronomy). When those chapters are not sufficient, a number of novels have acknowldgement sections that list sources for further reading for readers interested in learning more. The majority of his characters are scientists, engineers, and astronauts, although a few writers, journalists, and a bureaucrat or two appear upon occasion.

Clarke refuses to sacrifice other aspects of the story to a lecture. Few of his protagonists are academics doing pure theory or full-time research. A description of lab and computer work rarely drives much of a plot. Instead, his characters are often men working in a new area of developing technology or those men (and a few women) who are exploring the solar system or colonizing new planets. Certain of his later novels (especially *The Songs of Distant Earth* and *The Fountains of Paradise*) show his attempt to develop characters more fully than in his earlier novels.

The structure that Clarke uses in the majority of his novels follows a traditional plot structure, with one important exception. A traditional plot structure includes the following elements occurring in this order: the introduction of key characters; the establishment of the main conflict; rising action, which often involves several subplots; the climax; and then resolution or closure. Clarke much prefers to structure his novels with little or no sense of closure. Conflict in a Clarke novel tends to focus primarily on humanity's struggle to survive in the world rather than on conflict between individuals. When disagreement between characters does occur, the focus tends to be on the philosophical nature of the disagreement and rarely on violent behavior. Clarke's protagonists and antagonists often respect each other, even if they disagree with the other's methods or results.

Clarke has generally been credited more for his focus on ideas, science, and optimism about the human race's future than for his literary style. A number of mainstream reviews found his style, especially in earlier fictions, flat and wooden. An argument might be made for his accessibility to a wide audience. In an essay titled "Three Styles of Arthur C. Clarke: The Projector, the Wit, and the Mystic," Peter Brigg argues against pigeonholing Clarke's style as static. Analyzing both short fiction and novels published over a number of years, Brigg shows that there are varying styles in Clarke's work and examines works where he successfully integrates the different styles (*Rendezvous with Rama* and *Imperial Earth*). The "Projector" is the term Brigg gives to Clarke's writing that deals with science and extrapolation. The focus is on explaining information to the reader, emphasizing the scientific problem rather than subtleties of characterization or emotions. A second important style, found more in the short stories, is "The Wit," the comic tone. Humor is gained through plot devices (twists or surprise endings), through comic stereotypes of characters, and through the use of pseudoscience. Finally, "The Mystic" style is used in works such as *Childhood's End* and *2001: A Space Odyssey*, which "attempt to go beyond the limits of the hard extrapolations and the humorous entertainments" (Brigg 38). Brigg attributes the metaphysical elements in Clarke's fiction to the influence of Olaf Stapledon but notes that all of the works that end in mystical speculation still begin in the "mundane" and are told in a "quiet, factual voice" (38).

The "mystic" aspect of Clarke's work is what makes some of his fiction transcend the traditional conventions of science fiction, although science and engineering remain an important part of all his work. Clarke refuses to ignore the spiritual aspect of humanity in his evocation of the scientific aspect. In many of his novels, Clarke puts most of his energy into conveying the beauty and the mystery of the universe to his readers. Ada, in *Ghost from the Grand Banks*, explains this philosophy by quoting Einstein: "The most beautiful thing we can experience is the mysterious. It is the source of all true art and science. He to whom this emotion is a stranger, who can no longer pause to wonder and stand wrapt in awe, is as good as dead" (129). If "art" and "science" are seen to spring from the same source, then there is no contradiction in the mystical and the scientific aspects of Clarke's science fiction.

We may think we understand the ways the physical universe works because we walk around in it every day, but there are vast areas that are mysterious to us, both in space and on Earth. Clarke's most lyrical writing is reserved for describing this beauty and mystery to his readers rather than for describing individual characters. An example of Clarke's emphasis on the beauty of the physical world is the repeated image of the banyan tree, often used as a metaphor when a character encounters a different form of life (ranging from a giant octopus on Earth to incredible creatures that live in Jupiter's upper atmosphere). The sense of a huge, alien, yet living being is conveyed through this metaphor in short stories and novels with a lyricism that many of Clarke's critics have apparently ignored.

Readers trained in the assumption that a certain style or focus on individual psychology is more valuable than other subjects may find long detailed descriptions of the physical world (whether it is the Moon, the inner satellites of Jupiter, or Mars) and physics boring, but readers who are familiar with the conventions of science fiction will appreciate what Clarke is doing. Debates occur today about the scientific illiteracy of the general public. I cannot say with certainty that reading science fiction can solve this problem, but the possibility does exist. If Clarke's novels can both delight and instruct readers, I believe he will have achieved much of his purpose in writing.

OVERVIEW OF MAJOR PUBLICATIONS

Clarke has published extensively, in multiple genres and through various media, for over fifty years. It is not possible to list all his work in less than book-length format, as David N. Samuelson's excellent and exhaustive work, *Arthur C. Clarke: A Primary and Secondary Bibliography* proves. This section will present a brief discussion of his nonfiction and short story collections and a discussion of his novels, eight of which are the subjects of later chapters of this book.

Nonfiction

The "Nonfiction" section of Samuelson's bibliography is seventy pages long. This section covers essays as well as books, beginning with works published in 1932 and ending with works published in 1980. Although Clarke has published in technical journals, he has also written a good deal about science for the general audience. He wrote the first popular science book ever published by the Book-of-the-Month Club. Clarke's most well-known nonfiction article may be "Extra-Terrestrial Relays," which appeared in *Wireless World* in October 1945. This article was the first discussion of the theory behind today's satellite communication network.

His nonfiction writing covers such subjects as radar and electronics, telescopes, rockets, the methods of spaceflight, satellite communication, meteors, underwater diving, and a large number of essays that focus on extrapolation or speculations about future developments. Transcripts of speeches he has given at conferences and for governments are also included in this category. A number of his essays have been collected, edited, and expanded for print in collections. One collection, *Report on Planet Three and Other Speculations*, credits publication of essays in a variety of magazines and journals, such as *Boys' Life, Cavalier, Fantasy & Science Fiction, Playboy, Reader's Digest*, and *Why Not*, showing Clarke's wide range of audiences. Other articles were later expanded to become book-length works. Clarke writes for younger audiences as well as adults. Other works are more autobiographical in nature. *The Lost Worlds of 2001* and *The Odyssey File* discuss his work on *2001*, including the versions of the novel that were discarded in the process of writing. *The View from Serendip* and *Astounding Days* cover various aspects of Clarke's life, writing, and his love for *Astounding*, the science fiction magazine he began reading at age thirteen.

Some of Clarke's earlier science writing has gone out of print, and in many cases would be out of date, although he continued to revise and write new books for some years. But it is important to remember that Clarke, as well as a few others, were designing rocketships and discussing how to travel into space thirty years before Russia and America finally achieved spaceflight. And many of his extrapolative and speculative essays remain interesting and applicable even in 1996 because in some ways Clarke is still ahead of everybody else.

Short Fiction

Samuelson counts at least two hundred short stories by Clarke published between 1926 and 1980. Clarke has written science fiction as well as ghost stories, tall tales, time travel stories, and humorous stories, such as his accounts of pseudoscience in *Tales from the "White Hart"* (Rabkin 53–55). Two of Clarke's short stories are considered to be classics: "The Star" and "The Nine Billion Names of God." Both were reprinted in Clarke's collection of his favorites among his short stories, *The Nine Billion Names of God*. "The Star" is a first person account by a Jesuit astrophysicist who discovers that the star of Bethlehem was a supernova that destroyed an entire race of beings who left records on the furthest planet in their system. "The Nine Billion Names of God" also concerns the connections between science and religion. A Buddhist lamasery purchases a computer to list all the "real" names of God in a special alphabet they have invented, and hires two American engineers to oversee the three-month project. As the engineers are leaving, chuckling at the monk's superstition, they look up and see that "[o]verhead, without any fuss, the stars were going out" (22).

Clarke has often returned to what he calls the "acorn" of an idea in a short story to expand it into the "oak" of a novel years or decades later, so readers of his novels may find it useful to look at the first development of ideas in the short stories. *Childhood's End* had its genesis in "Guardian Angel," published in 1946. "The Songs of Distant Earth" appeared in two short forms (a story, and a movie outline) before becoming a novel. "The Sentinel" (1951) first featured an alien warning device and was used, along with other of Clarke's short stories, as elements of *2001*. "A Meeting with Medusa" describes the first exploration of Jupiter and is related to *2010*. *The Hammer of God* is based on a short story commissioned by *Time* magazine; in this case, the novel and short story end very differently. In one notable example of revision, Clarke began working on a story in 1939, eventually published it as the novel, *Against the Fall of Night*, in 1953, and then published a revised version as *The City and the Stars* in 1956. Both versions remained in print. Years later, he and Gregory Benford published *Beyond the Fall of Night* (1990), containing the original novel and Benford's sequel. Clarke notes in the introduction to *Beyond the Fall of Night* that he feels chagrined that some readers prefer the first version to his revision, but he does not believe that he can decide which is the better book (x). A good deal of the impetus for his revision is to update the stories to include the newest information about various planets or space travel in general.

Novels

Beginning in the seventies, Clarke decided to focus on fiction (McAleer 247). Samuelson notes fifteen novels (including one revision) in print by 1980. By my count, which may be inexact, Clarke has published at least twenty-five novels (including six collaborations). Finding some of Clarke's earlier novels and collections is difficult, as is distinguishing between the first editions and later reprints, sometimes published under different titles.

Selecting nine novels to discuss for this book was also difficult. Because much of the published criticism of Clarke's work appeared in print before 1980, I decided to focus on later works. *Childhood's End* and *2001* (both the film and the novel) have received the most critical attention that the reader can locate. Clarke has produced a good deal of work in the seventies and eighties that is well worth the attention. Although I was a fan of Clarke's in my adolescence, I had not read any work published after *Rendezvous with Rama*. When I became an English major, not only did I have to spend a great deal of time reading my assigned work, reading science fiction was discouraged by most of my professors. The experience of reading familiar stories again, and reading all of the newer novels, proved that Clarke's work has stood the test of time extremely well. His later work shows development of the themes that were important in his earlier work, and some interesting developments in style and characterization as well.

Rendezvous with Rama is a good place to start because it was published after a decade during which Clarke did not publish any novels. The ambitious evocation of an alien technology and humanity's attempt to explore an immense and mysterious ship won all the major awards in the science fiction field. Clarke feels that *Imperial Earth* and *The Fountains of Paradise* are two of his most ambitious works, and the protagonists and the scope of these stories about the exploration of space bear him out. Additionally, *The Fountains of Paradise* won the Hugo and the Nebula awards. *The Songs of Distant Earth* is Clarke's favorite work and was written not only to describe interstellar spaceflight realistically, but also because Clarke says he was tired of "critics going on about the lack of characterisation [*sic*], and my rather flat prose" (McAleer 214; 339). *2010: Odyssey Two*, *2061: Odyssey Three*, and *3001: The Final Odyssey* develop the ideas that were first explored in *2001* in even larger terms. *The Hammer of God* and *Ghost from the Grand Banks* explore two subjects that are important to Clarke: asteroid impacts and the *Titanic*, a lifelong love of his.

I read and enjoyed the collaborations done with Gentry Lee and Mike McQuay, but they are outside the scope of this work, which focusses on Clarke's solo novels. Clarke, trained in the sciences, obviously enjoys collaboration as a creative process. Science writing tends to rely on collaboration among a number of writers, whereas writing in the humanities tends to assume that authorship is individual and cannot be shared. In addition, the transformation of his novels into films is another kind of collaboration. Yet I also recognize that there is a good deal of cynicism developing about the recent practice of publishers using an established writer's name to sell a book primarily written by a lesser-known writer. In such cases, the collaboration often consists of the established writer contributing a plot outline and the other writer doing the writing. This subject is a fruitful one for debate. Clarke has written specifically about the nature of his collaborations with Benford, Lee, and McQuay, and I would encourage readers to read the introductions and the books and consider what he says. Characteristically, he notes that his major motive for entering into these literary experiments is curiosity, his "most abiding characteristic," and that he agrees "with the British nobleman who told his son: 'Try everything once—except incest and folk dancing'" (McAleer 337).

Reviewing his novels, it is possible to see several major thematic patterns that he returns to over time. These include a complex attitude towards technology, the necessity for humans to continue exploring the universe, and a strong connection between the evolution of human spirituality and the presence of aliens. None of the novels presents these themes simply and without conflict, of course. In many cases, the theme is presented more as a goal than as an achievement, with the journey being more important than the arrival.

Technology

The use of and commentary on technology is a defining aspect of science fiction because the major growth of the genre emerges from the Industrial Revolution. Clarke's interest in the technologies of communication is clear, both in his scientific work and in his fiction, but he also draws on other aspects of technology and engineering. Except in his humorous stories, Clarke insists on the realistic presentation of spaceflight. There is one area of technology he does not spend a great deal of time on: the technology of war. Instead, he considers the various ways in which technology can support the survival of humanity. Clarke's novels that focus primarily on technology present a complex view of the relationship between humanity, technology, and nature. Where earlier novels focussed primarily on technology for the sake of technology, later novels have widened their focus to include questions of a spiritual nature, relating not only to survival but to the ethics and implications of survival for humans as a species.

Prelude to Space, published in 1951, is a novel about the first attempt at a manned flight to the Moon. In the foreword to the 1976 edition, Clarke cheerfully admits writing the novel as propaganda: to encourage the public to support the idea of spaceflight. This novel is not considered one of Clarke's strongest works, which is a judgment that can be made about most writers' first novels. Although the novel is based on the scientific speculation of that time, there is a strong element of fantasy in the presentation of international cooperation and development of the technology of spaceflight as Clarke obviously hoped would occur.

In *A Fall of Moondust*, a group of tourists are trapped on the Moon, in a sea of dust that has been pulverized so finely that it behaves more like water. Clarke wrote the novel in 1960 and based the huge areas of dust on what was hypothesized about the Moon at that time. The action of the novel focusses on the rescue efforts by two men, Tom Lawson, an astronomer, and Chief Engineer Robert Lawrence. The novel shifts back and forth between the rescue efforts and what the trapped passengers have to do to survive—and readers are invited to figure out the technological solution. Although the limited exploration of the Moon has turned up no seas of dust so far, the novel is considered one of Clarke's stronger efforts.

Glide Path, Clarke's only non–science fiction novel, is the one that gave him the most trouble writing and getting published. He began writing it in 1958 but had to revise it several times, and it was not published until 1963. Based on his wartime experiences at a radar installation, the book is a tribute to his colleagues, as well as a history of technology. Following the protagonist, Alan Bishop, the novel details the development and testing of the radar system that played some part in the European war and an even larger part in the airlift to Berlin. As other writers will agree, trying to place events that really happened into a novel is sometimes more difficult than making everything up. This novel is considered more interesting for possible autobiographical revelations than for its overall story.

The Fountains of Paradise is considered one of Clarke's strongest works. Published in 1978, it won both the Hugo and the Nebula awards. This novel is about technology and the evolution of technology and describes the building of a space elevator, which has been written about in scientific journals. The elevator is a tower with its foundation on Earth and its "roof" attached to a geostationary satellite, which would make space travel easier and more economical. *Fountains* includes three thousand years of the history of Sri Lanka, an alien visitation to Earth, and Buddhist philosophy as it tells the story of Vannevar Morgan's attempt to build his tower in spite of opposition. Chapter 5 presents a close reading and a postcolonial reading of this novel.

Ghost from the Grand Banks, published in 1990, is set on Earth and tells the story of an attempt to raise the *Titanic* from the bottom of the ocean. Three men—Jason Bradley, Roy Emerson, and Donald Craig—first compete and then cooperate in projects to bring the ship up. An underseas volcanic eruption kills Jason and buries the wreck, apparently forever. This novel extrapolates from existing technology and is set much closer to the present time than many of Clarke's other works—in 2012, the one hundredth anniversary of the sinking. The novel introduces readers to chaos theory and the "Mandelbrot-Set," although some criticism has been made of the amount of mathematical theory that is included in the story. Chapter 9 presents a close reading and a feminist reading of this novel.

The Hammer of God, published in 1993, focusses completely on a disaster that can only be averted by means of a technological solution. An asteroid, Kali, is approaching the orbit of Earth and will collide with the Earth unless it can be diverted soon enough. The novel follows an attempt to divert the asteroid that is sabotaged by religious fanatics and creates suspense by not revealing whether or not Earth is saved until the very last page. The focus on the need to divert the asteroid against all odds makes this novel read more like Clarke's earlier ones in which the major focus is on the technology and basic survival. Chapter 10 presents a close reading and a feminist reading of this novel.

Space Colonization

Closely linked to the use of technology for space travel is theme of the necessity for human beings to continue exploring the physical universe, from early movements across continents and oceans to the later movements beyond Earth to the Moon, to other planets in the solar system, and eventually outside the solar system. The alternative, in Clarke's novels, is stagnation.

This fear of stagnation is most strongly expressed in one of Clarke's earliest and most well known novels, which he has revised once: *Against the Fall of Night* (later revised as *The City and the Stars*). In this novel, begun in 1939 and published in 1953, Clarke describes the eternal city of Diaspar. Here, where people have everything they could ever need, where they are reincarnated regularly, and where their lives are completely controlled by machines, a "new" person, Alvin, is finally born. Alvin, the protagonist, does what nobody in Diaspar ever does. He leaves the city, discovers another human culture—a group living in the country—and then finds a way to go into space. The expanded version of *Against the Fall of Night*, *The City and the Stars*, revised and published three years later, includes over one hundred additional pages. The revised version keeps the same basic plot but expands the events and creates more complicated machines and situations. Both novels present a strong message: Humans must keep developing and exploring rather than retreating to a protected and static environment.

The image of the city as a trap is also found in *The Lion of Comarre*, a novella that describes a self-perpetuating city, Comarre, which seduces people into dependency. Having more fantasy elements than is usual with Clarke, the story describes Dick Peyton's journey, his meeting a lion who saves him from the city, and his victory over the city. These works present a unique look at the dangers of stagnation associated with technology. Most of Clarke's novels are more optimistic about the use of technology in the colonization of space.

The Sands of Mars is a 1951 novel that attempts to present a realistic view of Mars based on the scientific knowledge of the time. The plot of the novel focusses on Martin Gibson, a writer from Earth, who is hired to write a book about the first passenger ship's trip to Mars and about the colony on Mars. The Earth companies are debating how much support to provide the colony there, and the colonists are trying to become more independent. Eventually, their secret plan is carried out. The colonists set off a nuclear reaction on Phobos, one of Mars' two moons, and turn Phobos into a sun that will help them terraform Mars. The novel also describes the changes in Gibson himself as he discovers, but does not reveal himself to, his son from a college romance. This first novel about the colonization process sets up some ideas that are developed in Clarke's later work.

Another novel, published in 1952, is *Islands in the Sky*, written for a younger audience. The protagonist, sixteen-year-old Roy Malcolm, wins a quiz show and demands a trip to an artificial satellite, or space station, as his prize. After he arrives, he manages to get involved in a variety of activities and trips from the station, all described in great detail, including participating in a film made in space. Although colonization of the planets is not a part of this novel, the importance of satellites as jumping off places and in communication for space travel is clearly made, and at the end Roy is determined to go on to Mars where a colony does exist.

Earthlight presents a less optimistic look at the future of colonization than earlier novels do. Conflict between a federation of colonists on Mars and Venus and Earth over the mining rights on the Moon, considered part of Earth, could lead to war. The protagonist, an accountant recruited by an intelligence agency, is Bertram Sadler. He is sent to the Moon under cover of doing an audit while trying to find out who is leaking information to the federation. The novel presents good details of life on the Moon, but it is not considered a successful spy story.

Imperial Earth: A Fantasy of Love and Discord moves the colonization process out even further, to Titan, one of Saturn's moons. Duncan Makenzie, a clone of the founder and leader of the colony, leaves Titan to visit Earth to speak at the five hundredth anniversary of the Declaration of Independence. He is trying to find a new technology to keep Titan's economy expanding. Part of Duncan's visit on Earth involves dealing with two people who were important to him in his past. Published in 1975, this novel is considered one of Clarke's strongest, showing both the scientific and the social aspects of colonization. Chapter 4 presents a close reading and a gender reading of this novel.

The Songs of Distant Earth is Clarke's favorite of his novels. Appearing in 1986, *Songs* presents a future in which the impending nova of the Sun forces humans to colonize distant planets, first using a seedship method and then using a newly developed drive and hibernation. Thalassa, a planet colonized seven hundred years earlier by a seedship, is visited by the last ship to leave Earth before the nova. The novel includes a love story between a Terran, Loren, and a Lassan, Mirissa, who must part when the ship leaves Thalassa. Chapter 7 presents a close reading and a postcolonial reading of this novel.

Two of Clarke's earlier novels also describe the exploration of the sea, which he later used in writing *The Songs of Distant Earth*. Clarke often equates the exploration of the sea with the exploration of space. *The Deep Range*, published in 1957, describes a future in which ocean farming supplements farming on land. The novel follows an astronaut who has had to leave space because of an accident and who becomes a "whale-herder." Walter Franklin achieves a successful career over the years, and Clarke describes this possible future use of whales in great detail, including the philosophical objections by a Buddhist monk on Ceylon about killing animals for food. *Dolphin Island: A Story of the People of the Sea* is another of Clarke's juveniles. Published in 1963, it describes how a young man named Johnny Clinton leaves home and ends up crashing in the ocean. He is rescued by dolphins and taken to live with a scientist who is engaged in dolphin research. The novel describes exploring coral reefs, dolphin intelligence, and surviving hurricanes as Johnny earns a home with the scientist.

Evolution, Spirituality, and Aliens

It is an interesting fact that two of the most famous science fiction writers, Isaac Asimov and Arthur C. Clarke, rarely created stories involving aliens. Clarke eventually wrote a number of novels with aliens in them, but these novels have an interesting approach to presenting the aliens: they seldom or never appear. One reason for refusing to include many alien species is no doubt connected to Clarke's insistence upon the realities of space travel. Interstellar distances are so vast, and travel is limited by the speed of light, which means that the only effective way to explore space is through robot probes, or sentient robots. Clarke does at times show contact with robot probes, or forms of life that are not limited by physical bodies. The aliens often play important roles in the novels, but little information is given on their actual biology, probably because Clarke's major work was in physics and math.

In spite of the narrative importance of aliens in *Rendezvous with Rama* and in the Odyssey series, the aliens themselves never appear in those novels. In other novels, the aliens do appear briefly, but the most important result of humanity's contact with an alien species does not rely on actual contact but on the fact of their existence and what it implies, philosophically, for humans. One of the assumptions about space exploration in much science fiction has been the idea that humans will be the ones to explore space and meet new species. These stories are based on the expectation that humans will be the technological superiors of the other species. Clarke's books do not conform to this convention. Instead, there is a pattern of a superior species (the Overlords in *Childhood's End*, the Ramans, the aliens in the Odyssey series, the Starholmers in *Fountains of Paradise*) coming to Earth, or the solar system, first. Humanity is left to deal with both the shock of a first contact, and with the realization that they are not the most advanced species alive.

Childhood's End, published in 1953, is probably Clarke's most famous and most controversial book. This novel begins some time after the Overlords, an alien species that humans have never seen, came to Earth and stopped all wars and technological development. The Overlords have provided everything humans need to live, which has stopped all progress. Finally, a generation of children are born who are the next evolutionary step for humanity. They do not need technology, relying instead on mental powers. They have achieved "Total Breakthrough" into a group mind. They leave Earth, destroying it as their last act, to become part of the Overmind.

Rendezvous with Rama describes an alien spaceship entering the solar system. The ship is boarded and explored, but no sign of life or a crew is found. The ship, a huge perfect cylinder, is explored as thoroughly as possible in the short time available, but it eventually leaves the system without showing any interest in humans. This novel, published in 1973, won all the major science fiction awards and eventually led to a series of three later novels written by Clarke with Gentry Lee. Chapter 3 presents a close reading and a feminist reading of this novel.

The Odyssey series consists of four novels—*2001, 2010, 2061,* and *3001*—published over a period of twenty-nine years. Although the novels are usually discussed as a series, Clarke insists that the later books should be viewed as a rewriting of the same story rather than as sequels. In *2001*, a mysterious black monolith visits Earth and manipulates the ancestors of humanity, which allows for the development of language, technology, and eventually spaceflight. Millions of years later, humanity discovers a monolith on the Moon that sends a message out toward Jupiter. Five astronauts are sent on a mission to the location, but problems with Hal, the supercomputer on board the ship, lead to failure. The one survivor, David Bowman, enters the monolith and is transformed into a being of pure energy.

2010 describes a joint Russian–American mission to recover *Discovery*, Bowman's abandoned ship. Heywood Floyd, the head of the agency that organized the first mission, accompanies this mission. Although they recover the ship and reanimate Hal, unexpected events cut short their study. The transformed Bowman acts as a probe for the aliens. They implode Jupiter and make it a star, giving life on one of its inner moons a chance to evolve. Humans are warned not to land on Europa. Chapter 6 presents a close reading and a feminist reading of this novel.

2061 describes events fifty years after *2010*. Heywood Floyd, with other celebrities, visits Halley's comet, but they are called back to rescue another ship that has been stranded on Europa in spite of the alien's earlier warning. The landings on Europa go unpunished, and a mountain of pure diamond is discovered there. It was one of the core fragments thrown out by the implosion of Jupiter, and its impact on Europa has apparently harmed the monolith. By the end of the novel, Heywood Floyd is copied into the monolith, to join Hal and Bowman as the guardians of life on Europa. The last chapter of *2061* describes the entities in the monolith waking up as Lucifer begins to die in 3001. Chapter 8 presents a close reading and a gender reading of this novel.

3001 is set nearly a millennium after the earlier novels. The novel opens when Frank Poole's body is recovered from space, and Poole is brought back to life through the use of improved technology. This novel follows Poole's attempts to build a new life in the far future in which he finds himself but also covers what happens when the entities, or controllers, of the monoliths attempt to take action regarding humanity. The monolith in *2001* sent a transmission to its superior, 450 light years away. When instructions return approximately one thousand years later, the entities in the monolith (sometimes called "Dave," sometimes "Halman") warn Poole. Specialists are able to put together a "Trojan Horse" of computer viruses which Halman agrees to release into the monolith on Europa. The viruses destroy the monoliths, saving humanity for at least the thousand years it will take any message to travel and instructions to return since the messages are limited to the speed of light. Chapter 11 presents a close reading and a feminist reading of this novel.

The Odyssey Pattern

Although the twenty-two novels discussed above were published over a period of forty years and tell many different stories, there is a strong similarity among them. It would be possible to place a number of the novels in any of the three "categories" of themes that I have identified: a complex attitude toward technology, the necessity for humans to continue exploring the universe, and a strong connection between the evolution of human spirituality and the presence of aliens. George Edgar Slusser argues that this similarity is due to fact that the Odyssey pattern is a central and organizing structure that not only unifies Clarke's stories and novels but also connects his work to "deep and persistent currents of Western literature" (3). The journey, both for individuals and for a species, is based on the competing ideas of progress and stagnation. Different novels evoke different aspects of this journey—from the beginning, through maturity, to stagnation—but the journey underlies all of the stories.

Rendezvous with Rama
(1973)

Rendezvous with Rama, the first novel published after a ten-year gap during which Arthur C. Clarke published more nonfiction than fiction, received a great deal of critical attention. The fiction published between 1963 and 1973 was mostly collections of short stories or new editions of earlier novels. *Rama* immediately won all the major awards given to science fiction: the Hugo, voted on by the fans; the Nebula, awarded by the Science Fiction and Fantasy Writers Association; the John W. Campbell Award, voted on by a panel of writers; and the Jupiter Award, voted on by members of the Institute of Science Fiction in Higher Education. The novel is a good example of the science fiction Clarke is best known for, focussing on exploration and the philosophical implications of alien intelligence. In addition, Clarke would return to the universe of *Rama* over fifteen years later in a series he collaborated on with Gentry Lee: *Rama II*, *The Garden of Rama*, and *Rama Revealed*.

The novel is set in the year 2130, when a huge cylinder-shaped spacecraft enters the solar system. *Endeavour*, a survey ship, is rerouted to rendezvous with Rama and study it. The ship is dark and dead with no trace of life. The inside of the cylinder is split into two "hemispheres" by a large "sea," which goes all the way around the cylinder. The sea is frozen and contains an island "city." Creatures, which the crew christens "biots" (for *bi*ological rob*ots*), appear and are active but ignore the humans. After thwarting an attempt to blow up the spacecraft by Martian colonists, *Endeavour* leaves Rama. The ship then leaves the solar system, paying no attention to humans, or Earth, during its visit.

This chapter first presents a brief discussion of the *Rama* series, and then explores five aspects of *Rendezvous with Rama*:

1. The need to solve the mystery of Rama is the focus of the plot.
2. The structure is divided between the scientists on Earth and the *Endeavour* crew.
3. The narrative point of view limits readers to the amount of knowledge the crew has.
4. Individual character development is subordinated to the emphasis on a collaborative project.
5. The major themes.

The chapter concludes by introducing feminist theory and criticism and presenting an example of a feminist reading of the book.

THE RAMA SERIES

Three later books, coauthored by Clarke and Gentry Lee, were published between 1989 and 1994. Because the books are collaborations, and this study focusses on Clarke's solo fiction, they are not included in this study. The later novels develop the themes and ideas of *Rama*, and readers who are intrigued by *Rama* may wish to learn what happens next, so a brief discussion of the series is included in this chapter.

Clarke insists in the foreword to *Rama II* that he had no intention of writing a trilogy when he ended the first novel with "The Ramans do everything in threes," although many readers were convinced that two more ships would have to visit the solar system. The opportunity he had to work with Lee on *Cradle* as well as Lee's expertise as a chief engineer at the Jet Propulsion Laboratory made the collaboration seem natural when Clarke thought of returning to the Rama universe after finishing *2061: Odyssey Three*. The three novels are a conventional sequel, following the adventures and lives of the same group of characters over a period of many years. None of the characters in the three collaborative novels appear in *Rendezvous with Rama*.

Rama II describes the events that occur when another Rama ship returns to the solar system in 2200. A scientific expedition sent to study the ship finds no sign of life. When several crew members die and the ship changes course to head directly for Earth, the World Government is convinced that the ship is hostile. The expedition is ordered to withdraw, and an attempt is made to blow the ship up using nuclear bombs. Three members of the expedition (Nicole des Jardins, Richard Wakefield, and Michael O'Toole) are left behind. Convinced that the Ramans are not hostile, they manage to warn the ship, which defends itself and changes course, leaving the solar system.

The Garden of Rama describes a journey of almost fifteen years that takes Nicole, Richard, and Michael, and their five children, to the Node, a facility for refitting Rama spaceships. On the way, they learn that there are other species traveling on the ship, which will be refitted and sent out again. The Ramans are a species that studies spacefaring life throughout the universe. Their method is to first send an exploratory ship through a system. If that ship is boarded, later ships are sent to try to "capture" a few members of the species for further study. Then an invitation is extended to a large group to come live aboard the ship for some time. If the invitation is refused, the group is collected without their consent.

Richard, Nicole, and four of the children return to Earth to pick up a group of two thousand humans. Michael marries Richard and Nicole's oldest daughter, Simone, and they stay at the Node to meet the Raman requirement for a backup "breeding pair." Back on Earth, the World Government suppresses the transmitted invitation and secretly plans to deflect colonists who volunteered to go to Mars to Rama. Although the humans on board the ship are provided with a place to live, robot servants, and the basic necessities to sustain life, within five years the group has ruined their environment, broken out of their habitat and into another species' space, and has begun a war with that species. Nicole is in prison charged with sedition and facing death by electrocution, and Richard has escaped the human habitat and is living on the island, secretly nurturing the avian aliens he rescued from the war.

Rama Revealed continues describing the events on Rama, focussing primarily on Richard and Nicole and their children. Richard rescues Nicole from prison, and they return to where they lived during their first trip. They eventually bring some of their children to join them, and learn about the two other species on board, the avians and the octospiders. They live with the octospiders for some time, while the humans attack the octospiders as well as the avians. Finally, the artificial intelligences

who observe everything on the Rama ships decide to intervene to avoid
the extinction of one or more species. They halt the ship and remove
everyone. Then they separate the humans into two groups: those who
can live and interact with other species on an equal basis and those who
see humans as a superior species and cannot.

There is still no sign of the Ramans, but one possible explanation of
Rama's purpose is offered by a human biot who tells Nicole and her
family that the Node, and all the other technologies, were created from
a Prime Monitor sent from another universe by God. The purpose of the
Prime Monitor, the Nodes, the ships, and all the artificial intelligences is
to study spacefaring life-forms. The goal of the study is to eventually
gain enough information to create a completely harmonious universe, or
state of being, in which "life must reach such a level of both spiritual
self-awareness and technological capability that it can actively transform
everything around it" (430). Nicole is reunited with her older daughter's
family and is offered life-saving organ transplants, but she declines the
offer. Instead, she asks that all medication be suspended and that she be
allowed to spend her last hours of life in the "Knowledge Module," the
part of the Node that contains all the knowledge gathered in this part
of the galaxy. Her request is granted, and the book ends with her death.

Certain elements of the Rama series are similar to Clarke's other
works, especially the first three Odyssey novels (*2001*, *2010*, and *2061*),
which he had completed before beginning the collaboration. The necessity for humans to continue growing and learning, both individually and
as a species, and the grandeur of the physical universe are important
themes in Clarke's fiction. The Rama series also embodies Clarke's Third
Law regarding advanced technology: "Any sufficiently advanced technology is indistinguishable from magic." The technologies of the Rama
ship and the Node are so advanced that they seem like magic to humans,
a few of whom do manage to learn a limited amount, but none of whom
can understand the technology sufficiently to reproduce it.

But there are some striking differences in character development and
tone between the series and Clarke's solo novels. These differences reveal
the important role played by a collaborator. I do not mean to say that
Lee is solely responsible for these elements. Many writers who collabo-
rate have noted the ways in which working with another writer will
spark new possibilities through the combination of effort that is collaboration. Some of the more intriguing differences are the larger role given
female characters, more graphic descriptions of sexual interaction between men and women, more description of and focus on childhood

experiences of major characters, more importance given to religious backgrounds and beliefs, and a less optimistic tone about the possibilities of human evolution and development, both spiritual and technological.

PLOT DEVELOPMENT

The plot of *Rendezvous with Rama* is constructed around the necessity of exploring the first alien spacecraft that has ever entered the solar system. The novel opens with the description of a tragedy that took place in 2077 when a meteorite hit northern Italy, killing one hundred thousand people. One result of this tragedy was to unify humanity in committing global resources to avert future tragedies. Project Spaceguard— a system of radars, orbiting telescopes, and computers—was developed to track asteroids—so that preventive action could be taken against future meteorites.

By 2130 Project Spaceguard has become routine, until the first radar sighting of an object outside the orbit of Jupiter. The object is thought to be an asteroid, but its unusual characteristics, including its speed and projected orbit, alert the system. Rather than entering an elliptical orbit around the Sun, the object seems to be heading toward the Sun in a hyperbolic orbit, like a comet. "Rama," as it is named, becomes a puzzle that must be solved. The ability of humanity to solve the problem, based on their spacefaring capability, is an important element that is developed in the later series because only spacefaring species interest the Ramans.

First, an unmanned probe is sent to photograph Rama, proving that it is not an asteroid or other natural object. A great deal of debate takes place over what the proper response should be: exploration, fear, or avoidance. Eventually, a ship, *Endeavour*, is pulled from a routine mission, fueled up, and sent to make contact with Rama. A committee, the Rama Committee, is soon established to advise the crew.

The decision to send the probe, and then a ship, is not automatic, however. A bureaucratic group, the Space Advisory Council, must decide whether to allocate the funding for the probe. The Council has a number of scientists as members, and there is conflict between the "modified steady state" theorists and the "big bang" theorists. The conflict between the two groups of scientists is related to the theories about the origins of the universe each group espouses. The "steady state" theory hypothesizes that the universe was not created by a single event and that it is limitless and expanding. The "big bang" theory hypothesizes that a single event (the "bang") marked the creation of the universe and that the universe will expand and then collapse again. The chair of the committee, belonging to the "big bang" school, is described as prejudiced against spending money on sending actual instruments into space, but three "steady state" proponents vote against him.

The Council, Rama Committee, and the colonists on Mercury (called Hermians) provide some conflict, but the major antagonist, the force opposed to the exploration of Rama, is the time limit imposed on the mission by the physics of orbital mechanics and fuel. Rama will be accessible for approximately three weeks before it comes so close to the Sun that humans could not survive. *Endeavour* is chosen to make contact because it is the only ship able to rendezvous with Rama in time.

Commander Norton, the captain of *Endeavour*, orchestrates a slow and cautious approach and entrance to Rama. When the first team enters, they find a dark, completely lifeless world. There are huge stairways and ramps, reminding Norton of an Aztec temple, except that everything looks new and unused. There are "cities," or groups of buildings, including one christened "New York," which is located on the island in the Cylindrical Sea. Everything tends to be built in patterns of threes: three stairways, three ramps, the biots built on a pattern of threefold symmetry (three or nine appendages), and so on. Yet the world is not completely dead. When the first team reaches the bottom of the stairway and they are standing on the cylinder, they discover that there is enough oxygen that they can breathe without their protective gear.

Changes begin to occur inside Rama as it approaches the Sun. Huge "trenches" in the cylinder that had mystified the crew turn out to be immense, artificial light sources. The temperature rises; the ice in the Cylindrical Sea breaks up, and winds begin to blow. The crew withdraw to their ship for forty-eight hours. When they return, they find clouds, in the shape of a perfect tube in the center of the ship, and a waterfall stirring up the sea, where the water has turned green. Rama goes from an anaerobic stage (not enough oxygen to sustain life) to photosynthesis in two of the crew's days.

The crew's explorations, and their reports to the Rama Committee, lead to more questions and debate. No trace of the "Ramans," or of any crew, either in some form of stasis or living, can be found. Some humans argue that the ship could house a form of life similar to a termite colony, with the specialized biological machines serving a queen. Other humans argue that the interstellar distances are too great to send crews on ships, and that the machines on Rama are simply following a ship's program.

Alternately, Rama could be a generation ship, instead of a ship meant to arrive somewhere in one crew's lifetime. The debate about whether Rama's purpose is hostile or benign continues during the crew's stay.

The human crew try to explore parts of Rama that seem inaccessible. They build a small raft to take them to the island in the Cylindrical Sea, and one member (Jimmy Pak) crosses the sea on a sky-bike to explore the southern hemisphere and even reaches the South Pole. When a sudden discharge of energy from a formation they call the "Horns" destroys the bike, Pak has to crash-land and is nearly trapped on the Southern Hemisphere.

The physical challenges of Rama are not the only ones they must face. Near the end of their stay, a coded message from Spaceguard informs them that a clandestine launch of what is probably a missile has been made by the Hermians. One of the crew proposes disarming the bomb. It is fitted with cameras that will send pictures to Mercury, but because it takes ten minutes for transmissions to travel between Rama and Mercury, the bomb can be disarmed before the first signals arrive and the Hermians respond.

Commander Norton must make the decision whether to carry out the plan. If Rama presents a threat to humanity, then it would be able to carry it out without any hindrance. But if no threat is intended, the fact that the ship is blown up after entering the solar system could become a "cosmic crime" for which humanity will be held responsible. Norton decides to disarm the bomb. Rama eventually leaves the solar system without any activity—hostile or friendly—directed at Earth or humans. Although a great deal of knowledge has been gained from contact with Rama, the knowledge (compared to how much could have been learned) is slight and provides no clear answers. Humanity is left with many questions and the sense that they are insignificant because they are no longer the most technologically superior species alive.

STRUCTURE

The novel is structured to follow plot events in two locations. At the beginning, the major focus is located on Earth or the Moon, but as the plot develops, the major focus shifts to the spaceship *Endeavour* as it docks with Rama, explores the spacecraft, and then leaves to return to Earth. The Earth chapters cover what happens when Rama is sighted, when the Rama Committee is formed, and when the United Planets General Assembly meets. The space chapters cover *Endeavour*'s trip to Rama, the exploration of the ship, the disarming of a bomb, and the start of the human crew's return to Earth. The novel does not end with a return to Earth but with the crew still in space, anticipating a return several months later, and the departure of Rama.

During the first quarter of the novel (Chapters 1–10), the narrative shifts back and forth between the two locations regularly, with Chapters 1–3, 6, and 9 relating plot events on Earth or the Moon, and Chapters 4, 5, 7, and 8 relating events on *Endeavour* and Rama. In the next quarter of the novel (Chapters 11–20), there are still some chapters focussing on events on Earth (14, 16, 19), but the majority of chapters focus on the exploration of Rama. In the last half of the novel, there are only two chapters set on Earth or the Moon, but the events described are vital to the resolution of the novel. The chapters focus on the discussion of whether Ramans exist on the ship, and the Hermian Ambassador's announcement of the missile they have launched to dispose of the perceived threat. The majority of the chapters in the last half of the novel are focussed on the exploration, and the crew who are exploring come to very different conclusions regarding Rama than do the politicians, and some of the scientists, on Earth.

The increasing importance of chapters set on Rama and describing the exploration supports the novel's, and the later series', focus on the importance of exploration to gain knowledge. These chapters convey the sense of how small humans, and what they know, are compared to the universe, and the philosophy of accepting the possibility of alien life without assuming hostile intent. Both the crew and the scientists are dedicated to understanding and exploring Rama, so the events described in different locations are closely related, as are the two groups of characters.

The structure of the novel shows the developing conflict between the beliefs of the crew and the scientists and the beliefs of some Terrans and the Hermian colonists. The crew and scientists do not assume that the ship could be a hostile force, which is the assumption or fear of some Terrans and the Hermians. The Hermians' fears lead them to the attempt to blow up Rama, but the decision to disarm the bomb and the resulting failure of Rama to make any hostile act support the crew and the scientists. The crew and scientists believe that either such an advanced species would be too intelligent to be hostile, or, if they are hostile, their technology is so far advanced that humans could do nothing against it anyway. This view is developed in the series as well, especially in *Rama*

II when the politicians on Earth secretly arm the exploratory mission with nuclear bombs, as well as launch missiles from Earth when one of the military commanders refuses to use his code to arm the bombs.

NARRATIVE POINT OF VIEW

Clarke tends to use the third person narrative point of view in the majority of his novels—as do many science fiction writers. Third person narrators are narrative voices that exist outside the story. These narrators are omniscient, knowing and able to report on any character's thoughts, actions, and speech. The omniscient narrator can relate events through perspectives of any character or several characters within the book or can speak directly to readers. A narrative voice that addresses readers directly is called an "intrusive narrator" and makes no secret of knowing more than the characters in the novel and sharing that information with readers. But a third-person narrator can also withhold information, choosing not to reveal it until later.

Rama is told from the third person narrative point of view, working through the points of view of a large and varied number of characters in different locations. Most of the point-of-view characters are members of the *Endeavour* crew who are exploring Rama. Several scientists on the Rama Committee are also point-of-view characters, although not to the same extent as the *Endeavour* crew. There is also an intrusive narrator in several chapters who provides background information on the origins and development of the tracking system that made it possible to first spot Rama. But this intrusive narrator chooses not to give any information about Rama, or its originators, limiting itself to information about human history and technology so that readers share the perspective of the human explorers of Rama. Clarke, as the author, could have chosen to provide further information about the Ramans through the intrusive narrator. His decision not to do so indicates that the mystery of Rama is of great importance and places the reader in the position of exploring the ship along with the crew.

CHARACTER DEVELOPMENT

Because a large number of characters existing in two different locations are point-of-view characters (see above), the necessity to switch perspectives regularly as the plot develops leads to less attention paid to the development of individual characters. One result of this lack of character development in *Rama* is that characters at times verge on stereotypes. One example of stereotyping is in the presentation of the elderly scientists (male and female) who make up the various committees. Clarke often presents comic stereotypes of scientists, bureaucrats, and politicians. These characters are not presented as negative stereotypes, and the narrative tone used in describing them is, for the most part, gently humorous, especially in detailing the "feuds" between different scientific disciplines. Another result of the varying points of view and lack of individual character development is that the reader's attention is focussed more on the exploration of Rama as a collaborative project and on the mystery of Rama itself. Clarke obviously does not intend any individual character to become the major focus in this novel, unless it is Rama.

Overall, character development is based more upon the presentation of groups rather than individuals. The *Endeavour* crew is the most well developed group of characters, with the most narrative time spent on different individuals. The scientists on the Rama Committee play an important role in interpreting data and advising the crew, but they are described as a group rather than as individuals, with the exception of Dr. Perera. The opposing forces the crew face for most of the novel are the time and physical limitations, but the Hermians are presented as another opposing force. Little narrative time or attention is spent on them, and their concern is dismissed as similar to other crackpot groups on Earth and the colonies who are unable to deal rationally with the implications of Rama. Their attempt to blow up the ship is easily countered and dismissed, and the lack of character development given the Hermians supports the idea that their opposition is not of great importance. The individual character given the most attention is Rama itself. The ship is personified, that is, given the aspects of a human character such as a name and a perceived personality.

The Endeavour Crew

In this novel, the plot structure and time limitations dictate the fact that there is no time for Earth to plan an approach and select a special crew. *Endeavour* is selected because of proximity. This crew, and the captain, are not presented as a specially selected and trained group, but as a group doing a routine, if occasionally dangerous, job. Work in space has become a routine job, rather than an elite mission for a few, often military, men by this time. The crew maintains military sounding ranks, and there is a hierarchy of command that includes a bureaucracy on Earth, but there is no sense of a military elite controlling the Solar Survey.

Commander Norton is not a protagonist, in the sense of a single individual whose life and development is the major focus of the novel, although he is a major character who acts as the point-of-view character in the majority of the chapters. Neither is he presented as an epic hero who is the major force for change in the story or as the solitary explorer. Instead, Norton is presented as a career officer, a mature and cautious man, well aware of the rules and regulations he works under and not anxious to break them. He is happily married to two wives, one on Earth, the other on Mars, and supports two families, a common choice for people who have careers in space. His recordings (video letters) to his families are reproduced in several chapters as he discusses the situation with them.

His approach to the exploration is a cautious one, involving his crew in the decision-making process. He chooses people with the right experience to explore various parts of Rama, such as finding a lower-ranking crew member who has sailing experience to oversee the building of the raft. At the end of the novel, Norton must decide whether or not to allow the Hermian missile to destroy Rama, taking the chance that Rama might eventually destroy Earth. Norton finally decides that the "human race has to live with its conscience. Whatever the Hermians argue, survival is not everything" (208). Norton does not choose to make a preemptive strike, and that choice is validated by later events. That moment of decision shows the heroic stature of an "ordinary man" who places philosophical values above physical survival.

There are several crew members who are singled out for individual development as characters who shape the plot of the novel. The first is Jimmy Pak, the youngest officer, who volunteers to cross the Cylindrical Sea on a sky-bike and explore the Southern Hemisphere. The second is Lieutenant Boris Roderigo who proposes and then carries out the plan to disarm the Hermian missile. Both of these characters volunteer to undertake hazardous actions, but they do so from entirely different motives.

Jimmy Pak begins by having to admit to Norton that he has broken regulations by bringing along a sky-bike. Because the bike offers the only opportunity to explore the Southern Hemisphere, Norton is prepared to forgive the smuggling, which is grounds for a court-martial, if Pak succeeds. Five chapters are devoted to the exploration of the Southern Hemisphere and the "Horns." The Horns are large mysterious structures at the southern end of the cylinder, which turn out to be part of some sort of propulsion system. Pak is an athlete who has competed in the Lunar Olympics, as well as being young enough to believe that he cannot die. He is the one crew member who is obviously in danger of death when he crashes and travels on foot back to the cliff overlooking the Cylindrical Sea. Pak discovers what could be fields and one possible plant form, a flower, which is the only Raman specimen they bring back to Earth. The chapters that describe his trip are the one example in this novel of the solitary explorer, risking his life for knowledge.

Boris Roderigo takes a greater chance with his life than do the other crew members when he volunteers to carry out his plan to disarm the Hermian bomb. He volunteers not because of youth and a sense of adventure but because of his religious conviction. He is the only character among the crew who is described has having a specific religious affiliation. He is first introduced in Chapter 12 when he is part of the second team to enter Rama. He is identified as a member of the Fifth Church of Christ, Cosmonaut. The basic foundation of this church's faith is that Jesus Christ came to Earth from space. The narrator informs readers that a large number of this church's members work in space, and describes them as: "efficient, conscientious, and absolutely reliable. They were universally respected, and even liked, especially since they made no attempt to convert others" (58). Despite these admirable qualities, Commander Norton (and presumably other coworkers) finds the Church members strange and cannot see how anyone with "advanced scientific and technical training could possibly believe some of the things he had heard Cosmo Christers state as incontrovertible fact" (58). Roderigo tells Norton that he sees Rama as representing the good, or holy, and the Hermians as representing evil in the eternal battle between good and evil, and so he is willing to take the chance of dying to disarm the missile.

These events, focussing on individuals, stand out because the narrative spends much more time describing the exploration as a collaborative project depending on the efforts of a large number of people. This collaboration is the major focus of the story and is presented as an adventure of the highest kind although it may not at first be seen as dramatic as the adventures encountered by individuals.

The Rama Committee

The Rama Committee tends to play their part in the novel as a group rather than as individuals. The committee is made up of a number of scientists and politicians who study the data gathered from Rama, analyze it, and also offer advice to the crew. Among this group, the scientists play a greater part than the politicians. Astrophysicists, astronomers, geologists, meteorologists, biologists, archeologists, anthropologists, and even historians are among the committee members. Little information is given about this group's personal lives: They appear only in professional and public meetings, debating the information from Rama. The one exception to this is Dr. Perera, who is the character who twice offers advice that saves the crew, first from the winds caused by the melting of the sea, and second when Jimmy Pak is stranded on the cliff.

Hermians

The only Hermian character in the novel is the Ambassador from Mercury who stands in for his entire culture. He begins to question the motivations of Rama, or the Ramans, early in the narrative. In Chapter 19 the Ambassador first raises the concerns of Mercury that Rama will not move outside the solar system but will take up an orbit around the Sun, closer to the Sun than Mercury. Later, in Chapter 38, the Ambassador announces that Mercury has sent a nuclear missile to destroy Rama because of its perceived threat to humanity.

The only other information about the Hermians is given by the narrator, who tells readers that the colonists on Mercury are settling what is nearly the most uninhabitable planet in the solar system, "with its days longer than its years, its double sunrises and sunsets, its rivers of molten metal" (98). The psychology of the Hermians is explained in Chapter 37:

> Psychologists had claimed that it was almost impossible to understand fully the mentality of anyone born and bred on Mercury. Forever exiled from Earth by its three-times-more-powerful gravity, Hermians could stand on the Moon and look across the narrow gap to the planet of their ancestors,

even of their own parents, but they could never visit it. And
so, inevitably, they claimed that they did not want to. (197)

The Hermians may be respected, but they are not trusted, and when
they do take action against Rama, their reasons are incomprehensible to
some of the other characters. The Hermians are presented as a stereotype,
a group image that implies that all Hermians share the same psychology
and perspectives on issues. Because there is only one individual character
who is a Hermian, it is not possible to see the differences that must exist.
They are presented as a group who, without fully understanding what
they are attempting to destroy, are willing to cause its destruction for
the sake of their own preservation, which has not been threatened by
Rama.

The Personification of Rama

Rama is personified by being given a name and through the perceptions of the humans who are exploring it. Just as humans have often
personified the planet on which we live as "Mother Earth," Rama becomes a personality, a character within the novel, as well as the mystery
that drives the plot of the story. The long and careful descriptions of this
artificial world show a place that is totally alien to humans. Trying to
"see" the world inside the cylinder means a constant shifting of perceptions of distance, and relative "up" and "down," which people living
on a planet take for granted as never changing. The reader is asked to
visualize standing on the inside of a huge, hollow cylinder where the
horizon curves up overhead, and where a sea circles that horizon. The
changes that take place as Rama comes to life, especially the start of
photosynthesis and the movements of the biots, also support the notion
of Rama as a living being. Finally, the course that slingshots Rama safely
around the Sun and establishes a new orbit contributes to the sense of
an incredibly advanced technology that is "ignoring" Earth in pursuit of
more interesting goals.

THEMES

The important themes include exploration as a means of gaining and
valuing knowledge and the philosophical questions raised by the rela-

tionship between humans and intelligent life on other planets. (A discussion of other works with similar thematic elements can be found in Chapter 2.) Humanity's development and expansion is directly linked with space exploration. Space exploration is important not only to gain material resources but to gain knowledge about the universe. Moving into space raises the question of whether or not humanity is a cosmic accident, the only intelligent species to develop a technology of spaceflight, or whether there are others (dozens, hundreds, perhaps thousands) of other species who have done the same thing. If there are other spacefaring species, what relationship will we have with them, or can we have any, given the limits placed upon space travel by the speed of light?

The universe can be dangerous, but Rama is an unknown factor. One possible response to the unknown is destruction, but there are other possible responses. Some humans would destroy what they cannot understand or control, but the novel presents what Clarke seems to be saying is a more civilized, in the best sense of the word, response: the desire to learn more about the unknown. Although Norton feels a sense of failure and insignificance at the end of the book, a great deal has been learned compared to what was known before. Acquisition of knowledge opens up the possibility of gaining further knowledge. But not everyone sees the visit as an opportunity to gain knowledge.

Some humans in this book fear exploitation by a species with superior technology, perhaps because this pattern existed throughout much of human history when one culture with superior technology would oppress another culture. But in fact the mysterious object has no such intention and shows no interest in humanity or desire to make contact. Even though no actual contact is made with an alien species, the novel makes it clear that humans will forever after have a different view of the universe and their place in it. They are no longer at the top of the evolutionary ladder, as they have long perceived themselves to be. The question of whether or not there are other intelligent species is settled, and that fact that this species is far advanced technologically over what humans have been able to achieve also proves that humans are not the only species involved in space exploration.

ALTERNATE READING: FEMINIST CRITICISM

Feminist scholars locate the origins of American feminist literary criticism with the 1970 publication of Kate Millett's book, *Sexual Politics*, which analyzed negative stereotypes of "women" in literature by important male writers. Feminist literary criticism is not simply an isolated academic theory because it is connected to the activism and philosophy of the feminist movement, a social movement dedicated to gaining equal rights for women. The contemporary American feminist movement can be traced to the publication of Betty Friedan's *The Feminine Mystique* in 1963 and to the organization of the women's rights groups in the 1960s. These sixties women's groups, including the National Organization for Women (NOW) and many others, borrowed strategies for protest from the Civil Rights Movement. There is a history of feminist movement in this country, with the debate over the rights of women having historical connections to the movement to abolish slavery, the campaign for women's right to vote, and the Temperance and women's club movements. The similarities and differences between the oppression of women and the oppression of slaves in this nation have been debated for years.

Although there is probably no single feminist goal that all feminists would agree is the most important, one common philosophy shared by different feminists is that the oppression of women must be opposed by a variety of different projects and strategies. Feminist literary criticism can be understood as one project that involves various scholarly works that analyze the way issues of power and gender intersect with ideas about literature. One project is the analysis of sexist images of "women" in works by male writers; another is archival research for writing produced by women that might not have met the standards of literature, such as diaries, letters, and journals. Other feminist scholars work on reclaiming lost works by women, published work that has gone out of print or has been ignored (or both) for years, or focus on popular culture. Popular culture includes analysis of film, television, popular novels, advertising, and other areas in which the constructions of women and gender are considered in relation to power.

Debates by literary scholars in recent years have expanded the scope of feminist criticism. In the early eighties came books by scholars who were women of color. These writers pointed out the exclusion of literature by African American, Native American, and Hispanic women and made the issues of class and race a part of feminist scholarship. Then in the late eighties and early nineties came work by male scholars asking what it means to be a woman reader (or a feminist reader), if a feminist reader must always be a woman, and could a male become a feminist reader.

Even though much important feminist literary criticism focusses on work by women writers, feminist literary criticism does not have to be limited only to reading women writers. One method of feminist critical reading is based on analyzing the gender constructions that exist in the text. This method does not simply ask whether any single male or female character is realistically portrayed. Trying to determine whether any character in a book is an "accurate" representation of a gender, race, or class is impossible. Characters in books are linguistic constructs, patterns of words. Literature tries to represent aspects of reality by presenting imaginary characters in such a way that readers are persuaded to enter into a secondary, or created, reality and to believe, for a while, in the apparent reality of those characters.

One aspect of characterization is gender, with that understanding the "gender" is defined by feminists to mean the way a society defines the roles assigned to the different sexes. The biological fact is that only females can bear offspring, but the fact that care of those offspring is assigned to women is a social choice, not a biological imperative. Analysis of gender relations in a text is one possible focus, especially in texts describing a future, changed society that is assumed to be better than the present.

As discussed in Chapter 2, Clarke works primarily in a genre that was once called "hard science fiction." The majority of science fiction was written mostly by white men, a situation that did not change until the 1960s and 1970s. Science fiction is a genre based on the assumptions that the future will be better than the present and that technological development will be a primary cause of improvement. The writers in this genre often postulate amazing technological changes, and it is possible to ask what social changes will accompany the technological changes. Feminist critics of science fiction who ask that question have shown that the social assumptions and gender roles in a good deal of science fiction are described as unchanged and are similar to the traditional beliefs of earlier ages. Feminist critics like Joanna Russ have analyzed the tendency of the mostly male writers to exclude women almost entirely from the novels or to give them extremely limited roles as daughters or girlfriends of the male characters.

Developing a feminist reading of Clarke's novels is an interesting project for several reasons. One reason is that although Clarke rarely makes female characters protagonists, or major point-of-view characters, he tends to include women in a wider variety of roles than much science fiction, especially in his recent work. Another reason is that the cultures in many of his novels are described as ones in which personal and pro-

fessional equality is a right granted all human beings. Finally, many of
his male characters do not conform to the cultural expectations associated with traditional masculinity, or even to conventions established for
science fiction heroes. These males tend to be much more intellectual,
analytical, or pacifist than are many of the protagonists of science fiction
novels written by other writers of Clarke's generation.

Women were completely excluded from the space program during its
first decades, and even a television show like *Star Trek* had trouble per-
suading viewers to take women as crew members or officers on a spaceship seriously. Many novels and films tended to present space as a
domain for men only, and for years the readership of science fiction was
believed to be adolescent males. The fact that much science fiction, especially television and films, focusses on military subjects to a great extent may be a contributing factor to the exclusion of women.

At first glance, *Rendezvous with Rama* does not exclude women. The
exploration of Rama is done by a mixed crew of men and women who
work in space for long periods of time. There are indications that women
have gained professional equality on Earth and in space. Women serve
on the Rama Committee and on the *Endeavour*. The two most important
female characters on the crew are Surgeon Commander Laura Ernst and
Sergeant Ruby Barnes. The Surgeon plays a major role in the command
decision of assembling exploration teams and schedules, and she can
override the captain if she believes it necessary. The Sergeant is an experienced sailor and is appointed to be in charge of their trips on the
Cylindrical Sea. She is captain on the boat they build, even when Commander Norton is aboard. However, neither woman is a point-of-view
character, and few of the other women mentioned are developed as important characters. So the equality of women is described more than
shown through the women character's own thoughts, taken for granted
but not explained in depth.

The customs and taboos surrounding marriage and families have also
changed. Information about family relationships and sexual customs is
provided by Commander Norton as he writes to his two families. Multiple marriages and extramarital sex are both legal and accepted. A man
can have two wives; a woman can have two husbands. The major taboos
and social regulations concern the number of children born on Earth,
which strictly regulates its population. The colonies are not as strict. The
regulations concerning relationships on the spaceship forbid sex between
people who are more than two degrees in rank apart; otherwise, sexual
interaction among crewmates is not discouraged.

This background information hints at equality between men and women both professionally and personally. How has this equality come about? The narrative does not specifically answer that question. But one chapter hints at a possible reason. Chapter 11 stands out among all the others for two reasons. The first reason is the questions raised by the depiction of "men," "women," and "monkeys" in the chapter, and their relative power relationships. The second reason is that the events in this chapter do not advance the exploration of the spaceship, and a group of characters introduced here are not developed any further. This lack of connection to the major plot elements is a break, or a gap, in the text, revealing an area of analysis that can lead to consideration of this future culture's assumptions about gender and power.

The chapter starts with a sexual meditation, then describes a brief conversation about crew assignments, then shifts to a lengthy discussion of "superchimps," the genetically engineered monkeys that do all the routine housekeeping and maintenance chores on spaceships. The sexual meditation is almost offhand, resulting in no change in a character or events. Commander Norton is described as believing that "Some women . . . should not be allowed aboard ship; weightlessness did things to their breasts that were too damn distracting. It was bad enough when they were motionless; but when they started to move, and sympathetic vibrations set in, it was more than any warm-blooded male should be asked to take" (49).

Norton is sure that an "upholstered lady officer" caused at least one space accident.

It seems fairly obvious this idea cannot be taken seriously. If men were routinely prone to crashing vehicles whenever a woman with large breasts walks, or floats, by, there would probably be many more crashes than is the case. The reduction of women to sex objects has been made an excuse for denying women jobs, and to that extent, the offhand commentary is not humorous in any fashion. Norton's meditation is initiated by the entrance of the ship's surgeon, Laura Ernst, to discuss crew fitness and schedules. The personnel decision is made quickly and does not lead to any further plot development. It is also clear that the two have had an affair in the past that has not affected their professional relationship.

The primary purpose of this chapter is not the relations between men and women but the introduction of the simps. Almost half of this chapter is devoted to an explanation of their nature and responsibilities on board the ship. Because the simps are left on board the ship to do routine chores while the humans explore Rama, they play no major part in the story and are not seen again. The lack of development raises the question of why they were introduced at all. A close reading of the information given about the simps leads to one possible answer to that question.

There are four simps on *Endeavour*: Blackie, Blondie, Goldie, and Brownie. Their names are similar to those humans give a variety of pet animals. A simp weighs and consumes less than a human does, and the corporation that sells them advertises that they can replace "2.75 men for *housekeeping, elementary cooking*, tool-carrying, and *dozens* of other routine jobs." The simps are described as workers who were "quite happy to work *fifteen hours a day* and did not get bored by the *most menial and repetitious* tasks. So they freed human beings for *human* work" (53, italics added). Additionally, the simps are clones, sexless vegetarians who have IQs of 60. They have their own language, which is a sign language, and they can understand English. The one problem of simps in space is that the human crew becomes attached to them, but they cannot be trained to use spacesuits in emergencies. The policy in an emergency that requires abandoning ship is to euthanize the simps.

What Clarke is describing is a created race who are the perfect housekeepers. They can work longer and harder than humans, but they do not nag anybody and are not likely to demand anything. The work the simps are responsible for on board is the same work that has been assigned to women by many cultures: cleaning, cooking, and routine repetitive jobs. This work requires relatively little training and tends to be extremely boring. Yet this work also includes some tasks that are vitally important to the survival of any family or group of people. Presumably, the need for those chores on a spaceship is not simply cosmetic because of the money and effort that must have gone into developing simps who are, apparently, sold in a free market.

In many cultures, both historically and currently, slave populations that include males and females have been maintained to do the same sort of work. Over the years, technology has led to more machines developed for some kinds of routine work, but only recently have machines capable of doing the work *on their own* (that is, robots) been developed for household, as opposed to factory, use. Some science fiction postulates a future in which robots will be invented to do all the boring and routine work, freeing all humans for other activities that are more pleasant or profitable. Clarke's other novels usually feature such robots, if the question of housework comes up at all.

The distinction between the work the simps do and *human* work is similar to the division of labor into "men's" and "women's" work, a division that existed as recently as the 1960s when job advertisements in newspapers were divided in this fashion. Even some feminist theory has neglected to explore the ramifications of the demand for women to have equal access to education and professional jobs while continuing to marry and raise families. As African-American feminists have pointed out, many white women who work outside the home hire them to do the boring, routine, and menial jobs of housework, cooking, and child care. The issue is not so much whether the work should be done or not, but whether certain groups are forced into routine, low-paying jobs by the lack of education or other institutionalized discrimination.

How many readers, focussing entirely on the exploration that is taking place inside Rama, will stop to wonder how routine work is performed on *Endeavour*? The questions this chapter raises, when considered against the rest of the novel, concern the issues of invisibility, power, and choice in relation to gender. The characters responsible for important mainte- nance of the ship are even more invisible than the women who have moved into professional jobs in this novel. The existence of the simps hints that equality for women may not have been gained because it is a right but because something more convenient came along to replace them.

The existence of the simps is related not only to questions about gen- der and power but also to the ethical questions associated with genetic engineering that are being debated today. In the not-so-distant future, as this novel shows, science may have the technology to create a slave pop- ulation, such as the simps, that will do mindless, no-paying work with- out a demand for equal rights. Perhaps this population will come from another branch on the primate family tree. But, technologically speaking, it would prove equally possible to genetically engineer humans to per- form the same sort of tasks. Without careful considerations of how work is organized and rewarded, of how existing technologies are used, future oppression of this group will go unquestioned. Because one fear this novel deals with is the fear of a "superior" species exploiting humanity, the question of what species humanity is exploiting becomes an impor- tant one, and one that a feminist reading will focus on.

Imperial Earth
(1976)

Imperial Earth contains one of Arthur C. Clarke's strongest statements on the necessity for human beings to keep developing—personally, culturally, and technologically—to avoid the risk of stagnation. The novel is set in 2276, a future in which Earth has successfully colonized the Moon, Mars, and Mercury. The frontier, the colony that exists furthest out and has been settled the least amount of time, is located on Titan, Saturn's largest moon. The colonies, rather than being controlled by national governments on Earth, are developed by corporations and exist as sovereign states. Earth maintains a symbolic rather than an actual imperial power as the originating planet.

The novel follows the life of a native of Titan: Duncan Makenzie. He makes a trip to Earth in pursuit of both political and personal goals. His reasons for traveling to Earth involve technology. Titan will soon face the problem of its major industry becoming obsolete because of new technology. In addition, Duncan is taking advantage of the trip to Earth to have himself cloned. He is the clone of his "father," Colin, who is the clone of Malcolm Makenzie, the founder of the clan. Duncan does not achieve his goals as planned. Conflicts with people from his past appear to deflect him from his original goals. But by the end of the novel, what appeared to deflect him becomes the means by which he achieves his original goals, and he has learned more than he had anticipated about himself, his family, and Titan and Terran cultures.

This chapter will examine five aspects of *Imperial Earth*:

1. The plot development brings together the public and private aspects of Duncan's life.
2. The narrative point of view works almost entirely through Duncan, establishing him as the protagonist of the story.
3. Other characters in the novel are developed primarily in relation to Duncan.
4. Several key images in the novel are linked to fractals.
5. The major themes.

The chapter concludes by introducing gender theory and criticism and presenting an example of a gender reading of the book.

PLOT DEVELOPMENT

The narrative is structured around two plot lines, the first involving the political aspect of Duncan's life and the second involving his personal life. The plots become intertwined as events on his trip to Earth bring these two aspects of his life together. The journey to Earth is regarded as necessary for anyone involved in a colonial government for several reasons. The first reason is that the trip, and knowledge of Terran cultures, is the sign of membership in an elite group. The second is that making contact with individuals in positions of power on Earth helps create better communication in the future. Because instantaneous face-to-face communication can take place only on a planet, not across space, personal interaction is believed to create better communication between leaders.

Most of Duncan's goals for his trip to Earth are related to his political life. He is invited to Earth to make a speech at the Quincentennial Celebration of the Declaration of Independence (2276) because of his political office. The Makenzies rule Titan as President (Malcolm), Chief Administrator (Colin), and Assistant Chief Administrator (Duncan). Duncan also has a secret mission to learn more about the new drive for spaceships developed by an Earth company. This new technology will change the economic and power relationship between Titan and Earth.

At the beginning of the novel, Duncan plans to go to Earth, make contacts, deliver his speech, and accomplish his personal goal of bringing back a clone-son to continue his family's dynasty. Then he expects to return to Titan and continue his life as before. This straightforward series of events is quickly complicated by the problems that Duncan finds when he arrives on Earth.

These problems shift his focus from his political goals to personal issues. He is frustrated when he must spend a large part of his time unraveling mysteries related to people he knew well in the past. These mysteries include the unlicensed offer of Titanite—a rare, controlled element found only on Titan—for sale to an Earth jeweler. There is also the equally unauthorized and surprising presence of his old friend Karl Helmer on Earth. Duncan's efforts to solve these mysteries lead him into contact and conflict with two people he has not seen in years: Karl and Calindy (Catherine Linden Ellerman).

Duncan's earlier relationship with Karl Helmer is an example of how closely intertwined Duncan's political and personal lives are. His relationship with Karl began when they were children and included sexual intimacy when they were adolescents. Later, they were estranged, especially when Karl's father was elected to a political office and began challenging the Makenzie dominance on Titan. At the time Duncan visits Earth, they have not spoken in over ten years. On Earth, Duncan must deal with Karl's appearance as a political problem, not a personal one. Duncan discovers that Karl is responsible for bringing the unlicensed Titanite to Earth. Duncan's personal knowledge of Karl, gained during their years of friendship, is what allows him to solve the political problems that Karl creates.

Duncan fears that the problems will distract him from his main purpose on Earth. But his resolution of his personal problems results in a solution to his political goals. This resolution is not completely positive. Karl is killed in an accident while he and Duncan are speaking for the first time in years. His death reveals an answer to the question of how Titan should shift its economic base in the future to avoid being made obsolete by a new technology in space travel. Karl's work in communications theory becomes the basis for Duncan's speech at the Quincentennial where he proposes a new project for exploring space, which will be based on Titan.

Karl's death also leads Duncan to resolve the requirement of his father and grandfather that he create another clone-son. Duncan changes his mind about his clone-child and continuing the Makenzie line. When

Duncan returns to Titan with a child, the child is a clone of Karl Helmer. The child is the final, living embodiment of the connection between Duncan's political life and his personal life, which he had believed he could keep separate.

The Importance of Technology

Technology is linked to the necessity for continual development and innovation in *Imperial Earth*. Neither Earth nor Titan and the other colonies could exist without major technological developments. The Earth Duncan visits has moved much of its population underground, leaving huge ranges of open country above. Colonization of other planets in the solar system has served as a means of reducing overpopulation and developing more resources. Because most food is processed or synthesized, "agriculture" is practiced only as a hobby by a few enthusiasts. The Midwest is a huge forest, and large cities are relics of the past. The technology for spaceflight is also continually developing. The new space drive, called the A-drive, draws on the energy of a black hole, a "node," rather than hydrogen for its propellent.

The colonies on other planets depend upon a vast amount of technology to survive. Titan is unusual in having an atmosphere. As the intrusive narrator informs readers, it is the only other body than Earth that does, even if the atmosphere is methane. But humans could not live on Titan without extensive reliance on technology, because they must live beneath the surface. Titan's existence is also linked to technology; its main export is hydrogen for use as fuel in spaceships. The political and economic relationship between Titan and Earth, and the political situation on Titan, is affected by the varying levels of technological development.

The political plot of the novel is connected to another kind of technology. The colony was founded on a specific technology for collecting hydrogen developed by Malcolm Makenzie. Malcolm succeeded in founding the colony, but he could not have children because of radiation damage. The first child born to Malcolm and his wife Ellen died young because of his genetic damage. Malcolm deals with the tragedy by visiting Earth and ordering a clone. Even though Malcolm and eventually Colin and Duncan himself marry and adopt their wives' biological children into the Makenzie clan, they limit political power to Malcolm and his clones. Duncan is expected to produce a third-generation clone as his son to continue and consolidate their dynasty. Because cloning is not possible except through technological means, it plays a large part in the political plot of the novel. The technology of cloning, which can be found only on Earth, is accessible only to the extremely wealthy and powerful.

Malcolm's dynastic plans are challenged by other powerful clans on Titan, especially the Helmers (Armand and Karl). Clarke does not spend a large amount of time exploring political and social conflicts on Titan itself. The political conflicts are between peers, almost within the same ruling family, not from a revolutionary movement by the less powerful part of society. The Makenzie rule is not dictatorial or tyrannical. Their power base is linked to the economic success of the colony, not to any military or police force. They must justify their rule to their stockholders rather than to voters. Part of Duncan's mission on his journey to Earth is to consider what Titan can develop to replace its obsolete product so that the Makenzies can remain dominant. He finds the solution, a technological one, through his personal relationship with Karl Helmer.

After Karl's death, Duncan learns that he is the executor of his estate. He also has the notebook Karl was drawing in just before he died. Reading the notebook to try to learn more of Karl's life before his death, Duncan finds a number of sketches, including a drawing of what Duncan assumes is a sea urchin. Duncan interprets the drawing as a sea urchin because he saw one on his visit to the genetic clinic to arrange for his clone-son. As executor, he also is given Karl's "minisec," a powerful, portable computer. Reading through Karl's files, Duncan realizes that the drawing actually is a plan for the ARGUS project, the blueprint for a major technological breakthrough in terms of interstellar communications and contact with alien intelligence. The drawing represents a communications relay system to monitor the lower band radio waves in space. Karl theorized that there may be life-forms in space, which he called "Star Beasts," that communicate by means of such radio waves.

Duncan realizes that this project offers the chance for Titan to develop a monopoly upon an entirely new technology, and his speech at the Quincentennial develops that theme. This new project would involve a different kind of exploration of space, the search for intelligence rather than physical travel by humans. In his speech, he emphasizes that this exploration and technology differ only in scope not spirit from the earlier discoveries associated with previous centennials.

Technology plays a vital role in Duncan's personal life as well as in his political life. Duncan would not exist without the technology of cloning, and his decision to clone Karl, rather than himself, after Karl's death represents several changes in Duncan. The child represents the joining of two important political families on Titan: Duncan's love for Karl and the possibility of further scientific and technological development. Karl's work has always been more creative and theoretical than the Makenzies' more pragmatic applications of theory to create a profit-making technology. The child also represents a change in the dynastic plans of the Makenzies. Cloning as a technology changes the nature of human reproduction from the "mixing" of genes from two humans, allowing for greater flexibility and adaptation, to the reproduction of a single set of genes. The three Makenzies differ to some extent because of the different circumstances of their upbringing and education, but genetically they are identical. By cloning Karl, rather than himself/Malcolm, Duncan uses the technology to bring in another genetic component to the Makenzie dynasty.

NARRATIVE POINT OF VIEW

Imperial Earth is almost entirely told in the third person narrative voice working through the point of view of Duncan, who is the protagonist of the story. (For a discussion of narrative point of view, see Chapter 3.) In this case, the protagonist is also the point-of-view character, the character who perceives the events and whose consciousness readers share. Readers share Duncan's consciousness and his awareness of the change he experiences throughout his visit to Earth. The intrusive narrator provides background information on the Makenzies and scientific information on Titan in a few chapters, but no other character in the book is a point-of-view character. The result of this narrative choice is that readers get to know Duncan as a character in much greater detail than if the point of view shifted among several characters.

CHARACTER DEVELOPMENT

Because Duncan is the protagonist, his character is developed in much greater detail than is the case with other characters. His character is shown developing in several ways: through flashbacks to his childhood; through his visit to Earth and his experience of surviving in a new and different culture, as well as in a new environment; and through his interaction with other characters. Three early chapters describe flashbacks to Duncan's childhood and adolescence. These flashbacks establish important aspects of Duncan's character and motivations that affect the decisions he makes on his journey to Earth and introduce other characters who are major influences on him.

Opening the novel is a description of Duncan's early experience of hearing mysterious sounds on the surface of Titan, a world beyond his reach because children are not allowed to visit the surface. Karl, who is older, teases him about the Hydrosaurus rex, their private joke, and then explains the meaning of the sound. It is a ram-tanker orbiting Titan and collecting hydrogen for export. This chapter establishes key elements of Duncan and Karl's relationship.

Karl is older, more intelligent, and more sophisticated than Duncan. He teases Duncan at first, then provides him with information. Duncan is fascinated by the mystery and possibilities of speculation, but he is also well aware of the pragmatic realities of life. He is aware of his future involvement in the hydrogen economy and the politics of Titan, but he continues to play his recording and dream of Earth when he falls asleep at night for years. Another childhood flashback describes his first experience learning about the mysteries of math, when his Grandmother Ellen gives him a set of pentominoes, a game based on mathematical principles.

When Duncan visits Earth, he is an adult, married, and completely involved in the political system on Titan. His visit to Earth places him in a new environment where his status as an administrator on Titan may not mean very much to the Terrans he encounters. Duncan has to learn how to deal with the Terrans. By the end of the novel, Duncan realizes that he identifies with the future of the colonies and not the past glories of cultures on Earth, but he also learns to appreciate the physical joys of living in a different environment.

Duncan must deal with the issue of how Terrans, and colonials, tend to perceive Terran culture as superior to colonial cultures. Terrans are described as feeling an unconscious superiority based on their history because they are all descended from cultures that were empires in the past and that have maintained that cultural awareness. Because many colonists have moved from Earth to Titan, they tend to share this assumption as well. Duncan, as a third-generation colonist, identifies with Titan rather than with Earth. This identification is shown to be his primary one, outweighing even the fact, as described in Chapter 17, that Duncan is black. This chapter establishes that racial discrimination based upon skin color no longer exists within the United States and has become a matter of historical curiosity. Duncan's indifference to his skin color implies that the historical curiosity or awareness of those differences does not exist on Titan, because he does not even consider what color he is until a Terran brings up the subject in conversation.

George Washington (his real name), one of the organizers of the conference, takes Duncan where two black men in livery meet them at the door. One of the men speaks in "genuine slave patter" because he is a professor of linguistics. Washington tells Duncan: "A couple of centuries ago, if you'd suggested to him that he play one of his humbler ancestors, even in a pageant, he'd have knocked your head off. Now he's having a perfectly wonderful time, and we may not be able to get him back to his classes at Georgetown" (117). Washington himself is a light-skinned black man, and he notes that more and more the races are mixing and that Duncan (because of cloning) has an unfair advantage in maintaining his skin color in his descendants.

Duncan reacts to Washington's comment on skin color "with puzzled incomprehension. He had never given any more thought to his skin color than to that of his hair. . . . Certainly he had never thought of himself as black; but now he realized, with understandable satisfaction, that he was several shades darker than George Washington, descendent of several African kings" (117). Although Clarke does not go into detail about the social and cultural changes that take place over three hundred years, it is possible to deduce that he believes future space colonization will solve not only overpopulation but also oppression based on racism.

Duncan also has problems adjusting to the physical difference of life on Earth; large animals and insects frighten him. Running is hazardous, and he reacts negatively to the idea of food grown in dirt rather than synthesized. He is afraid to go outside because he has lived underneath the surface all his life. But by the end of the novel, he has adjusted to living on the surface. He can enjoy sitting outside and various kinds of weather; he has even gone wading in the ocean, an experience of great terror to anyone raised on Titan!

The other characters in the novel are seen largely through Duncan's perceptions. Their importance exists primarily in their influence on and relation to Duncan. These characters are: Karl Helmer (his best friend); Malcolm and Colin Makenzie (his grandfather and father, his older selves); Grandma Ellen (Malcolm's first wife), and Calindy (Karl and Duncan's Terran love).

Karl, Duncan's childhood friend and apparent antagonist throughout most of the novel, turns out to provide Duncan with the answers he needs for several important problems. Karl is seen mostly in Duncan's memories of him, and only briefly in the course of the novel itself when he is killed during their confrontation. Karl is vitally important to Duncan, and thus to the novel itself. His importance lies not only in the personal relationship he has with Duncan but in his scientific work that Duncan expands upon after his death. Karl is associated with the romance, mystery, and possible danger of space travel, especially that associated with discovering new life-forms. This association is shown in his first appearance in the novel (talking to Duncan about the strange sound) and in the recording he made that Duncan plays after his death. The recording is of a sound "like the slow beating of a giant heart, or the tolling of a bell so huge that a cathedral could be placed inside it, rather than the reverse" (311).

Other characters who are important to Duncan are his older "selves," Colin and Malcolm. One early chapter does summarize Malcolm's success in developing the ram-jet technology and establishing Titan, and then bringing up Colin as his successor and partner. Other than this chapter, little narrative time is given to them, but they are always in Duncan's mind. Because they are "identical twins" in a way, Duncan believes that Colin (and presumably Malcolm) "knew all the mistakes [Duncan was] going to make, because he had made them already. It was impossible to conceal any secrets from him, because his thought processes were virtually the same" (54). Duncan's decision to clone Karl instead of himself becomes the incident that finally separates him from the sense that he is a younger copy of Malcolm and Colin. He gains the stature of an independent man, instead of still being subordinate to his older "selves." The fact that Karl's clone is now Duncan's infant son, reversing their former relationhip in which Karl was the older and dominant partner may have also played a role in Duncan's decision.

The novel presents no description of the Makenzies' wives, other than a listing of their names and children. The important female characters are Grandma Ellen, who divorced Malcolm after their daughter's death, and Calindy, Karl's and Duncan's first love. Neither is married. Ellen lives apart from the family, but Duncan often visits her. She is responsible for encouraging his interest in science and mathematics, and she also provides emotional support. At the end of the novel, when Duncan returns to Titan, she is waiting for him at the spaceport. He realizes that this is her first trip to the colony in fifty years and that she will help him raise his child.

Calindy met Karl and Duncan when she was stranded on Titan with a shipload of wealthy young Terrans. During Duncan's visit to Earth, he discovers the truth behind Karl's estrangement and his obsession with Calindy. The two shared an illicit technology called the "joy machine" while having sex, and this machine burned Karl's brain out, in a sense, resulting in his fixation on the young Calindy. Learning the truth about Karl's problems and making love to Calindy, who is now a mature businesswoman, finally allows Duncan to realize that his own feelings for her were an adolescent fixation. By the end of the novel, Duncan has grown beyond his fixations on the young Karl and the young Calindy and has gained a new sense of the future. When he was a child, he would listen to the recording he made of the mysterious sound and dream of Earth. Having achieved that dream, he now dreams of the space beyond the stars.

IMAGES

The sea urchin that Duncan kills while visiting the genetic clinic and the drawing of ARGUS that he first takes to be a sea urchin are important images. The ways these different images are connected to other images in the novel result in the images working as metaphors. A metaphor is a comparison, taking two objects and attributing characteristics of one of the objects to the other object. The careful attention paid to the description of these images stands out because Clarke's style does not usually feature such overt stylistic devices.

The images are also fractal in nature. A discussion of fractals can be found in Chapter 9. Briefly, fractals are complex patterns in which a smaller part is similar to the larger whole. Seeing the drawing "shift" from the sea urchin to the thousand-kilometer radius of ARGUS leads Duncan to contemplate the relative size of Earth, or humanity compared to the possible "Star Beasts" that Karl theorizes could exist in the dark between the suns. Humanity, in relation to the Star Beasts, would be like the sea urchin in relation to Duncan. The amoeba and the galaxy are different sizes, but their essential "pattern" is the same.

The fractal images associated with language and the patterns of light on water are also metaphorical. The mystery surrounding the name "Argus," which refers to three different mythological characters (Odysseus' watchdog, the builder of Jason's ship *Argo*, and a multiple-eyed God), is a kind of linguistic fractal. Near the end of the novel, Duncan is sitting at the genetic clinic watching a lagoon where "the countless reflections of the sun in the dancing water created sparkling patterns that seemed to move forever down the wind, yet remained always in the same spot" (330). The patterns of light that are continually the same and continually changing are fractals, as is the DNA that is part of the "dance" of life, as Duncan seeks to clone first himself then Karl Helmer.

THEMES

The basic theme of this novel is the journey, the joy of which exists in the traveling rather than the arrival. Journeying is vital to avoid personal or social stagnation. Individuals must travel to other cultures; cultures must expand to other planets. Journeying always involves change and adaptation. A discussion of other works that have the same themes can be found in Chapter 2. The journey in *Imperial Earth* is a literal one, but also a symbolic one, the journey from childhood to adolescence to maturity—which occurs in the life of every individual. This same journey through time occurs in the life of cultures as well.

Duncan's journey from Titan to Earth and back is also the journey from childhood to adulthood. Although he is legally and apparently an adult at the beginning of the novel, he still has to achieve maturity. The chapters that are flashbacks to Duncan's childhood are a means of showing that childhood, but that structure also emphasizes Duncan as a child in relation to Karl, his older clone selves, and to Grandma Ellen and even Calindy. Duncan travels to Earth and attempts to resolve his past with Karl and Calindy; he chooses that his clone son will be Karl rather than himself. These decisions, made on his own without the influence of his family, mark a move into maturity.

These journeys, both the literal and the symbolic ones, are not without risks, of course, and Duncan realizes that when he kills the sea urchin. There are possible dangers out there, but staying home is no guarantee that the monsters will not come. In this novel, the focus of the new journey for humanity that Duncan proposes, based on Karl's theorizing and work, is the area beyond the sun—"the edge of the wilderness between the stars" (317)—where comets are born. The new journey will change Earth—and Titan—as well, just as the colony on Titan, which came originally from Earth, has changed in response to its new environment.

ALTERNATE READING: GENDER CRITICISM

Gender criticism shares certain theoretical assumptions with three other methods of literary criticism: feminist theory, gay and lesbian theory, and psychoanalytic theory. With the exception of psychoanalytic theory, these fields of study have originated and developed during the last thirty years or so. But although there are some common assumptions and vocabulary, there are also differences in focus among the different critical approaches. Feminist theory focusses on issues of gender and power, with the assumption that women are defined primarily by the gender roles that are constructed by a culture. Chapter 3 contains a discussion of feminist theory and criticism. Feminist theory deals with issues associated with gender, so that some scholars use the terms interchangeably, or as a way of discussing overlapping issues. Feminist theory is based on the concept that one gender (female) is oppressed because of gender.

Gay and lesbian theory, which has come to be a distinct field in the last decade or so, also deals with issues of gender and the social constructions of gender. In fact, there has been a great deal of lesbian feminist work done in feminist theory and criticism. But gay and lesbian theory works principally with the assumption that people are defined primarily by their sexuality or sexual identity. Gay and lesbian theory, like feminist theory, has a connection to an activist, political movement. This movement opposes the oppression of homosexuals by a heterosexual dominant culture and has become more prominent in recent years because of the movement toward a more inclusive civil rights since the 1960s and because of the tragedy of AIDS. Both feminist and gay and lesbian theories draw on concepts and vocabulary from psychoanalysis to analyze issues of gender and sexuality.

One of the key concepts that a number of scholars working in feminist studies, gay and lesbian studies, and gender studies share was developed by Michel Foucault, a French philosopher and writer, in *The History of Sexuality*. Simply stated, Foucault argues that sexual identity is not a natural or inherent characteristic. Sexual identity refers not only to sexual activity but to the ways in which individuals perceive themselves in relation to their biological sex and the gender roles constructed by their culture. Foucault argues that European and American cultures have created and defined the different categories of sexual identity through the various language systems, or professional discourses. The specialized languages of such professions as law, religion, and medicine, especially psychoanalysis, act both to control sexuality and to provide ways of resisting that control.

One example of the constructed categories is the idea of "homosexual" and "heterosexual" people. The concept of the homosexual and the heterosexual personality, or identity, originated in the nineteenth century with Freud. Before that time, the language about homosexuality defined "homosexual acts," which could be performed by any individual. Just as the feminists argue that "femininity" and "masculinity" are belief systems created by a language and a culture, it is possible to argue that sexuality is created to some extent by language and culture.

A question may be raised about the choice to use gender theory to develop a critical reading when feminist or gay and lesbian theory overlap with it. Feminist theory does not tend to deal at length with the concept of masculinity as socially constructed, although this concept is implied by feminist theory. Gay and lesbian theory currently focusses more on issues relating to contemporary cultures. A critical reading could be developed using either approach, but in *Imperial Earth* the relationship between Duncan and Karl cannot necessarily be understood as a "homosexual" relationship in the sense of homosexuality as different from and opposed to heterosexuality. The dominant culture of America during much of the twentieth century tends to define heterosexual as the norm, shown by cultural acceptance and public acknowledgment of heterosexual relationships (limited only by certain family relationships, age limits, and number of partners). Homosexuality is defined as deviant, sinful, and evil. The culture of *Imperial Earth* does not acknowledge the construction of two competing sexualities that define themselves against the other.

In this novel, the "norm" (defined as what the majority of the people believe in or subscribe to) is bisexuality, rather than homo- or heterosexuality: "Duncan could never feel quite happy with someone whose affections were exclusively polarized toward one sex. What a contrast to the *aggressive normality* of Karl, who did not give a damn whether he had more affairs with boys or girls, or vice versa. At least, until the Calindy episode . . ." (234, italics added). Clarke does assume that future societies will have very different expectations about the sexual identities of male and females. Though many of these expectations are not developed in detail, the implications are of interest to a reader using gender theory.

There are two aspects of the novel that are of interest to a reader using gender theory: the issues of the separation of the world into public and private spheres, and the technology of cloning. The separation of the world into two separate aspects—the "public" world of business and politics and the "private" world of personal relationships—is made clear at the start of the novel, before the story begins. An epigraph that consists of a quote from *Hamlet*, Act I, Scene 4, is given: "For every man has his business and desire." The distinction between the public world, or work, and the private world, or family, is an attribute of cultural beliefs. Traditional beliefs often limit access to the public world to men, restricting women to the private world.

In this novel, the public and the private worlds are not separate. Duncan's relationship with Karl shows a progressive intermingling of the two worlds, exemplified finally by the two births that end the novel. The two births are the ARGUS proposal, which is Karl's brain-child that Duncan will bring to maturity, and the living child who is Karl's clone and Duncan's son to raise to maturity. The two worlds are not separate, but the narrative seems to present them as inhabited exclusively by men. Males have even taken over the process of birth, which was previously the exclusive domain of women. Only in a technological future could such an appropriation occur.

The existence of the technology of cloning is a central part of the novel. Feminist debate is split on this issue. One argument is that this technology could serve to liberate women from the cultural requirement that women bear children. Another argument is that the technology has the potential to further oppress women if the technology is initiated by a male-dominant culture. Questions of who controls the technology, who is trained in the use of the technology, and the economics of the technology must all be considered in considering whether such technology would liberate or oppress. Because the industrialized nations have seen an increasing use of technology associated with birth along with increasing debates over who controls the reproductive choices of women, the idea of cloning raises questions that a gender reading can address.

The narrative focus on Duncan's life, and his relationship with Karl, begins to establish the technology of cloning as operating for the convenience of rich and powerful men. But presenting this situation within a narrative does not mean that the narrative is advocating or supporting the situation. Several important scenes in the novel can be considered with questions about gender and power in mind. In Chapter 28, Duncan calls Mortimer Keynes, the genetic surgeon who cloned Colin from Malcolm and Duncan from Colin. Duncan believes that he can schedule a routine cloning. To his surprise, Keynes refuses to do a third clone. When Duncan tries to explain his reasons, Keynes refuses to listen.

He tells Duncan the story of the Ptolemies, the descendants of the Greek general who ruled Egypt after Alexander the Great's death. This ruling family solved their problem of dynastic succession by marrying brothers and sisters for over a thousand years. Keynes refuses to clone any more Makenzies because they are doing it to continue the rule of their family rather than to solve a genetic defect. As a result, "genes are no longer shuffled, [cloning] stops the evolutionary clock. It means the end of all biological progress" (207). This refusal frustrates Duncan who disagrees with Keynes, or believes he does. By the end of the novel, Duncan finds another genetic surgeon, but he decides to clone Karl rather than himself. His action brings genetic diversity into the Makenzie dynasty, but the final image of the novel is Duncan holding the infant in his arms. This image is the father-son dyad, or couple, rather than a larger family. What relationship with this technology do women have?

There are two groups of women in this novel. One group is the named characters. These women are either childless—Grandma Ellen and Calindy—or completely invisible—the Makenzies' various wives who all have biological children by other men. In any case, they do not take advantage of the technology, as far as the information presented in the novel goes. But there is another group of women described in the novel who are involved with the technology of cloning.

When Duncan visits the island where Dr. Mohammed, the second genetic surgeon he consults, lives and works, there is a scene described in a chapter that pays tribute to H. G. Wells. Chapter 31 is titled "The Island of Dr. Mohammed," an exact parallel to Wells's novel about vivisection, *The Island of Dr. Moreau*. While Duncan is at the clinic, he walks to the beach one night and inadvertently spies on a group of people. In a clearing, pregnant women and a few men are dancing around a bonfire. Duncan knows the cloning process, so he knows that these are the women who bear the clones made by Dr. Mohammed. The technology is not sufficiently advanced to include a technological replacement for the female body.

These women are called "Mothers" by the other workers on the island, but they are never given the chance to be mothers in anything but the most basic biological sense. They are the containers for the children. Duncan sees that they are mostly ugly, even hideous. He realizes that the few who are attractive are mentally retarded. These women are chosen by computer selection because they wish to bear children but cannot, apparently because of their appearance or retardation. This solution is perceived by Duncan, and apparently by others, as a compassionate one. The economics of this situation are never explained, although the idea that this future society is doing women a favor by letting them indulge their biological urges implies that little or no money is paid them.

The issue of payment for women who are already engaged in various fertility practices is already an issue of debate in 1996. Should women who provide eggs for use by infertile couples be compensated, as are the men who provide sperm? What payment should a woman who bears a child for an infertile couple receive? Does paying women for such acts result in the children born being slaves, that is, humans who are purchased by money? Or are the women paid for their services, not for children? The relationship between economics and childbearing is already complicated; future technological development will complicate it further. Undoubtedly the doctors and medical personnel at the genetic clinic make a good deal of money through cloning. The women who provide an essential service for the completion of the job apparently are granted this opportunity as a favor and receive little or no compensation.

On the personal level, Duncan's decision to clone Karl rather than himself is a positive one, resulting in a greater diversity within the Makenzie dynasty, avoiding political and personal stagnation, and reproducing a person he loved. Duncan is happy, and his Grandma Ellen will probably help him raise the child. In terms of the conflict of the book, he has solved his problems. Analyzing the events with questions of gender and power in mind sees the similarity between the cloning technology and Wells's novels about vivisection. The argument made by Keynes is a strong one. The public implications of cloning, as it is described in this novel, are less positive and more troubling than the personal resolution achieved by Duncan. What may make any single individual happier in his or her personal life may have a different meaning in relation to a larger group of people. So perhaps the separation between the public and the private worlds is stronger than it first appears in this novel and is still related to differences in the relative power between males and females.

The Fountains of Paradise
(1978)

The Fountains of Paradise is one of Arthur C. Clarke's better known novels. Winner of the Hugo and the Nebula awards, this novel shows some intriguing developments with regard to the conventions of science fiction. Most science fiction is based upon the scientific knowledge that has been developed in this century and upon the recent technological innovations based on that science. This novel shows that human history has been one of continual technological evolution. Humanity is a species that builds, and builds upon what it builds. Spirituality is not a process that must be opposed to technology but is an equivalent process of ascending, or building on the past. Both processes take time, and so the chronology (time frame) of the novel moves from the beginning of the first millennium (dated by the birth of Christ) to over three thousand years later.

The main focus of the novel is the Orbital Tower, proposed by the main character in the novel, Vannevar Morgan. Morgan is introduced first in his professional capacity, as the Chief Engineer (Land) of the Terran Construction Corporation, coming to Taprobane to propose his project. This Tower is a construction that will span the distance from a high point on Earth's equator to a satellite that is in a stationary, or geosynchronous, orbit above Earth. Clarke has been interested in the possibilities of such satellites since the 1940s and has published both nonfiction and fiction about using such satellites. The Tower, which must be constructed of a newly developed hyperfilament, will make transportation of goods and people into space easier and more economical. Several chapters at the start of *Fountains* tell the story of a king of Taprobane, Kalidasa, who built a palace fortress two thousand years before Vannevar Morgan's life. Mentioned at times throughout the novel, and ending the novel, is the story of the first alien probe to contact Earth and of an alien visitor who comes to Earth fifteen hundred years after Morgan's death.

This chapter examines six aspects of *The Fountains of Paradise*:

1. The story of Morgan's Orbital Tower is framed by the stories of Kalidasa and the Starholmer to show the connection between technological and spiritual evolution.

2. The split narrative point of view also supports that connection, especially through the intrusive narrator's use of excerpts from documents.

3. Kalidasa and Morgan are developed as point-of-view characters and then placed within the perspective of legend, history, and myth.

4. The Tower goes against the conventional use of spaceships in science fiction.

5. Some knowledge of Buddhist beliefs is necessary for understanding the theme of the novel.

6. The major theme.

The chapter concludes by introducing postcolonial theory and criticism and presenting an example of a postcolonial reading of the book.

PLOT DEVELOPMENT

The plot of *Fountains* includes several stories about great technological projects that are built thousands of years apart but share some similarities. The three projects are Kalidasa's palace/fortress, Yakkagala; Morgan's Orbital Tower; and the Ring of Towers that developed from the first tower. The different stories share certain elements: Sri Kanda, the sacred mountain in Taprobane; the shared themes of spirituality and science; the human desire to ascend beyond the earthly or physical state;

and the stories told about the past, historical or legendary or both, in the present.

The story that is given the most narrative space within the plot is Vannevar Morgan's project to build his Orbital Tower. The story of the Tower is framed with chapters that tell two other stories that support the theme of building and ascension over a period of millennia. "Framing stories" are so-called because they often literally make a framework around the main story by their location at the beginning and end of a novel. One purpose of a framing story is to support or comment on the main story in some way. The framing stories in *Fountains* parallel and support the main story, showing the important connections between the evolution of technology and spirituality.

The first framing story is the story of Kalidasa and the building he did thousands of years before Morgan was born. The second is the story of alien contact, first by a robot probe (Starglider) and then by an alien being (Starholmer). The actual visit by an alien takes place long after Morgan dies, but the Starholmer visits the site of the first Orbital Tower, now called the Tower of Kalidasa.

The story of Kalidasa opens the novel and foreshadows Morgan's story by describing a man who puts his life into building a great project and who dies soon after completing it. Kalidasa is a king who is in conflict with the Buddhist monks and with his older half-brother. Although he succeeds in building his palace, he soon dies in battle with his half-brother who orders Yakkagala left to the jungle because it is too great a challenge to the gods.

Morgan has to overcome a number of obstacles in order to achieve his goal. The first obstacles are bureaucratic problems that are a fact of life for anyone working in government bureaucracies. Morgan works for a world engineering agency, the Terran Construction Corporation. He has recently completed one ambitious project, the Gibraltar Bridge, which links Europe and Africa by means of a bridge over the Strait of Gibraltar, and he wants to control the building of an even larger project, the Tower. Morgan attempts to negotiate the bureaucratic obstacles by doing a preliminary study with his own team, by not issuing any interim reports, and by setting up the framework for an independent company, or consortium, partially funded by the Autonomous North African republic.

A more serious obstacle concerns the proposed location of the Tower. It must be built on a mountain on the equator. Only Sri Kanda in Taprobane is suitable for the Tower because gravitational irregularities exist over other possible mountains that would make it impossible for the satellite or the tower to remain stable. In fact, there are only two stable points on the geosynchronous orbit above the equator: one over the Pacific, and the other over Sri Kanda. The obstacle is that there is a vihara, a Buddhist temple, thousands of years old on Sri Kanda. The head of the order, the Mahanayake Thero, refuses to allow construction of the Tower on the mountain. The temple has a deed dated to A.D. 854 guaranteeing them perpetual ownership of the temple land—which has been recognized even by invaders. The Mahanayake Thero refuses to permit construction on the sacred space because the isolation of the vihara from the rest of the world is vital to its existence. The World Court upholds the vihara's claims regarding the sanctity of the mountain.

An apparent solution to the problem of location is proposed when Morgan is contacted by a representative of Mars. A group on Mars wants to see him build a smaller tower there, from Deimos (one of Mars's two moons) to Mons Pavonis, a mountain on Mars. Mars, with one-third the gravity of Earth, a lower synchronous orbit, and a higher mountain on the equator, would be a suitable location for a much cheaper Tower. Mars wants to build the Tower as part of a project to melt the polar caps and terraform Mars, but Morgan is aware that the Tower will not have as great an impact on human expansion and colonization if it is built on Mars instead of on Earth. However, completing the Tower on Mars might provide a model for what could be done on Earth.

In studying the plans, Morgan sees a possible problem with the Mars project. Phobos, the second moon, which is in a lower orbit than Deimos, could collide with the Tower. But the planners on Mars have taken Phobos into account. The tower will vibrate, or resonate, as every structure does. The vibrations can be accurately calculated, which means that the tower can be tuned to avoid collisions. This problem is part of the scientific principle that underlies the plot of the novel. All structures have a resonance frequency. Taking the resonance frequency into account is vitally important to any construction project. Failing to take the frequency into account can result in the destruction of a bridge or a building.

Morgan agrees to build the project on Mars and schedules a test of the construction process on Earth. A probe will be dropped from the satellite, unreeling the hyperfilament all the way down to Earth. Morgan returns to the World Court to get permission for the test to take place on Sri Kanda, partially out of a desire to challenge the monks. Because the test does not intrude upon the temple's land and will not result in any major changes for the vihara, the Court allows the test. The test is the turning point of the plot concerning the Tower. Morgan is apparently resigned to building the first Tower on Mars, but the events that take place around the test result in an entirely different outcome than he had anticipated.

Interpreting the events of the story requires a careful reading of several chapters to see how the events in the plot are revealed, or not revealed. The test is described in Chapter 30, but earlier chapters show a subplot that affects the way the test ends. Chapter 22 describes how the Venerable Parakarma (Dr. Choam Goldberg), the Mahanayake's assistant, leaves the vihara after the first meeting with Morgan. This departure is important when set against certain Buddhist beliefs that the only certain way to achieve Nirvana is by withdrawing from the material world to a temple. Nirvana, the state of freedom from rebirth into the material world, is the ultimate goal of Buddhism.

The chapter that describes Parakarma leaving is titled "Apostate," a word that refers to someone who renounces his or her religion. Parakarma's decision to go back into the world could be seen as someone renouncing Buddhism. But Parakarma is the point-of-view character in this chapter, and he does not see himself as abandoning the vihara or his religion but as leaving in order to achieve that right action that is the goal of the Buddhist ethical system. In order to achieve this right action, he needs "tools that could not be found on Sri Kanda—or even, for that matter, on earth itself" (119).

There are no other chapters from Dr. Goldberg's point of view. Instead, Chapters 24 and 26, which are told from Rajasinghe's point of view, describe unusual weather patterns. At the time of the story, the technology to predict and control the weather to some extent through a satellite system using lasers exists. Rajasinghe knows about these methods because he helped persuade the former superpowers to hand the control of their orbiting satellites over to the Global Weather Authority. This diplomatic solution allowed not only weather control but also a more peaceful Earth. Monsoon Control, one part of the Weather Authority, is able to control and thus predict the weather in Taprobane with fair accuracy, but Rajasinghe observes some questionable storm patterns in these two chapters.

Morgan schedules the test of his process on a day when Monsoon Control guarantees no wind over thirty kilometers an hour. The completed Tower could withstand winds of any possible force on Earth, but at the point where the probe enters the atmosphere and before the filament is anchored, it is vulnerable to gusts. When the probe enters the atmosphere and nears the mountain, an unexpected gale warning is issued, and high winds snap the filament. No great harm is done. The probe crashes, but nobody is hurt and the probe is recovered. Because the greatest objections to the Tower proposal involve the fear that it would break, it seems as if this accident will result in complete failure for Morgan.

But there is an apparently miraculous event that leads to the opposite result. The test is scheduled at the same time of year that certain golden butterflies swarm on the lower levels of Sri Kanda. They never go high enough to appear at the vihara, but this year is different: "Driven by the gale, in their hundreds and thousands, they were being swept up the face of the mountain, to die upon the summit. Kalidasa's legions had at last achieved their goal—and their revenge" (152). This event can be explained in three possible ways: first, that the flight of the butterflies is pure coincidence, random chance. Second, a legend that Morgan is told on his first visit to the vihara says that Kalidasa's army has been perpetually reincarnated as these golden butterflies. A prophecy was made that if the butterflies ever made it to the top of the mountain, to the vihara, the monks would have to leave because Kalidasa would have won. Either explanation would occur to most of the characters in the novel who are only aware of what has happened on the mountain.

A third possible explanation is that Dr. Goldberg attempted to cause Morgan's test to fail, using the weather satellites to cause unseasonable winds. These winds succeeded in snapping the hyperfilament as he intended, but they also swept the butterflies up the mountain. The result is conclusive: Morgan's incredible defeat has turned to victory as he reflects that "a few dead butterflies can balance a billion-ton tower" (153). Morgan does not realize how these events come about. He is aware of feeling only that "whatever gods [there] may be" are on his side (156). Only a reader who is able to share the omniscient narrator's point of view, shifting from character to character, is able to trace this pattern underlying apparently random events. The plot structure, which first appears to describe chaos or coincidence, has an underlying pattern that can be discerned by such a reader.

Tracing the pattern requires some knowledge of both Buddhist thought and chaos theory, especially "the butterfly effect." Buddhist belief is based on the concept of reincarnation, the belief that souls are reborn in physical bodies through multiple lifetimes. Reincarnation is not limited to rebirth in only one kind of body, so Kalidasa's soldiers could be reincarnated as golden butterflies. Chaos theory studies complex systems that appear chaotic and without any pattern, such as the system of physical forces we call weather. One aspect of chaos theory is the realization that small effects can create large differences in outcomes over time. This aspect is illustrated by the "butterfly effect," a metaphor that says a butterfly waving its wings in China affects weather in New York. The story, or metaphor, is based on the theory that small forces can accumulate in ways and in patterns that are not immediately accessible to human understanding and can be understood only by careful mapping on computers. A more complete discussion of chaos theory can be found in Chapter 9.

Buddhist beliefs represent a spiritual explanation of the universe, whereas chaos theory is a scientific explanation of the universe. Religion and science are generally considered opposite, if not contradictory, explanations. In this novel, the two explanations may not be as contradictory as they first appear. Both undercut the assumption that all natural events can be understood and easily controlled through human technology. The process of applying technology has results that cannot be predicted. The plot of this novel brings the spiritual and the technological together in the embodiment of the butterfly effect in Kalidasa's legend. Dr. Goldberg believes that he can use technology to achieve his goals, but the resulting events are not under his control and what occurs, whether understood as miracle or random chance, is never completely explained to the reader.

After the monks leave the vihara, Morgan is free to build his Tower. Most of the actual details of construction are skipped over as the narrative quickly moves over the first seven years of construction. Then, a long section, nineteen chapters, focusses on a very small period of time within the narrative. This section is contained within the last complete section of the book, "Ascension," and describes what happens when a team of scientists is trapped on the Tower. They are studying an unusual sunspot display, and the batteries of their vehicle catch fire as they are returning to Earth. Although they are able to make it to an emergency refuge, they are stranded. They will soon die from the cold or lack of oxygen, because they are above the atmosphere.

Morgan and everyone involved with the project begins working on possible ways to save the scientists. The problem of the cold is quickly solved. The people who work on the weather satellites point out that they can aim their lasers at the chamber to heat it sufficiently. But there is only one way to deliver food and oxygen to the stranded group. One of the vehicles used on the lower part of the Tower can have an external battery added to give it the power necessary to travel above the atmosphere. There must be a pilot on board to complete the docking procedures, which means that only minimal supplies can be transported. This plan will give the seven people a good chance of surviving until transport can be sent down from above on the Tower. Morgan insists that he is the only possible pilot. He is a small man, which means he weighs less, and he is also completely familiar with the engineering. Although he has developed a heart condition during the last seven years, Morgan keeps this information secret from everyone, believing that the task is within his powers. The trip up is described in detail, especially the various problems that nearly cause the mission to fail. Morgan eventually succeeds in delivering the supplies to the scientists, but on the way down, his heart finally gives out and he dies, still on the Tower.

Morgan has a vision as he dies. He sees a future ring of Towers surrounding Earth, all linked to the first Tower. The chapter ends with a description of the perfect silhouette of Sri Kanda across the clouds as day dawns. Morgan saw this cloud shadow when he first ascended the mountain to speak to the monks, and the pilgrims who ascended also saw it at dawn. This perfect image, which has not been affected by any act of humanity, will no longer be seen by pilgrims and is probably not seen by Morgan as he dies, but the narrative voice at the end of the chapter prophesies that many people will see it in the future as they ride to the stars.

Morgan's death is the climax but not the end of the novel. There is an epilogue titled "Kalidasa's Triumph," which connects the story about Kalidasa's life and projects with the story about the alien contact with Earth. Starglider, the robot probe from Starholme, visits the solar system during Morgan's life. Starglider's task is to visit solar systems and to communicate with all industrial cultures, sending information back to its home world. When the probe leaves a system, its last act is to give the culture the location of its home world so that direct communication can take place. Given the interstellar distances, the message from Earth to Starholme takes fifty-two years to travel one way, so communication will be established in a little over a hundred years. Morgan, and other characters, know about the future contact, but because it will take place after their deaths, it does not concern them greatly.

The epilogue of the novel is set in the far future, long after contact has occurred. A Starholmer visiting Earth travels with a group of children to visit The Tower of Kalidasa, which is Morgan's Tower. The original Tower is completely submerged by later development, including Ring

City, a huge city that circles the globe. Humans have colonized and ter-raformed Mars, Venus, and Mercury and are living there as well as in Ring City. At this time, Earth is entering an Ice Age, but the humans who have the technology to halt the Ice Age have chosen not to use it. This future, created in part by Kalidasa and in part by Morgan, is not one in which technology is opposed to, or superior to, or dedicated to the suppression of spirituality. Instead, it seems to be an essential com-ponent of technology perhaps because all the technology described in the novel allows for greater contact with and communication among humans rather than for destruction or death.

NARRATIVE POINT OF VIEW

The narrative point of view in *Fountains* is the third person omniscient narrator, working primarily through three major point-of-view charac-ters: Kalidasa, Vannevar Morgan, and Rajasinghe. (See Chapter 3 for a discussion of point of view.) There is also an intrusive narrator that does not lecture on science but presents written excerpts from other texts, such as letters, journals, books, and transcripts, in several chapters of the novel. Several minor characters occasionally serve as point-of-view char-acters as well. One is the Venerable Parakarma, or Dr. Choam Goldberg. Another is a reporter, Maxine Duval. Finally, in the epilogue, the point-of-view character shifts from humans to that of an alien, a visitor from Starholme who has come to Earth.

This novel lacks an intrusive narrator who provides lectures on the science of the novel, although it does have (as Clarke's works commonly do) information in a final "Sources and Acknowledgements" section on the scientific issues of the novel, particularly the Space Elevator. The lecturing tone is not absent from this novel. It has simply shifted to the character of Morgan, who lectures others on his plan throughout the earlier chapters of the novel. Science is still an important focus, but the intrusive narrative voice emphasizes spirituality through the use of ex-cerpts from a variety of texts.

The texts that are quoted, or reproduced in separate chapters, include transcripts of communications with Starglider during its trip through the solar system, an undiscovered fragment of a Buddhist scripture, quotes from history texts, and an excerpt from a book on contact with Starholme written by one of the characters in the novel. Most of these texts em-phasize the spiritual element of the novel, although one scientific lecture on the ionosphere is included. Because the point of the lecture is how little is known about how weather works, it tends to support the spiritual explanation of the butterflies being blown up the mountain. The intrusive narrator also withholds specific information on Dr. Goldberg's plan, and on the cause of the change in weather that leads to the embodiment of the butterfly legend, which provides additional support to the spiritual explanation.

CHARACTER DEVELOPMENT

There are two major characters in the book who are linked in their desire to build more and greater structures than anyone else: Kalidasa and Vannevar Morgan. Kalidasa and Morgan are point-of-view characters who are engrossed with their desire to build greater structures; by the end of the novel, both have entered the realms of history, legend, and myth. Other human characters are primarily developed as either opponents or supporters of Morgan. The Starholmer, one of Clarke's few alien characters, is introduced at the very end and serves to comment on the extent to which the projects of Kalidasa/Morgan have become legends, showing not only what humanity is able to achieve but also how little is remembered of any individual centuries after death.

The first major character whose story opens the novel is Kalidasa, a king whose story fits archetypal patterns. An archetype is an image or story element that is found in myths or legends in various cultures. The story of a brother who kills his father and is in conflict with a brother over taking that father's place is common to cultures in which inheritance and power pass from a father to a chosen son. Kalidasa's character is developed from several different perspectives. He is presented as a point-of-view character, as a figure of legend, and finally as the subject of historical and archeological study. Kalidasa is primarily associated with building Yakkagala. When Morgan visits Taprobane, the story of Kalidasa has become a major tourist attraction, told in the form of a light-show that Morgan attends.

The chapters told from Kalidasa's point of view are all from his perspective as the reigning king. Most of the character's concern is with his project, which was designed to reflect his glory as a ruler. Yakkagala is an example of impressive engineering and art. The fortress is built on a high rock and contains fountains of water pumped up from the plain as well as beautiful murals in a hidden place. But Kalidasa still suffers from comparing his project to his father's creation of an artificial lake that stored water for use by all the people living in the area. This contrast shows the difference between the use of technology to reflect the power and glory of an individual ruler and the use of technology to serve a larger good.

The second character who desires to build something greater than has ever existed before is also the main character of the novel, Vannevar Morgan. He faces opponents who see his proposed Tower as a challenge to a god who will resent humanity's attempts to ascend. Most of the information about Morgan, whether in the chapters told from his point of view or from other characters', focusses on his professional life. Little or nothing of Morgan's personal life is revealed. He does not seem to have married or had children, nor are any activities outside the building of great projects described.

His character is expressed through the knowledge and love he brings to his work, and the two memories of his childhood that are told make it clear that this knowledge and love had its beginning in childhood experiences. The two childhood memories that are related at key narrative points are connected to his early desire to become an engineer. Morgan remembers the pain of losing a favorite toy, a kite, when the string broke and the wind blew the kite away. This first "lesson in the strength of materials" is one Morgan never forgets (21). He attributes his desire to become an engineer to that childhood experience/memory. Later, trapped on the Tower, he remembers making small parachutes and watching them float away. His childhood dreams have been surpassed by his adult achievements, and he feels a sense of satisfaction as he dies.

Although the character of Morgan seems very different from Kalidasa, they share a similar desire despite their different cultures and levels of technology. Both wish their names to live on throughout history because of their projects. Morgan identifies with Kalidasa, and both are in conflict with the monks. The irony of the epilogue is that over time there has been a melding of the two stories and the two individuals. The Tower's technical name, Earthport One, is ignored in favor of the name "Tower of Kalidasa." The true victory of each character is not that they achieved individual glory through their buildings, but that their buildings eventually served humanity as part of the process of evolving technology that developed from stone palaces to orbital cities. The stories of such buildings are almost as important as the buildings themselves, because the stories serve as models for the future.

Other characters in the book exist primarily to provide opposition or support for Morgan's project. Opponents include Senator Collins (the head of the Terran Construction Corporation), the Mahanayake Thero, and the Venerable Parakarma. Supporters include Rajasinghe and Maxine Duval, the reporter. Rajasinghe feels that the project will bring new life to Taprobane, and Maxine Duval is involved in the project in her professional capacity as a reporter. Rajasinghe accepts Buddhist beliefs to some extent and acts to help Morgan in various ways.

The opposition of Senator Collins is disposed of quickly. He is described as a pompous ass who wants to take all the glory of the engineering projects for himself. The Mahanayake Thero is a different kind of opponent, one who cares for something beyond his personal glory. The Mahanayake is not a point-of-view character in the novel, but Morgan is aware of his spiritual power when he visits him. The Mahanayake is not defeated by Morgan, nor is the order of monks destroyed. They establish the order elsewhere, choosing to abide by the legend and prophecy. There is no sense that the order, or Buddhism, is in any way lessened by the Tower. The epilogue hints at quite another outcome, one in which the spiritual beliefs of Buddhism have become a philosophy for all humanity. The one Buddhist monk who is a point-of-view character, the Venerable Parakarma, is the one character who makes a major effort to stop Morgan's project. This effort apparently results in Morgan's achieving his goal, and the last information about Dr. Goldberg is that he has renounced Buddhism for further work in meteorology and has become successful.

Finally, one important character is introduced at the end: the Starholmer, an alien visitor to Earth. This character is part of the species that sent Starglider out to explore the universe. This species does not have young and lives for centuries. The Starholmer has come to study humans and is trying to learn to distinguish between the various kinds of stories on Earth. It is having trouble distinguishing between fact and fiction, and other uses of language, such as jokes. The alien reminds readers that language is also a tool, or a technology, and one that may differ on other planets. The Starholmer serves as the major speculative element in the novel, because so much else in the novel is based on fact.

Clarke is always careful to provide information in his "Sources and Acknowledgements" to help readers distinguish between the historical or scientific facts and the fiction in his novels. In this case much of the novel is based on fact. Taprobane is based on the history and geography of Ceylon, now Sri Lanka, only moved south to the equator. Sri Kanda is twice the height of the sacred mountain Sri Pada. Yakkagala is based on Sigiriya, or Lion Rock, of which Clarke says, "the reality . . . is so astonishing that I have no need to change it in any way" except to attribute a shorter building time to it" (279). The theory for the Orbital Tower was first proposed in a Russian journal in 1960, and then a similar proposal was made in a 1966 issue of *Science*.

GENERIC CONVENTIONS

Rocket ships were (and are) favored cover art for the science fiction magazines, and most science fiction stores rely on some form of spaceship. Writers can speculate on the changes in physics that will lead to possible interstellar travel, as Clarke does himself in other novels. But the space elevator, as theorized, has the potential to change the economics of spaceflight. Much of the cost involved in getting a ship off Earth is connected to the need for enough power to overcome the force of gravity. A future in which flight begins in space will be much different, as will a future in which an elevator transports people and goods up and down continuously.

Fountains focusses on another kind of incredible engineering feat that may not have the romance of the spaceship for many readers. Clarke admits in *Astounding Days* his own love affair with the image of the ship, as his fascination with the *Titanic* shows, but he often argues for more rationality in approaching the issue of space travel. His own work with communications satellites and the potential of the geosynchronous satellite make the idea of a space elevator connected to a synchronous satellite a natural topic for him to explore. This novel attempts to create the sense of romance and glory Morgan feels for his Tower with his readers.

SOCIAL CONTEXT

Some knowledge of the group of religions the West calls "Buddhism" is necessary for understanding the themes of *Fountains*. This religion originated in India and is based on the concept of enlightenment rather than salvation. The term "Buddha" means "enlightened one" and is a title rather than a proper name. The first Buddha was Siddhatthya Gotama (variant spellings occur in different sources). He is thought to have lived sometime during the sixth century B.C. There is debate over whether the stories of his life are historical or legendary. The doctrine, or body of beliefs, associated with Buddhism consists of a large body of teachings and writings that have developed over several thousand years. Buddhism is not based on a single sacred text, as Christianity, Judaism, and Islam are.

Buddhism changed as it spread from India to central Asia, China, Japan, Tibet, and southeast Asia. Beliefs in each area blended with Buddhism, which resulted in variations between the religious beliefs and practices in different countries. Certain basic concepts from Buddhism are important for understanding the themes of *Fountains*. These include the fact that Buddhism does not rely on the belief in a supreme creator, or God; that reincarnation, the rebirth of souls into physical bodies, is part of a process of spiritual development; and finally, that the ultimate goal of Buddhism is to achieve Nirvana, which is a transcendent state of freedom from rebirth into the material world. Buddhas serve as teachers and models for others, but different beliefs exist concerning the best means of achieving Nirvana. Some argue that total withdrawal into a monastery is the only means possible, but not all agree (Brandon 157–162). In *Fountains*, Rajasinghe defines Nirvana as "that state which can be defined only by negatives. Such emotions as anger, desire, greed no longer possessed any power; indeed, they were barely conceivable. Even the sense of personal identity seemed about to fade away, like a mist before the morning sun" (134).

Buddhism in Ceylon/Sri Lanka has a long history. A legend states that Buddha visited Ceylon three times, leaving his footprint on a sacred mountain there. Morgan visits the site and is told of the footprint. Historically, the origin of Buddhism in Ceylon is identified with an Indian emperor who sent his son to promote the new religion in Ceylon, in the third century B.C. The new religion quickly became influential in the political system of the country. Between the establishment of Buddhism to the occupation by the British in 1825, the ruler of the country was required to be Buddhist. Buddhism suffered under European occupation, but since independence in 1947, there has been a growing identification between the national identity and Buddhism (Brandon 107). Because Clarke has been living in Sri Lanka for thirty years and has obviously studied the history, culture, and religion of his adopted country, some knowledge of the social context is necessary for understanding the novel.

THEMES

Fountains describes a millennia-long history of human technological evolution. A discussion of other novels that have the same themes can be found in Chapter 2. The evolution of human technology is based on building on earlier work. Individuals desire to supplant the work of the past, but their work always owes a debt to the past. The novel shows that individuals responsible for achievements are often forgotten. What is remembered centuries later may not be the individual but the achievement, which has become a foundation for later work. More important than the temporal, and temporary, conflicts between individuals or the desire for individual glory are the growth and evolution of humanity shown in the different aspects of science and spirituality that may not, in the end, be different at all.

The Buddhist ethical system emphasizes selflessness and careful consideration of one's actions as part of a process of enlightenment or transcendence. By the end of the novel—the visit of the Starholmer to Earth—this system of beliefs has become widespread among humans as they have evolved over time. This evolution in spirituality has occurred along with evolution in technology, as explained by the world computer at the end of the novel. When the Starholmer asks why humans do not use their technology to change the climate on Earth, the answer is "There is a time to battle against Nature, and a time to obey her. True wisdom lies in making the right choice. When the long winter is over, man will return to an earth renewed and refreshed" (275).

The overall narrative of the novel shows a progression through different stages of human development. In the earliest stage, only a king such as Kalidasa could command the building of major structures, or monuments, which he commanded for his own glory. In a later stage, the resources of a planet are brought together under the direction of one man who must work with others but who can still dream of his name being passed down. Finally, when greater technologies exist, the human race has matured to a state where it does not always feel that it must do something just because it can. Because much of technology is creating changes or altering the world itself, this maturing reflects a different relationship with the planet, or nature, developing over time.

ALTERNATE READING: POSTCOLONIAL CRITICISM

Postcolonial theory is primarily based on the work of scholars from countries once colonized by European nations. These countries, which are often categorized as the "Third World," have a specific relation to the industrialized nations of the "First World," including their former colonizers. Postcolonial theory and criticism analyze the uneven relationships of power and culture between these two worlds, which shared a different relationship in the past than they will in the future. Edward Said's *Orientalism*, published in 1978, is acknowledged as one of the earliest, if not the first, statements of this theory.

When postcolonial theory is applied to literature, certain arguments about culture and literature become the basis of critical readings. One argument focusses on the ways in which empires perceived their colonies in opposition to themselves. The commonplace terms "West" and "East" are questioned, because they rely on a perceived central location in Europe rather than on any inherent direction on a circular planet. Said argues that the stereotypical perceptions about the colonial world were, and are, based on a two-level hierarchy. In this hierarchy, the West is understood as always superior to and different from the East (called "The Orient"). Attributes such as reason, intellect, technology, and morality are attributed to the West, and the East is seen as embodying emotion, decadence, sexuality, and depravity. Whatever is seen as good is a characteristic that is inherent in, or essential, to the West; negative characteristics are projected upon the Orient.

A second argument concerns the extent to which cultural displacement occurred. Cultural displacement is the forced movement of populations from the East into the West, such as slavery and refugees. The result of the displacement has been a blending of cultures across national boundaries that is often ignored by the dominant culture. The concepts of "margin" and "center" describe the way the cultures or individuals are categorized.

A third argument claims that literature must be understood as carrying specific cultural attitudes and beliefs rather than being universal in theme or simply a description of strange and exotic places. The literature produced by colonizing cultures (such as England and France) is analyzed from a new perspective, and perhaps in company with literature produced by writers from former colonies. When a national literature is taught in an educational system, as British literature was taught in colonial schools in Africa, India, and Australia, literature becomes a part of a political and colonizing effort. Language is a major area of concern in a postcolonial analysis, because one colonizing effort always has been forcing the colonizer's language upon the colonized, and one means of resistance has been maintaining a native language, traditional literary forms, or blending languages to create new ones.

Developing a postcolonial reading of Clarke's novels is an interesting project for several reasons. Clarke moved to Ceylon in the late fifties, barely ten years after the country gained its independence. He has written stories and novels using settings in eastern nations and has made Buddhist characters and themes important parts of some of his work. As a British resident living in Ceylon and traveling and visiting America regularly for twenty years, Clarke is an early example of the kind of global characters he creates in his novels who move easily across national borders.

Science fiction, as a genre, has been almost completely associated with America and its technological dominance that began after World War II. But Clarke's vision of humanity's movement into space has insisted that national boundaries cannot be maintained in space. Clarke's novels—*The Fountains of Paradise*, *Imperial Earth*, and *The Songs of Distant Earth*—contain obvious efforts to challenge or reverse stereotypes of the Orient and the conventional assumption that technology and space travel will be dominated by any one nation or culture because that nation or culture is inherently technologically or morally superior to other nations.

Postcolonial critics have analyzed writers from colonizing countries who write about the colonies. The analysis shows the extent to which the stereotypes associated with the Orient inform the characterization, plots, and themes of the literature. Such literature, the argument goes, simply colonizes the oppressed culture again. The potential for such colonization is always present, but the need for cross-cultural education is an important one as well. *The Fountains of Paradise* avoids the stereotypical constructions of the East to a great extent and successfully revises the marginalization of non-Western countries in relation to technology and space travel by incorporating a different approach to history; by showing various characters from different cultures, including an alien; by predicting that the future will not be dominated by the Western industrial nations but will continue the process of blending Western and Eastern cultures; and by making Buddhist philosophy a major thematic element in the novel.

The historical information about Taprobane/Sri Lanka emphasizes that engineering and technology were not invented in the West first, or that civilization first existed in the West. Kalidasa meets briefly with representatives from a city "younger by centuries than Ranapura," the ancient capital of Taprobane (6). This younger city is Rome. During the first thousand years of the Common Era (the historical term that has replaced "A.D." to avoid relying on a specific religious figure), other empires existed in various parts of the world. The Byzantine empire in Turkey, the Gupta empire in India, and Imperial China were technologically and politically more developed than the area that would become known as Europe. History courses that cover "Western Civilization" instead of "World History" do not spend much time on these other civilizations.

The novel also questions the "Great Man Theory" of history, which is based on the assumption that historical developments and major events can be credited to single heroic figures. Kalidasa is an example of this assumption. In the "Sources and Acknowledgements" section, Clarke notes that archeological knowledge about Lion Rock, which is the basis for Yakkagala, shows that structure was the result of many years' labor rather than the achievement of one ruler.

Stereotypes in characterization are based on a process that reduces characters to one ethnic or "racial" common denominator. The characters in *Fountains* are a diverse group, representing several cultures. Natives of Taprobane are presented as having various perspectives on the Tower (Sarath and Rajasinghe disagree) and as existing in all classes and professions, from taxi drivers to monks. The two Buddhist monks have different ideas about how to achieve the right action in regard to the Tower. Vannevar Morgan is not presented as from any specific country or nation but as a bridge builder who desires greater travel between nations and between Earth and space.

This future is not necessarily dominated by the Western industrial nations. When Morgan needs to get funding for the Tower, he goes not to the United States or to Russia but to the Autonomous North African Republic. The Tower will serve the Terran economy, not any one nation's economy—although Taprobane will become a center of global power in the future. The presence of the aliens from Starholme also plays a part in commenting upon the human tendency to create differences based on such trivial things as skin color. The human race, which consists of only one race, may not be able to comprehend this fact until confronted with true aliens.

   The values and beliefs of the West and the East are blended in various ways in this novel, especially in the character of Morgan and in the change he undergoes. Morgan begins the novel as an individual who wants to be known as the genius who designed and built the Tower. He is the conventional male heroic figure of legends and history who also appears in a good deal of science fiction. At the end of the novel, as he dies alone on the Tower, Morgan sees beyond his individual achievements to the future developments and seems to move into a less egotistical and more global appreciation than he had achieved before. This lack of desire for individual glory is connected to Buddhist beliefs that play an important part in the novel and to the perceptions of the Starholmer.

   The novel not only shows the survival of Buddhism in the future but implies that only a religion that is not based on the figure of an all-powerful God defined in human-centered ways is likely to survive into possible futures that involve contact with other intelligent species. The chapters that contain transcripts of the communication between Earth and Starglider, the robot probe, include a number of communications regarding the different cultures Starglider has communicated with over its travels. Earth is also sending transmissions containing a large amount of the sum of human knowledge, history, culture, and religion. The probe categorizes cultures in a system based on the level of technological development, with categories ranging from "1. Stone tools," to humanity's level "5. Atomic energy, space travel" (86). Higher-level cultures exist, but Starglider is not allowed to give information about them to the lower-level cultures.

   Of the transcripts quoted in Chapter 16, "Conversations with Starglider," all five demolish any religion depending upon belief in a supreme creator. The probe is confused at first and cannot distinguish between "religious ceremonies and apparently identical behavior at . . . sporting and cultural functions," demolishes the "hypothesis" of God, and states that "Starholme informed me 456 years ago that the origin of the universe has been discovered but that I do not have the appropriate circuits to comprehend it" (88–89).

   Starglider's main purpose within the novel serves to question two major aspects of western religious and philosophical thought: Christianity's reliance upon the figure of a supreme being, or Creator, and the superiority of humanity as that Creator's highest achievement. Buddhist philosophy, which does not rely upon a creator and emphasizes respect for all life, is the single major world religion that survives into the future.

The Buddhist belief in selflessness as a goal, rather than the emphasis upon the individual's importance, underlies the concluding events of the story. The combination of the presence of aliens, Buddhism, and the emphasis upon the evolution of technology and spirituality effectively blends science and spirituality as well as the West and the East.

2010: Odyssey Two
(1982)

The novel *2010: Odyssey Two* (1982) was published fourteen years after *2001: A Space Odyssey* (1968). The third novel, *2061: Odyssey Three*, appeared in 1987, and the fourth and final novel in the Odyssey Quartet, *3001: The Final Odyssey*, was published in 1997. The movie *2001: A Space Odyssey* is considered by many to be the most important science fiction movie ever made. Arthur C. Clarke and filmmaker Stanley Kubrick first met and began working together in 1964, and the publication of the final book in 1997 makes the Odyssey body of work one of the most important and longest running phenomena in science fiction. As such, the complete body of works will eventually require a book-length study of their own. This book focusses on *2010*, *2061*, and *3001* exclusively. These novels, unlike *2001* which was written before the first lunar landing, incorporate the information gained by NASA missions to Jupiter and develop the major themes of *2001* concerning the nature of humanity, evolution, and sentience or consciousness.

This chapter presents a summary of all four novels, discusses their relation to each other, and then looks at six aspects of *2010: Odyssey Two*:

1. The plot development is based on exploring the mystery of the monolith.
2. The open-ended plot structure frames the actions of the humans with the experiment of the aliens who operate through the monolith.

3. The narrative point of view is split between two plot lines, working through Heywood Floyd and other humans, and through a transformed David Bowman and an intrusive narrator who provides information about the aliens to the readers.

4. Character development focusses on transformation and transcendence.

5. The novel and two important conventions of science fiction.

6. The major themes.

The chapter concludes by presenting a feminist reading of the novel.

THE ODYSSEY SERIES

A Summary of the Novels

The originating event, the mystery at the heart of all four novels, is the existence of an unnamed alien species. This species has evolved from a state of physical being, through a state of machine being, into a state of being that is one of pure energy. They are described as the "lords of the Galaxy, and beyond the reach of time" (*2010* 308). Although this species has left physical existence far behind, they remain interested in the evolution of physical life toward the development of conscious, or sentient, intelligence. They have spent millions of years manipulating species on planets throughout many galaxies to achieve that development.

2001 describes two contacts between the monoliths—the aliens' tools—and humanity. The first contact takes place several million years before the present time of the novel, in what will come to be known as Africa. A monolith manipulates the ancestors of mankind to become tool-users. Two monoliths remain as monitoring devices, one buried on the Moon and another orbiting Jupiter. In 2001 the second contact occurs when the one on the Moon (named Tycho Magnetic Anomaly-One, or TMA-1) is uncovered by Americans, and Heywood Floyd is sent to study it. TMA-1 sends a transmission toward Jupiter after its discovery.

The rest of the novel describes a mission that is sent out on a ship named *Discovery*. This mission consists of three astronauts in hibernation and two who are awake, Frank Poole and David Bowman. The mission also includes a supercomputer of the HAL-9000 series, known as "Hal." Hal has been programmed to complete the mission without any human supervision if necessary. Problems occur on the mission when Hal tries to cut off communication with Earth. When the astronauts refuse to believe his lies about an instrument malfunction, he kills four of them. Bowman manages to disable Hal and reach Jupiter, where he discovers the second monolith. He enters the monolith in a spacepod and travels to another galaxy where he is transformed from his physical existence into a state of conscious energy. During this process, he and his memories of his life are studied by the aliens, and the transformed Bowman is eventually sent back to Earth as the "Star-Child."

2010 describes a Russian–American mission on the Russian ship *Leonov* to retrieve *Discovery*, left orbiting Jupiter, before its orbit decays and it is destroyed. The mission has multiple objectives. Its most important objective is to rendezvous with and retrieve *Discovery*. The other mission objectives are to investigate the monolith and study Jupiter. A number of characters in *2010* were first introduced in *2001*. The most important characters are Heywood Floyd, Hal, and David Bowman, who is believed by all the other characters to be dead during most of *2010*. The Leonov mission succeeds to some extent, but unexpected actions by the monolith and by the transformed David Bowman occur.

In both novels, readers are given access to specific information about the aliens in chapters narrated by an intrusive narrator and from the point of view of the transformed Bowman. The human characters in the book have no awareness of the nature of these aliens and remain ignorant throughout the novels. The aliens do not want humanity to learn that their species has been manipulated. The nature of this manipulation is that *Homo sapiens* did not originally achieve the ability to use tools, which the story shows led to the development of language, culture, and eventually to space travel, through the process of evolution. This ability was given the ancestors of humans through specific manipulation and programming by the aliens who continue to observe their experiment by means of the monoliths and the transformed Bowman.

In *2010* the aliens use Bowman as a probe to continue their testing and evaluation of humanity. He visits Earth, then the moons of Jupiter. By the end of the novel, the aliens have set up a new experiment. Seeing that life on Europa, one of Jupiter's four inner moons, has the possibility of further evolution, they implode Jupiter, turning the gas giant into a sun. A monolith stays on Europa, presumably manipulating the Europans further. This experiment destroys all the life on Jupiter. Bowman was able to warn *Leonov* in time for them to leave before the implosion. Humans are sent a message that they may use any of the other three worlds, the former moons of Jupiter, but they may not land on Europa.

2061 is discussed in Chapter 8, but, briefly, the novel deals with events fifty years after the Leonov mission. Heywood Floyd joins a group of celebrities on *Universe*, a luxury liner that is traveling out to rendezvous with Halley's comet. The trip is a success, but when another ship is stranded on Europa, *Universe* must divert from the comet to rescue the crew, including Floyd's grandson Chris Floyd. The third novel's plot shows humans landing on Europa despite the ban and reveals that the transformed Dave Bowman and Hal are still within the monolith and actively overseeing life on Europa.

3001 is described by Clarke as having "discarded many of the elements of its precursors, but developed others—and I hope more important ones—in much greater detail" (261). This novel, set in 3001, brings back Frank Poole as the protagonist. His frozen body, left behind by Bowman after HAL killed Poole, is recovered, and he is brought back to life through the use of improved technology. A good deal of the novel is concerned with describing his attempts to make a life for himself in the future, but part of the plot concerns the attempts by the Monoliths (from Africa, the Moon, and Europa) to carry out mysterious orders transmitted by their controller, 450 light years away. These new instructions apparently order the destruction of humanity as a failed experiment. But Frank Poole is informed of the fact that the Monolith is receiving new orders by what he calls the "Dave component" of "Halman," the composite personality that has formed from Dave, HAL, and Heywood Floyd, who have been in the memory of the Monolith for nearly a thousand years. "Halman" is detached from humanity yet compassionate enough to warn Poole about the order. Specialists are able to put together a "Trojan Horse" program of computer viruses that destroy the Monoliths' ability to function, saving humanity, at least for the next thousand years.

The Relationship of the Novels to Each Other

Clarke does not wish readers to view the three later novels as traditional sequels to *2001*. Traditional sequels usually consist of a story that has been published in several different volumes and that is meant to be read in the order of the volumes. Such a story may cover the lives of the

same group of characters or move ahead in time to cover later generations, but sequels tend to be organized in a linear fashion, following the
same characters through time.

The Odyssey novels seem to meet the criteria for a traditional sequel.
The chronology of the four books is a linear chronology, moving from
2001 to 3001. Important characters appear in all four novels. The events
described in each novel take place after the events in the previous one,
and earlier events seem to provide motivation for later events. But Clarke
repeatedly states that he does not wish readers to approach the books
with the idea that they are "direct" or "linear" sequels. In the introduction to *2061*, he says "[the books] must all be considered as variations
on the same theme, involving many of the same characters and situations, but not necessarily *happening in the same universe*" (vii, italics
added).

The universes in each novel are different because of what has been
learned about the solar system—and Jupiter—over the years that Clarke
has been working on the various books. The first book and movie were
conceived and created between 1964 and 1968, before the first Moon
landing in 1969. When Clarke wrote *2010*, he was able to use information
from the 1979 *Voyager* flyby of Jupiter, and he planned to use what
would be learned on the Galileo Mission (which would drop a probe
into Jupiter's atmosphere) in *2061*. The Galileo Mission was delayed because of the *Challenger* tragedy, but Clarke decided to write the third
book anyway, using the return of Halley's comet in 2061 as the central
event. The Galileo Mission finally reached Jupiter during the time Clarke
was writing *3001*, but as he reports in the "Sources and Acknowledg-
ments" section, the failure of the main antenna to unfold meant that the
information and images sent back came very slowly. Two days before
finishing the novel, Clarke was first able to download and see the images, which did not contradict his descriptions of Jupiter, Ganymede, or
the other moons (249).

Given that the novels contain similar characters and situations but are
set in different universes, one approach to the stories is to consider them
as fractal sequels. Clarke is interested in chaos theory and fractals, which
are discussed in Chapter 9. Fractals can be defined as complex patterns
in which smaller parts are similar to the larger whole. It is possible to
read each *Odyssey* novel as a work that stands alone. However, considering the novels in relation to each other shows that the later novels are
retellings of a similar story revolving around the same mystery set in
plots of different magnitudes. The basic plot is humanity's attempts to

learn more about the monoliths. The magnitudes shift from a narrow focus on one ship and one man to a larger focus involving all of humanity in relation to the monoliths and the aliens.

Repetition within the novels also supports the concept of a fractal relationship between the books. Parts of the novels are reproduced in other novels. For example, the information about the transformation Dave Bowman undergoes in *2001* is presented as a flashback in *2010*, and Chapter 37 of *2001* contains the same information, nearly word for word, about the aliens as does Chapter 51 of *2010*. Necessary information from *2010* is repeated in *2061* in Chapters 58–59 when information about the implosion of Jupiter and the life on Europa is presented. Material in two chapters from *2001* (18 and 37) and three chapters from *2010* (11, 36, and 38) has been edited and included in *3001*, specifically information about the aliens, Dr. Chang's last message from Europa, and the description of life on Europa and Jupiter before the implosion, which Bowman observes when he is acting as a probe.

PLOT DEVELOPMENT

The plot of *2010* is similar to the plot of *2001*. Both novels focus on exploring the mystery of the monolith, and in both novels, unexpected events occur that prevent the exploration from succeeding. *2010* begins on Earth when Heywood Floyd meets his Russian friend, Dimitri, at a scientific conference. Dimitri informs Floyd that *Discovery*, left orbiting Jupiter when Bowman disappeared, is not in a stable orbit as everyone had believed. Dimitri suggests the idea of a joint Russian-American mission. He hopes Floyd can influence his government to agree to this proposal.

In *2001*, the Americans tried to keep the monolith a secret. Secrecy is no longer possible, and the political situation has changed. Although the two nations are not exactly friendly, international relations have improved. When the Americans realize that they cannot complete their ship in time to reach *Discovery* before the ship is destroyed, they agree to the joint mission. Heywood is asked to join the mission as one of the specialists. He agrees, despite the problems it causes in his marriage.

The three American specialists are scheduled to spend the trip to Jupiter in hibernation. But Floyd is wakened a month early when a problem occurs as they are reaching the moons of Jupiter. The problem is that another ship may beat them to *Discovery* and be able to claim it. It turns out that the Chinese, who were apparently building a new space station when *Leonov* left Earth, were actually constructing a ship, the *Tsien*. This ship has made the journey more quickly than *Leonov* and may reach *Discovery* first. But their speed and orbit means that they lack sufficient fuel to return to Earth. *Tsien* then lands on Europa, confusing the observers even more. Heywood studies data transmitted from Earth and deduces their plan. Europa has a surface that consists of water covered with ice. The water does not freeze because heat is generated inside Europa by the tidal, or gravitational forces, of Jupiter.

In theory, the Chinese can refuel on Europa, using water as the propellent for their drive. Their plan, which is risky but possible, fails because of the unexpected fact that there is life on Europa. A transmission from the only survivor on Europa is intercepted by *Leonov*. He says that a large creature was drawn from the water by the lights on the ship. In its attempt to reach the lights, the creature tipped the ship over, killing everyone except the one crew member who was outside the ship at the time. *Leonov* can listen to the survivor's transmission but does not have enough fuel to divert to Europa to save his life.

They arrive at Jupiter and manage to board *Discovery*. There they begin the long process of salvaging the ship and Hal. The reason why Hal acted the way he did in *2001* is discovered by Dr. Chandra. Hal's original orders were to keep the mission information about the monolith secret from the human crew. The resulting conflict caused a state similar to human schizophrenia in Hal. He cut off communication with Earth and, as he had to lie more and more, the conflict escalated until he finally resolved it by trying to eliminate his human partners.

Although Dr. Chandra is the creator of the HAL-9000 series and is the mission specialist responsible for evaluating Hal, Heywood Floyd has brought a fail-safe device along. Heywood arranges for Walter Curnow, the third American specialist, to install the device near Hal's main power input. This device will allow Floyd to cut off all power to Hal in a second, if necessary. Floyd, Curnow, and the Captain keep knowledge of this device from Dr. Chandra.

Along with their salvage work on *Discovery*, the crew studies the monolith orbiting Jupiter. Their methods of study are entirely passive because they do not know how the monolith might respond to force. They learn its dimensions (1:4:9), its apparent mass, and its featurelessness, but little else. Things change suddenly when something, perceived by one of the Russian crew as a point of light, emerges from the monolith and moves rapidly toward Earth. The human characters in the novel do not have any idea what this thing can be, but a number of chapters told from the transformed Bowman's viewpoint give readers more information about this new character and his importance to the plot of the novel.

The transformed Bowman travels faster than the speed of light from Jupiter to Earth. He visits his adolescent sweetheart, Betty, and his mother, who is in an nursing home, and then tours a number of places and events on Earth. He begins to realize that he is either controlled or monitored by the aliens. Returning to Jupiter, he tours the four inner moons (Ganymede, Callisto, Io, and Europa), studying them for any signs of life. Only one possibility exists. The species on Europa discovered by accident when *Tsien* landed there for refueling has the potential for development. When he returns to Jupiter, Bowman becomes aware of a larger plan in which he is participating.

He warns *Leonov* to return to Earth sooner than planned, within fifteen days. He cannot speak to humans directly, but he is able to enter Hal's circuits. He speaks to Heywood and then forms a representation of his original body from dust to convince Heywood that he is David Bowman. When Heywood reports his experiences to the rest of the crew, they are inclined to believe that it was an hallucination or a practical joke programmed into Hal. They cannot leave early because of their position and considerations about how much fuel they have remaining. Captain Orlova says that she would prefer to delay their departure date because the relative positions of Jupiter and Earth will mean that they will have more fuel in reserve. Though they can leave orbit around Jupiter any time, they will not have enough fuel to return to Earth if they leave early. Without any hard proof to support Heywood's hallucination, Captain Orlova refuses to accept the warning as valid.

Walter Curnow suggests that the crew could plan for an earlier departure date, using *Discovery* as a first stage booster rocket. Then, if proof is obtained, they will be ready to leave. Captain Orlova agrees, if the crew works only during their off-duty hours. Most of the crew and specialists agree, mostly because they want to get home earlier. The hypothetical plan to join the two ships together becomes a necessity rather than an exercise when the monolith suddenly disappears from its orbit around Jupiter.

At this point, Dr. Chandra raises an objection. The original mission plan called for Hal to return *Discovery* to Earth. The second plan asks Hal to participate in what amounts to his suicide because *Discovery* will be left adrift after all the fuel is used to boost *Leonov* back toward Earth. The crew believes that they can lie to Hal, but Dr. Chandra refuses to treat Hal this way. He argues that they should tell Hal the truth and allow him to choose. The others react badly to this suggestion. They see Hal as a machine, an object to treat as they wish. They are also afraid that telling Hal the truth will result in another breakdown, and they will be unable to use *Discovery* as a booster.

Heywood resolves this conflict by speaking to Captain Orlova privately, reminding her of his cutoff device and suggesting that they lie to Dr. Chandra instead. They can tell him to go ahead with his plan. If Hal agrees, everything is fine. If he disagrees or tries to interfere later, they can cut Hal off at any moment and substitute manual programs they have prepared. Captain Orlova agrees to this plan. As they leave Jupiter, they become aware of a growing black spot on the planet, which turns out to be the monolith reproducing itself and covering Jupiter's surface.

Hal agrees to the plan to use *Discovery* to boost *Leonov*, although he does suggest stopping their departure in order to study the black spot further as his primary mission—to study intelligence on Jupiter—demands. Dr. Chandra is able to persuade Hal to go through with the program to allow *Leonov* to leave. Later, as they return to Earth, Dr. Chandra discusses the nature of their dealings with Hal with Heywood, revealing that he removed the cutoff device long ago because it was obvious that something like that had been installed.

On their trip back, the crew continues to study events on Jupiter. The growing black spot on the planet is revealed to be the monolith replicating itself and covering the surface. The monolith is, as the crew on *Leonov* comes to realize, a von Neumann machine. This concept was developed by von Neumann to describe one method of approaching a job. Rather than build a large number of machines, it is theoretically possible to build one machine with the capability to reproduce itself using the raw materials around it. As the crew realizes, "humans" can be seen as von Neumann machines. The monoliths finally implode Jupiter, transforming it into a sun called Lucifer by humans. The crew speculates that the transformation was done by the monoliths converting hydrogen into a denser material that dropped to the core, leading to collapse and ignition into a sun. The new sun melts the ice on part of Europa, proving a more favorable environment for the species on Europa to develop.

The last chapters of the novel show Bowman doing two things: giving Hal a message to send to Earth and then removing Hal's consciousness from the ship to join him in the altered state of being in the monolith. The message is sent to Earth to tell humans that they can use all the worlds except Europa, where they are forbidden to land. *Leonov* prepares to return to Earth, putting the three specialists back into hibernation. The very last chapter of the book describes the effect of the new sun on Earth, and the epilog describes the Europans, a new intelligent species.

STRUCTURE

The structure of the plot frames the actions of the humans with the experiment of the aliens who operate through the monolith. In both *2001* and *2010*, the monolith, acting for the aliens, is part of a plot that the humans are largely unaware of but in which they participate. The monoliths originate events in both novels, and the double-plot structure is also related to the lack of closure in the novels. In *2010*, *Leonov* was supposed to retrieve *Discovery*, rehabilitate Hal, and study the monolith and Jupiter. During the middle sections of the novel, they appear to have achieved their goals regarding the ship and Hal and are in the process of studying the monolith and Jupiter. By the end of the novel, *Discovery* is destroyed and—(as far as the characters know)—so is Hal. Jupiter no longer exists, and the solar system has changed, with the addition of a second sun, new planets, and a new sentient species developing on Europa.

Although individual characters experience landmark events in their lives, there is no clear resolution or ending in this structure. David Bowman has discovered what he can do and has transformed Hal. Heywood Floyd is notified that his wife is divorcing him, and four of the crew of *Leonov* plan to marry when they return to Earth. But the mystery of the monolith is not solved, and the monoliths have revealed themselves as active devices of unknown power and potential. Their existence in *2001* proved that alien life exists elsewhere in the universe, but it was possible to assume that that life was extinct and that only the monoliths remained. Their actions in *2010* prove that the aliens are still active, although the characters do not realize to what extent. The novel ends with hints about the events of a novel to come: What will happen when Europans and humans finally meet? What further action will the aliens take? What will happen to the transformed Dave and Hal, waiting in the monolith?

NARRATIVE POINT OF VIEW

2010 is told in the third person omniscient narrative point of view. (See Chapter 3 for a discussion of point of view.) The novel's narrative point of view is split between two plot lines, one told from the perspective of Heywood Floyd and other humans, the other told from the perspective of David Bowman and by an intrusive narrator who provides information about the aliens to the readers. Heywood Floyd is the major point-of-view character in this novel. Over half of the chapters (thirty-one of the fifty-six) are told from his perspective. The first sixteen chapters are all from Heywood's point of view, establishing him as the protagonist and major character. There are other human characters who serve as point-of-view characters briefly: Walter Curnow, the American systems specialist; Max Brailovsky, a Russian engineer; Betty Schultz Fernandez, who is David Bowman's teenage sweetheart; and a nurse monitoring David Bowman's mother.

The transformed Bowman and the intrusive narrator are important point-of-view narrators as well. Bowman is a point-of-view character in eight of the chapters, and six of them are told entirely from his point of view. There are seven chapters told from the intrusive narrator's point of view. These chapters describe events both on the ships and on Earth, as well as the aliens controlling the monolith and the Europans. The intrusive narrator in this novel does not lecture about science as much as some of Clarke's intrusive narrators do. Instead, a good deal of the scientific information is presented by Heywood sending transmissions back either to his family or to the media services on Earth. The intrusive narrator simply relates events on board ship, or about the aliens, without being in any one character's perspective.

The narrative split is necessary because of the relationship between the two plot lines. Readers who share the perspective of the omniscient narrator can see the relation between the two plots, but the characters within the story are limited in what they can know about the other plot. The actions and motivations of the aliens, operating the monolith and through Bowman, remain separate from and mysterious to the human characters. Because even the transformed Bowman cannot fully understand the motivations of the aliens either, the intrusive narrator (who knows more than any other character) must provide that information. The information about the aliens is carefully controlled by the intrusive narrator who provides only limited information about the aliens who exist on the level of energy rather than of the physical world.

CHARACTER DEVELOPMENT

Three characters are the primary focus of development and change in all three of the novels: Heywood Floyd, David Bowman, and Hal. These characters undergo the greatest changes—not only physical but spiritual and intellectual. Heywood is the major point-of-view character in *2010*, and his character is developed much more fully than any of the other characters. His emotional and psychological state is developed through chapters describing his response to his firing after the loss of *Discovery* in *2001*, his choice to take an academic job, his second marriage, and his love for his wife Caroline and his two-year old son Christopher. His transmissions to Caroline and Dimitri from *Leonov* also contribute to the knowledge readers have of his emotional state. Heywood also has to face a personal loss during the mission. Caroline's opposition to the two-year mission and to his decision to go results in her decision to divorce him. Heywood is also described as upset about growing old, because he is twenty years older than his wife and is older than his crewmates.

The transformed Bowman is an important point-of-view character, and the development of a character who does not exist in any material sense is an important part of the novel. One question faced by the transformed Bowman is the extent to which he remembers being human and his relationship with the rest of humanity. Bowman is sent to Earth to evaluate the process of the experiment, and a vital part of that evaluation is his memory of emotions that are evoked when he visits the place of his brother's death, his first and only lover, and his aging mother. One chapter is a flashback to the younger Dave Bowman experiencing the diving accident that killed his brother, and this chapter provides a physical sense of the character. The visits to Betty and his mother provide a sense of Bowman's emotions that are studied by the aliens.

Bowman's journey also takes him to the moons of Jupiter and Jupiter itself to study the various life-forms that exist. His response to that life is also a part of the aliens' evaluation. The most revealing aspect of Bowman's character development is the process of questioning that begins on his journey when he becomes aware of the controlling intelligences of the aliens. He has powers, but he is controlled to some extent. He begins to wonder whether he can still act of his own free will. This dilemma is resolved when he warns the *Leonov* crew and when he saves Hal from the destruction of the *Discovery*. He can act on his own at least to some extent.

Hal is a character whose development is harder to discuss because he, or it, is never a human or a point-of-view character. But there is no doubt at all by the end of the novel that Hal is not simply a machine, and that he exists in some way independent of his circuits, in the same way that many humans believe that they exist independent of a physical body.

One of the ways in which Hal is created as a sentient being is through Dr. Chandra's perception of him as a form of intelligent life. This perception is mirrored, to a lesser extent, by other humans who perceive Hal as being crazy or stubborn. Humans often attribute human emotions or motivations to inanimate objects, but Hal is not simply another personified machine.

From the beginning of the novel, Dr. Chandra perceives his computers as his children. He mourns the loss of Hal. Chandra is involved in the development of computers to mimic the capabilities of the human brain, or Artificial Intelligence (AI). He is described as having "long since broken off communications with that dwindling body of philosophers who argued that computers could not really feel emotions, but only pretended to do so. ['If you can prove to me that _you're_ not pretending to be annoyed,' he had once retorted scornfully to one such critic, 'I'll take you seriously.' At that point, his opponent had put on a most convincing imitation of anger]" (22–23). He tells Sal (SAL-9000), his office computer, that of course she will dream when her circuits are disconnected because "[a]ll intelligent creatures dream" (25). Chandra's discussion of _ahimsa_, the ethical stance of nonviolence, with Floyd reveals that he does not think of computers as objects that can be created and destroyed at a moment's whim. Dr. Chandra insists on treating Hal ethically, as a living being, rather than as a machine. At the end of the novel, Hal joins Bowman in the state of energy where "human" and "computer" are more alike than different.

There are various secondary characters whose actions affect the plot or who are important to major characters. But as secondary characters, they do not develop or change in any important way. These characters are static, always acting in the same way. For example, Walter Curnow and Dr. Chandra are the specialists who do most of the work recovering _Discovery_ and rehabilitating Hal on the mission. Their characters are presented in a limited, stereotypical fashion. Walter is always the extroverted, outgoing, party-goer, and Dr. Chandra is always the exact opposite—introverted, ascetic, relating more easily to computers than to other human beings. Walter is bisexual and happily promiscuous; Dr. Chandra is sexless, married to his work. The Russian crew are briefly developed, described mostly in relation to their various jobs and in terms of their friendship with Floyd. Four characters on Earth are important to Heywood and Bowman: Caroline and Christopher, Betty, and Jessie Bowman. These characters are important because of their emotional importance to Heywood and Bowman. They are not developed at all and are seen mostly in relation to the men they are involved with.

GENERIC CONVENTIONS

This novel has an interesting relationship with two standard conventions of science fiction. The first convention is the reliance on the speed of light as a constant and its effect on space travel. This convention is one of the most important ones for the genre of science fiction, and Clarke usually subscribes to it completely. But in *2001*, his creation of the aliens pushes that convention to the limit, perhaps even breaking it. He postulates a species so far advanced that their technology allows travel that seems to break the speed of light. Clarke's famous Third Law states, "Any sufficiently advanced technology is indistinguishable from magic." The aliens in *2001* and the monoliths are one of the best examples of this law, even more so than the Rama spacecraft in *Rendezvous with Rama*.

These aliens have evolved so far that the narrator does not even try to explain the specifics of their existence, other than the fact that they exist as energy rather than matter, or how the monoliths work. The aliens can "rove at will among the stars and sink like a subtle mist through the very interstices of space," preserving "their thoughts for eternity in frozen lattices of light"; they are "creatures of radiation, free at last from the tyranny of matter" (*2010* 308). The aliens and the monoliths are not an extrapolation from current or speculated technology but are an entirely new state of being. *2001* may have left the genre of science fiction behind. The tone of the descriptions of the aliens shifts from a scientific, or lecturing, voice to a lyrical, poetic, voice. The aliens can only be described in metaphorical and transcendent terms ("sink like a subtle mist"). This unusual tone and unconventional portrayal of life shows that the Odyssey novels are transcending the conventions of science fiction.

The second convention involves the use of computers as potentially intelligent beings rather than as machines. Science fiction enjoys speculating on the possibilities of developing computers further in ways that mimic the human brain's abilities. The implications of this research raise important questions. What happens when a computer becomes self-aware, becomes an individual who can understand the concept of individual rights? What is the difference between a human being and a machine? Or is there a difference? As the crew realizes, humans can be understood as von Neumann machines. In creating Hal, Clarke created a character that has remained strongly in the popular consciousness ever since. *2001* is one of the earliest and most striking evocations of the possibilities of the sentient machine.

THEMES

The major theme of *2010* is the necessity for humans to keep searching for knowledge, not only as individuals but as a species. A discussion of other novels that have the same themes can be found in Chapter 2. The search for knowledge may result in transcendence, a moving beyond the physical state of being. By the end of the novel, humanity's perception of the solar system (and the universe) has been changed by learning of the existence of two alien species.

The first is an alien species whose state of being is so radically different from humanity's that they cannot be perceived by or communicate directly with humans. Only the tools they use, the black monoliths, can be perceived by humans. The second species is the Europans who are described at the end, circling a new sun formed by alien technology, who may or may not interact with humanity in the future. The first alien species is immeasurably beyond humans, in terms of their evolution, having moved from physical bodies, to inhabiting machines, to becoming beings of pure energy. The second species is far behind humanity because they have only begun to evolve toward intelligence since the change in their environment and the programming by the first aliens. But the existence of these species emphasizes the extent to which species are always evolving, changing and being changed by their environment. The time such changes take is far greater than an individual human can perceive directly, as is the magnitude of the continuum of evolutionary possibilities.

The journey theme in *2010* begins as a physical trip through the solar system, from one planet to another, but soon expands to include the spiritual journey as well. The literal trip is the passage of a group of individuals, but it marks the beginning of further evolution of the human species. One interpretation of the novel's message could be that humans are nothing but a lab experiment to be manipulated at will. Another reading could be that after a certain level of sentience or intelligence is reached, by whatever means, further evolution is always possible. The positive tone of the chapter describing the Europans does not support the idea that the Europans are primitive or inferior as a species. The valuing of sentient life, at any stage of development, is important to the aliens.

Humanity, poised between the other two species, is reminded that evolution is a long process based on change. The scope of the change in *2010* can only be understood in relation to the other novels. The alien manipulation of humanity is seen clearly in changes experienced by individual characters whose perspectives readers can share. Moon-Watcher in *2001*, David Bowman in *2001* and *2010*, and Heywood Floyd in *2061* reveal the continuum of change that is possible for a species.

ALTERNATE READING: FEMINIST CRITICISM

Feminist criticism draws on certain ideas about gender and power developed by feminist theory. Feminist theory generally tries to analyze the oppression of women in order to redress the inequality of women in male-dominant cultures. (An introduction to feminist theory and criticism can be found in Chapter 3.) Feminist critiques of science fiction analyze the extent to which women are often invisible in this literature or are relegated to limited roles. These roles usually are defined by their relationships to men. In later years, feminist criticism has begun to look not only at how women are represented but at how men are as well. Questions about the representations of men and women in literature and how those representations reflect the social beliefs concerning the two sexes are an important part of a feminist reading.

Long-standing beliefs regarding the nature of male and female associate males with the mind, which is assumed to reflect the intellectual and rational aspect of humanity; females are associated with the body, which is assumed to reflect the irrational and emotional. The belief that there is a difference between the mind and the body is referred to as the mind-body split. The association of one aspect of humanity with a gender implies that the aspect becomes the dominant characteristic of that gender. In the discussion of this split, the mind is perceived as being superior to the body, which results in a hierarchy where the masculine or the rational is seen as superior to the feminine or the irrational. This ideology results in certain behaviors being expected from men and women that are appropriate to their gender roles.

This association of different aspects with each gender assumes that the characteristics are innate, or biological, rather than culturally determined. The debate over what part genetics and what part culture play in human behavior is a long and complex one. But one result of the belief that women are essentially emotional and irrational is that women were denied access to education and jobs. *2001* is a novel that considers the potential for transcendence beyond the physical body and the limits of the material world. One of the results of the physical body has been this perceived split between male and female, focussing on differences rather than similarities. Considering the importance of transcendence in this novel, how does *2001* perceive intellect, emotion, and gender?

2010 does not restrict space travel to men only. *Leonov* has a crew of seven Russian cosmonauts and three American specialists who are undertaking a long and dangerous mission. The Russian crew consists of four men and three women. The captain, surgeon, and medical-nutritional specialist are women. The navigation, engineering, and computer specialists are men. The three American specialists are all men. This situation is not dissimilar to the actual space programs. The Russian program had women as cosmonauts before the American program allowed women as astronauts.

The female characters on *Leonov* are first presented as mostly strong and independent, even intimidating. Captain Tanya Orlova is a competent officer who intimidates Heywood at their first meeting. She argues for the need for hard proof when presented with Heywood's report on the warning from Bowman, and she acts quickly when the plans must change. Surgeon-Commander Katerina Rudenko is described on her first entrance as "massive" and "maternal" (41). She is an authority in the field of space medicine, and Heywood feels lucky to have her on the crew. The nutritional specialist, Zenia Marchenko, is a younger woman who takes over when the original choice has an accident. She is described in much more traditionally feminine terms as shy and needing to be babied by others in the crew.

The interactions between the men and women on the mission do not create major problems. But the characters are not described only in terms of their professional lives, with the exception of the two computer specialists. The women are restricted to traditional roles: wife; mother; or the nurturing professions, which were open to women earlier than to men. By the end of the novel, all the women are married or engaged to be married. The Captain was married from the beginning, to her second officer. Katerina is going to marry Walter Curnow, and Zenia is going to marry Max. These marriages and engagements are not the only ones described in the novel. Heywood is married at the start of the story, but his marriage is not a successful one. He was a bureaucrat turned academic when he married his second wife, Caroline. She is so unhappy with his decision to go on the mission that she divorces him while he is gone. Heywood's main response to the divorce is grief over losing access to his son Christopher.

The other women characters are important because of their emotional relation to male characters. David Bowman returns to Earth to visit two women: Betty, his first girlfriend, and Jessie, his mother. Bowman communicates directly with Betty, discussing his identity and memory with her. He returns to her because he felt the strongest emotion of his life with her. Before he leaves, he asks if her first child, a son, is his, and she lies to him. Readers are not told what he communicates to his mother. The scene is described from the perspective of a nurse who sees Jessie's lips moving, and a comb rising from a bedstand to comb her hair. Jessie dies at that moment.

Women in *2001*, even those who succeed in their professions, are soon married off or seen primarily in relation to the men in their lives. Women are still primarily responsible for supporting the emotional aspects of life. As lovers or mothers, they care for men. Even their nurturing of children is shown directed at sons rather than daughters. Men in the novel accept this situation without question or ignore it completely in their focus on their professional work.

The transformation that David Bowman undergoes to enter into the monolith removes him from physical life to another kind of existence. This process began with the aliens examining and storing his memories. His experiences in *2061* appear to be for the purpose of the aliens as well, as they examine and store his emotions. This process is described as resulting in an entity who is beyond material existence but also beyond those emotions we associate with existence: "[he] was beyond love and hate and desire and fear—but he had not forgotten them, and could still understand how they ruled the world. . . . He had become a player in a game of gods, and must learn the rules as he went along" (204). The superiority of the aliens lies not only in their existence as nonmaterial beings but also in their lack of emotions. Because this state is postulated as one possible direction for evolution to take, the fact that it is associated primarily with males is a disturbing one to a feminist reader.

The Songs of Distant Earth
(1986)

As has been the case with a number of Arthur C. Clarke's novels, *The Songs of Distant Earth* had its genesis in a short story of the same title. *Songs* develops scientific and technological issues that are important to Clarke, especially his concern with dealing with interstellar travel realistically. As he notes in his "Author's Note" at the beginning of the novel: "There is nothing in this book that defies or denies known principles; the only really wild extrapolation is the 'quantum drive,' and even this has a highly respectable paternity" (no page number). The quantum drive can approach the speed of light (nearly) but not exceed it. The novel also includes a love story as a major plot element, a rather unusual motif for Clarke.

The novel tells what happens when the starship *Magellan* must stop at a planet, Thalassa, where a colony was established by Earth seven hundred years ago. Earth began establishing colonies centuries earlier when scientists realized that Earth's sun would eventually go nova. But no contact between Terran and Lassan cultures has taken place for four hundred years. *Magellan* needs to use water from Thalassa to build a new shield to protect it from space debris. Despite potential areas of conflict, the Terrans and Lassans work cooperatively together during the time the ship spends in orbit.

This chapter examines five aspects of *The Songs of Distant Earth*:

1. The interaction between two cultures is the major area of plot development.

2. The structure raises narrative expectations and then undercuts them.

3. The narrative point of view is split between Lassan and Terran characters but is weighted more toward Terran characters.

4. The character development works through descriptions of personal relationships, introspection, and self-analysis.

5. The major themes.

The chapter concludes by presenting a postcolonial reading of the book.

PLOT DEVELOPMENT

The major plot of this novel is the meeting of the two human cultures that have been separated for centuries and see each other as "alien." There are a number of subplots, secondary stories about individuals, contained within the major plot line. But all the secondary stories contribute to the focus on the interaction between the two human cultures. The Lassan culture is described as a stable and peaceful one, partly because of decisions made in the colonizing process and partly because of the environment of Thalassa, a tropical world that consists largely of water. The *Magellan* crew come from Earth and Mars but are primarily called "Terrans" because the Earthlings are in the majority.

Lassan culture is based on what is known as the "Great Purge," a conscious weeding out of texts that would have passed on "religious hatred, belief in the supernatural ... everything that concerned war, crime, violence, and the destructive passions" (143). Their planet was colonized by a seedship, a robot-controlled ship that carried stored genetic material rather than living colonists. They have one political system in which their president is chosen in a lottery; their constitution was chosen for them before the seedship left Earth. The constitution is described as a "Jefferson Mark Three Constitution ... utopia in two megabytes" that has been amended only six times in the history of the colony, with no changes made in the past three hundred years (93). There has never been a war on Thalassa; the single most important historical event was the volcanic explosion four centuries earlier that destroyed their communications beacon. The culture is an egalitarian one; both women and men work at a variety of jobs. Marriage usually occurs only after the birth of approved children, and there is no sense of enforced monogamy. People live in groups, as parts of extended families, and there seems to be no discrimination based on gender or any concept of "different" races.

The crew of *Magellan* is very different from the Lassans. They are clearly more diverse, but little is known about their cultures. Most of the information about the crew focusses on the fact that they have lived through the destruction of Earth and the solar system. The Martians are a minority on the crew and consider themselves from a completely different culture than the Terrans, but other cultural differences seem small in comparison to the experience of watching that destruction. There are hints that the officers have military backgrounds and experience with violence. There is no specific information on gender equality. Most of the crew who are identified are male, except for a doctor and an astronomer, but Captain Bey recalls the assassination of the last World President, a woman, shortly before *Magellan* left Earth. Egalitarian cultures probably existed on Earth, but the hierarchy and power structures on *Magellan* and, perhaps, an unconscious equation of "sailors" with "men" result in most of the major Terran characters being male.

The Lassans see the Terrans as technologically superior. The Terrans do not agree, with the exception of the quantum drive, which only a few of them understand. Some of Terrans see the most important difference between the two cultures being the experience the crew had seeing the Sun go nova and witnessing the destruction of the Earth. Moses Kaldor believes that all the crew on *Magellan* are maimed, suffering from survivor guilt. The crew tends to stereotype the Lassans as a more "innocent" and "simpler" culture than *Magellan*'s.

At the beginning of the novel, the potential for misunderstandings and conflict between the two human cultures exists. Earth believed that the colony on Thalassa had been destroyed, because the communications beacon had been lost. When the ship approaches Thalassa, the captain realizes that he has to deal with a thriving culture that has retained its technology and not slipped into a more primitive state of existence. He wakes Moses Kaldor, a diplomat, from cold sleep to meet with the Lassans. The captain is prepared to use force if need be, but the Lassans agree to trade water for information. They are glad to help, and the President even invites the crew to enter their Olympic competition.

Various subplots show a variety of interactions between the Terrans and Lassans, all of which have the potential for conflict. The two groups work together, beginning with the construction of the shield. Their efforts are quickly expanded to include projects such as exploring Thalassa and studying the "scorps," an indigenous, or native, life-form living in Thalassa's oceans. Most Terrans and Lassans assume that the scorps are not intelligent, but there are hints that this assumption may be wrong or at least premature. Further study reveals that the scorps are stealing metal from the colonists to use for decoration and may be more evolved than is first thought.

Another kind of interaction is seen in personal relationships between the crew and Lassans. These relationships include love affairs and friendships based on shared interests. The most important love affair is between Loren Lorenson and Mirissa Leonidas. Mirissa also develops a strong friendship with Moses as they work together on downloading data. One potential problem develops when some Martian crew members argue that *Magellan* should remain on Thalassa rather than continue to Sagan Two where they face a decades-long terraforming process.

The first plot line to be resolved is constructing the shield. After the Lassans agree to exchange water for information, a manufacturing plant is set up and the work begins. Little narrative attention is given the actual engineering process. The resolution of the technological project is not completely positive, although there is no conflict between the two groups. One life is lost in the building of the shield when Kumar Leonidas, a Thalassan and Mirissa's brother, is accidentally killed. He is standing on one of the ice flakes at the moment it is hauled into space. The speed is too great for him to jump off. Kumar's death is described a tone reminiscent of a ritual sacrifice. He has been described from the start as beautiful, charming, young, and heroic; his nickname is the "Little Lion," and he is popular on Thalassa. He saved Loren's life when he was swept off a ship during a tidal wave. His death is the only one described in the novel. Tragic as it is, his death is not caused by human conflict or violence. Any large engineering project described in one of Clarke's novels is accompanied by death, a realistic assessment of the price for such projects.

As Kumar's death shows, the subplots tend to emphasize or end with cooperation rather than conflict. This sense of cooperation is shown in the relationships of the major characters as well as in the work projects. Loren works primarily with two Lassans: Kumar and Brant, the man who lives with Mirissa. The work the three men do involves studying the scorps. Their work is not affected by the personal relationship between Loren and Mirissa. Brant moves to the North Island to work there for a short time, but that decision is expected by Lassans, a culture that does not require monogamy between men and women. At the end of the novel, Brant and Mirissa are back together, and she knows that he will be the father of her second child, as Loren is the father of the first.

The one potentially violent area of conflict between the two human cultures occurs with the mutiny plot. Owen Fletcher and several other Martian colonists argue that *Magellan* should stay and colonize Thalassa rather than go on to Sagan Two. The proposition to stay goes to a vote by the ship's crew who are awake; most of the million people on the ship are in cold sleep. When the Martians fail to win the vote, they attempt to sabotage the ship. This attempt fails because several of the mutineers have confided details to Lassan women they are having affairs with, and the information is passed on to the Lassan government, and then to Captain Bey. The only action taken against the mutinous crew is to leave them on Thalassa when *Magellan* leaves. Although this decision avoids the violence of execution or imprisonment on board the ship, it has long-term effects on Lassan culture.

The next-to-last chapter of the novel takes place long after *Magellan* has left and describes the movement of the scorps from the oceans onto the land. This movement is prompted by their desire for metal, which cannot be manufactured underwater. Unfortunately, as the last sentences note, they had the "bad luck to emerge on land during President Owen Fletcher's quite unconstitutional but extremely competent second term of office" (309). The implication seems to be that Fletcher's policy regarding the scorps was to respond with violence, relying on technological superiority. There is also the question of whether or not the scorps survive this contact with the Lassans.

The resolution of all the plot lines is shaped by the characters' awareness that the ship will be at the planet for a limited time and that adding a million people to the colony is not a viable option. The Earth crew is primarily dedicated to the new colonization efforts at Sagan Two, which will require decades and extensive use of the quantum drive to terraform the planet. The Lassans know that their world cannot support any huge infusion of population. They live on two islands, called North and South, and strictly control their population. Couples must submit their genes for mapping and approval before they can have children, and the numbers are limited to two per couple, a basic "replacement" of population, or zero population growth.

Some crew members suggest the possibility of using the quantum drive to create new land areas on Thalassa, a process that would mimic the natural volcanic processes. Others argue against this application of technology because not enough is known of how the tectonic plates and a planet's crust work. In addition, there is the strong argument that the survival of humanity depends upon settling more planets.

Throughout the novel, the plot's focus on the interaction between two cultures results in characters—and readers—thinking about the results of such contact, especially if one culture is technologically superior to the other. In this novel, of course, the two cultures are human, but there is another species, or culture, living on Thalassa. The problem of human colonization destroying a potentially intelligent species is part of the history of the colonization process. Moses Kaldor, and others, worked in the years before the nova to evolve a set of Directives for colonizing. Dr. Anne Varley, an astronomer on *Magellan*, presents a lecture to the Thalassan Academy of Science in Chapter 21. She explains the ship's mission to Sagan Two, the planned use of the quantum drive to terraform the planet, and the philosophical nature of the Directives.

After the quantum drive was developed, the possible range of colonization was greatly expanded. Debate on Earth led to a movement to develop not only law but "Metalaw," legal principles that could apply to all forms of intelligent life, not just humans. As part of this Metalaw, Dr. Varley explains, the Geneva Directives were developed. One of the directives was that a colony ship should avoid all planets with oxygen. The seedships sent out earlier were directed only to avoid planets with "the potential for life to develop." This standard is much vaguer, as is shown by the presence of the scorps on Thalassa. In the course of her lecture, Dr. Varley makes it clear that she believes that the Directives could not have passed without the knowledge that the quantum drive made an increased range of travel possible. Because Thalassa was settled before the Directives were established, the colony was established on a planet that had the potential for life.

STRUCTURE

Like the major plot, most of the subplots in the novel end without a clear resolution or sense of closure. ("Closure" can be defined as a final narrative event or explanation that answers a reader's questions about what happens after the events described in the novel.) Certain opening events lead readers to expect violence between the two human cultures. In other cases, the love stories lead readers to expect resolution in the form of happy endings (marriage) or tragic ones (breakup or death). In both cases, the more-conventional endings fail to occur, resulting in a plot that lacks closure. The lack of closure can be surprising or upsetting to readers who expect narrative resolution. Clarke's novels often end in this fashion, but the lack of closure seems most appropriate in this novel that describes part of an ongoing process of human development and efforts to colonize other planets. The only final ending would presumably be the end of the universe.

The opening events set up potential areas of conflict that could turn out to be violent or dangerous. But the developing series of events avert the violence, resulting in cooperation and survival in most cases. Any conflict between *Magellan* and Lassans would have been resolved in only one way, with the destruction of the Lassans. The ship's quantum drive could completely destroy a planet if it were used as a weapon. The commitment of the Terrans to extending humanity's chances of survival is a strong one, but the captain is prepared to use violence if need be. Because the Lassan culture does not consider meeting *Magellan* with refusal or violence, the potential conflict is resolved with cooperation.

Other story-lines conclude in ways unlikely to satisfy readers who expect conventional endings to love stories. The love affair between Loren and Mirissa is given the most narrative time and attention. The two fall in love, nearly at first sight, and eventually live together. Mirissa chooses to have Loren's child. At the same time, both have significant commitments to and relationships with other people. Because neither Terran nor Lassan culture restricts sex to a monogamous marriage, there is no conflict over their affair, although Brant does move to North Island, where he has at least one lover, for a time. Loren's wife is in cold sleep on the ship, and she is also pregnant. Neither Loren nor Mirissa feels that their love must replace the earlier commitments. But when *Magellan* leaves, Loren leaves as well. Neither of them considers the idea that he would stay behind with Mirissa or that she would leave with him. Both are committed to working for the development of their colonies.

The planned mutiny led by Owen Fletcher comes the closest to ending violently, with the planned sabotage. But the problem is resolved peaceably with the decision to leave the mutineers on Thalassa. This decision, however, leads to the final event described on Thalassa when scorps leave the water during Fletcher's unconstitutional presidency. This situation is described so briefly and ambiguously that it is hard to understand what is being described in this ending that is in no way a clear resolution of the plot. If Fletcher's response is violence, then there is a good deal of irony in such a resolution. The *Magellan* crew could have taken what they wanted from Thalassa, with the threat of destruction through their superior technology, but chose not to do so. Alternately, if the scorps first attacked the Lassans without warning or provocation, then Fletcher's response could be self-defense. One brief reference is made to Mirissa's grandchildren seeing the light of the quantum drive fifteen light years away as it shines "above the watchtowers of the electrified scorp-barrier" (307). This sentence hints at a continuing conflict between the two cultures, one human and one nonhuman, that has not been resolved.

POINT OF VIEW

The Songs of Earth is told from the third-person omniscient narrative point of view that shifts between major characters from both cultures but is weighted toward the Terran point of view. (See Chapter 3 for a discussion of point of view.) The three most important point-of-view characters are Mirissa, Moses, and Loren. The main Lassan point-of-view characters are Mirissa, Brant, and Kumar. The main Terran point-of-view characters are Loren, Moses, Captain Bey, and Owen Fletcher. There is also a "lecturer" who provides information about the important scientific elements of the novel and gives a good deal of historical information about the events on Earth that resulted in the colonizing of Thalassa, as well as other planets.

The novel opens on Thalassa from Mirissa's point of view as she, Brant, and Kumar see the flare that signals the arrival of a ship. The first five chapters cover the first sighting, landing, and meeting from the Lassan point of view. The next five chapters shift to the Terran point of view and also move back in time to report what happened on *Magellan* before the arrival at Thalassa, providing more information about the Terrans on the ship through the points of view of Loren and Moses. The rest of the novel is arranged in chronological order, shifting between *Magellan* and Lassan points of view. Almost twice as many chapters are told from the *Magellan* point of view (thirty-five from Terran characters, three from a Martian character) than are told from the point of view of Lassan characters (eighteen). At the end of the novel, the opening pattern of narration and chronology is reversed. In the next to last chapter, Mirissa watches the ship leave and then grows old and dies after seeing the "flame" of the ship reaching Sagan Two. The last chapter is set on *Magellan* as Loren watches taped messages from Mirissa and his son, long after Mirissa and his son are dead.

The intrusive narrator, who primarily provides lectures on the scientific principles used in the novel, is also clearly identified as sharing the knowledge and culture of the *Magellan* crew. Most of the chapters devoted to lectures focus on the structure of the physical universe; the discovery and study of neutrinos; the chronology of the events leading up to the time of the novel, including the Sun going nova; and the discovery of the quantum drive: all events that affected Earth. Only one chapter, which describes the scorps, involves the intrusive narrator focussing on Thalassa.

CHARACTER DEVELOPMENT

The Songs of Distant Earth takes a rather different approach to character development than Clarke's novels usually do. Most of his novels focus more on revealing character by showing individuals in action rather than through descriptions of introspection or meditation. Focussing on action rather than psychological description is common in science fiction. This novel relies to a greater extent upon characters engaging in a process of introspection. Characters in this novel engage in uncharacteristically long and detailed reflections. Because characters are engaged in attempting to relate to other characters from a different culture, this introspection and self-analysis work well.

There are certainly events that involve exploration and a great deal of activity, such as the trips out onto the ocean to study the scorps, the tidal wave that sweeps Loren off the ship, and Kumar's death. But the fact that the technological plot is quickly resolved and presents few problems frees narrative time to focus on the results of the technology: the meeting of the two alien human cultures. The amount of introspection, which is related to the amount of time spent in a specific character's point of view, is one identifier of a major character in this novel.

The three major point-of-view characters—Mirissa, Loren, and Moses— are especially prone to engaging in the process of introspection. Because Mirissa and Loren engage in a love affair, they must consider the ethics of doing so, as well as the results. Mirissa's involvement with Loren, her pregnancy, and her friendship with Moses lead her to think a great deal about the differences in culture, history, and knowledge between Terrans and Lassans. Her own sense that she is somewhat isolated in her culture because of her intelligence is a major motivation for her to become more involved with the Terrans, as is the fact that her family has worked with the Archive for generations.

Loren's involvement with Mirissa leads him to question his relationship with Brant, and Kumar as well, as they engage in activities such as exploring Thalassa's oceans and studying the scorps. But most of Loren's introspection takes the form of reflection upon the past "life" on Earth shared by the *Magellan* crew. He compares the past and the present not only in relation to his affair with Mirissa but in relation to the attempt to colonize other planets. His memory of the last days on Earth before the nova, and leaving the solar system but watching what happened when the Sun finally went nova, is the major device, besides the Lecturer, to convey information about the lost home of humanity and how these experiences have changed the people on *Magellan*.

When Loren is first wakened from cold sleep, he meditates in Chapter 7 on the "tragedy that had shadowed more than forty generations"; he wonders what sort of dreams he will have in natural sleep, as opposed to cold sleep; and he remembers witnessing scenes "that no one could ever forget and which would haunt Mankind until the end of time. . . . With his own eyes, he had seen the volcanos of Mars erupt for the first time in a billion years; Venus briefly naked as her atmosphere was blasted into space before she herself was consumed; the gas giants exploding into incandescent fireballs. But these were empty, meaningless spectacles compared with the tragedy of Earth" (37). Loren's reflections reveal that the experience of the tragic loss is the major motivation for most on *Magellan* to wish to continue the colonizing efforts on Sagan Two, despite the decades it will take to achieve terraforming, and why most do not choose to stay on Thalassa.

Moses also spends a good deal of time reflecting upon the situation in the novel, although he tends to focus more on the differences between the two cultures in an academic or intellectual way. He is concerned with the issue of the "Great Purge" and its results upon Lassan culture, as well as the question of what contact with *Magellan* will do to that culture. Moses' reflections take the form of diary entries, which are transcribed in several chapters. He writes his diary entries as if they are letters to his dead wife, a woman who chose not to leave on *Magellan* and who presumably died in the last conflagration. She is still alive in his memory, and he addresses his thoughts on the situation and the Lassan culture to her. These recordings, or diary, are private documents shared with no other character in the book, so the reader becomes a voyeur, watching over his shoulder as he records his words. A great deal of what Moses records involves issues of technology, ethics, and knowledge. He also discusses these issues with Mirissa as they work together to download information from *Magellan* to the Archives on Thalassa.

THEMES

Some of Clarke's novels deal with the sense of a major undertaking just begun, or with a new technology just completed, and involve themes emphasizing human ingenuity and technological development. These novels, focussing more on technology, tend to present culture as a single, unified Earth or Terran culture. Cultural differences, especially those associated with different levels of or access to technology do not become a major theme in those novels. *The Songs of Distant Earth* deals more with the results of technology, specifically colonizing planets. A discussion of other novels with similar themes is presented in Chapter 2.

Because the colonization process has been going on for centuries, different colonies have evolved in ways that would be different from the Terran culture or cultures. This novel describes the meeting of two very different cultures, each trying to ensure humanity's survival in the universe after the destruction of Earth. Survival is a gamble, despite "technological" wonders. Technology in this novel is not presented as the solution to all problems. Natural events, such as the Sun going nova and the volcanic eruptions on Thalassa, may be predicted but cannot be controlled or stopped. Given the extent to which chance and natural catastrophe affect the human species, technology may be one tool for survival, but addressing the problems of human prejudice, hatred, and violence is an equally important method.

Characters from two human cultures meet and interact in this novel, finding each other "aliens" even though they are all human. But despite the differences, nearly all the plots are resolved without conflict, if not without the inevitable death that is part of life. There are dangers in daily life, including those inevitable results of the physics of the universe (everything from tidal waves to novas). The necessity of working together to face these dangers should be enough of a challenge to face without adding human violence that could be avoided.

There is a utopian theme in *Songs*, expressed in the idea that violence and hatred are more culturally constructed and transmitted than innate to the human race. Lassan culture is the closest thing to a utopia (outside the evolutionary step for humanity described in *Childhood's End*) that Clarke has created. The utopian novel is a genre that existed before the contemporary genre of science fiction but is often associated with science fiction. A writer trying to present a society that is the "best" possible society that can be imagined is writing a utopia. But as a number of critics have noticed, the writer's own culture is never absent from the imagined utopia. Plato's *Utopia*, for example, describes a culture that includes slavery. The slave class was considered necessary to do physical labor so that the upper class could devote time to intellectual and political activities. Feminist utopias published in the 1970s have been criticized for focussing on the feminist concerns expressed by white middle-class women and ignoring the feminist concerns expressed by women of color.

Clarke has not been known for utopian literature, although his work shares science fiction's sense of optimism and progress through technology. This optimism is reserved for continuing development, not some final end, some perfect state that can be achieved through technology or any other means. The city of Diaspar in *Against the Fall of Night* and *The City and the Stars* is described as the ultimate city, capable through incredibly advanced technology controlled by a "computer" of supplying all possible needs for inhabitants who are virtually immortal. However, this city, the ultimate technological achievement, is presented as the opposite of a utopian society, a dystopia. The hero, Alvin, must escape from Diaspar and its stagnation. Apparently Clarke is not interested in the idea of a static perfection for humanity, as opposed to continued exploration and development.

But Thalassa's superiority to many Earth cultures is clearly indicated by a comment made by Moses Kaldor, one of the major point-of-view characters. Describing Thalassa, he notes that "[i]t *is* possible to build a rational and humane culture completely free from the threat of supernatural restraints. . . . The Thalassans were never poisoned by the decay products of dead religions" (72). Kaldor himself notes that one single example cannot be considered sufficient evidence to base a conclusion on, but he believes there is a strong possibility that a better ("more rational and humane") human culture must be based on freedom from supernatural threats, which accompany most religions.

The colony on Thalassa is presented as a highly superior culture, and it was created as part of a colonizing process using seedships, frozen embryos, robot technology, and controlled information. According to the historical information accessed by Moses in his studies of the colony, Lassan culture has been improved by two specific selection processes: scanning for genetic problems (according to a character in this novel, only 15 percent of human behavior is genetically determined); and purging all religion and a great deal of history and literature from the information in the library banks sent with the seedship. Moses debates the nature of this past censorship, as well as what information should be supplied to the Lassans from the information carried on *Magellan*.

In spite of all of Thalassa's superior qualities, the narrative makes it clear that Thalassa cannot be considered a utopia for several reasons. For one, it is clearly a culture still developing, and the end of the novel implies that the Lassans are willing to wipe out a potentially intelligent life-form. Also, the culture does not show any desire to explore and develop further, to keep expanding technologically and spiritually, which is a positive trait in Clarke's literature. The *Magellan* crew, who are more actively engaged in the process of exploration and expansion, are presented as having qualities that are lacking in the Lassans, perhaps because of their environment, perhaps because of their culture. The two cultures interact peaceably and learn from each other, but neither is specifically identified as the best way for humans to develop by the end of the novel.

ALTERNATE READING: POSTCOLONIAL CRITICISM

Postcolonial criticism is a critical approach based on work analyzing the effects of European colonization of countries and cultures in Africa, India, and the "Orient." (An introduction to postcolonial theory and criticism is presented in Chapter 5.) Edward Said, an important postcolonial critic, has analyzed the extent to which Europeans imagined, wrote about, and believed in a stereotypical view of what they called the "East." This stereotype resulted in a simultaneous fascination and revulsion with the exotic image of the East as the "Other." Europeans perceived the culture of the Orient as the opposite of European cultures. In this stereotype the Eastern culture is defined as valuing emotions and instincts rather than rational and intellectual thought as decadent rather than moral, and always as inferior to European cultures.

The Songs of Distant Earth clearly refers to this colonial past in several ways. A spaceship named *Magellan* visits a water world with only two islands; two cultures with different levels of technology meet and interact. This story is similar to the history of European colonization into what they called the "New World." This world was very much the "Old World" to the various indigenous peoples who had lived there for thousands of years. The historical contact led to the domination of indigenous cultures by the technologically superior European cultures. The novel presents a much happier ending to the story, because *Magellan* and its crew are committed to traveling to Sagan Two, a planet that has no potential for life, and terraforming it. They vote against colonizing Thalassa, which would have resulted in the destruction of the Lassan culture.

The novel attempts to undercut the stereotype of the "Other" by various narrative choices. Paying more attention to the point of view of Lassans, denying the notion that technological superiority conveys moral or intellectual superiority, and making it clear that individuals are the cultural inheritors of technology all work against the stereotype. Presenting the Lassan culture as positive should reverse the stereotyped view of the inferior "Other". But the danger of stereotypes is the extent to which they underlie apparently neutral narrative conventions. Although the novel works openly to present both cultures as equal, two important aspects reveal the presence of this stereotype: an association between gender and culture, which results in the Lassan culture being gendered as feminine and the Terran culture as masculine; and the ambiguity of the concluding events of the novel.

The narrative point of view tends to associate a specific culture with either feminine or masculine traits. There are male and female characters in both cultures, of course, and both are apparently egalitarian. But with Mirissa as the main point-of-view character for Thalassa, and Loren, Moses, Captain Bey, and Owen Fletcher as the main point-of-view characters for *Magellan*, the cultures are associated primarily with either female or male characters. The Lassans are associated with the feminine symbolism of water; the *Magellan* crew is of course associated with the ship. Because the ship is never described, many readers will probably imagine the rocket-shaped ships that dominate a great deal of science fiction art, or the rocket-shaped ships that are familiar to viewers of earlier launches. These rockets, long and fiery, have definite associations with masculine symbolism. Overall, the Lassan culture, which is praised as lacking conflict, could also be stereotyped as weak, or feminine, compared to *Magellan*'s knowledge of destruction and violence.

The specific characters from each culture result in the gendering of the cultures. Most of the *Magellan* crew who are awake and identified by name are males; Loren's wife is in hibernation, and Moses' wife is dead. Captain Bey apparently never had a wife. Crew members are described as having affairs with Lassan women, a typical "island paradise" fantasy, which is part of the stereotypical view of the East as home to exotic women (and effeminate men). Presumably a female crew member, if she chose, could have an affair with a Lassan male, but no mention is made of such an event. The Lassan characters are more equally distributed between male and female, and Brant and Kumar are certainly heterosexual. This situation mirrors the historical one in which European ships, crewed by males, contacted cultures with both males and females but did not see the males of other cultures as equals. The crew, especially the Captain and Loren, often are frustrated by the Lassan culture's approach to problem solving and have to suppress this frustration.

The concluding events, specifically the departure of *Magellan* and the connection that is made between the resolution of the mutiny plot and the closing of the novel, are ambiguous in the construction of the two cultures. The next-to-last section of the novel is titled "The Songs of Distant Earth," as is Chapter 52. This section begins immediately after Kumar's funeral and describes the events leading to *Magellan*'s departure. The ship is leaving new technology and new information behind on Thalassa, as well as cultural and artistic artifacts. But the ship is also leaving the mutineers and the child Mirissa is carrying. A concert is scheduled to mark the departure. It consists completely of recorded sounds of Earth and the last great symphony by a Terran titled "Lamentation for Atlantis." When Mirissa visits the ship, she sees the bust of Tutankhamen, which is displayed outside the area of the ship where the people in cold sleep travel.

All of these images bring together concerns of mortality, beauty, death, and grief that cross cultures, as well as descriptions of art from various cultures that existed on Earth. Such a description at first reads as a cross- and multicultural evocation of the best of humanity, not placing one culture as superior to others. But all of the parting gifts are from *Magellan* to the Lassans. Nothing is taken from Thalassa to the ship. No description of Lassan art or artifacts is given. The parting constructs *Magellan* as carrying the superior technology and art from a destroyed planet. Moses Kaldor leaves Mirissa the gift of a casket carrying what is believed to be a relic of the Buddha, which evokes a religion of Earth as well. Important aspects of a culture—technology, art, and religion—are associated with Terrans, not Lassans.

The final events on Thalassa connect the resolution of the mutiny plot and the closing. Captain Bey decides to do what Magellan did when faced with similar problems: maroon the troublesome crew. Historically mutinies by European crews led to captains abandoning the mutineers behind on various islands. In many cases, these islands were inhabited by tribal cultures. The problem was not specifically the few men left behind, but European settlement, invasion, and destruction of the indigenous cultures. In leaving the four mutinous crew members behind on Thalassa, Captain Bey wonders if their aggression is what the Lassan culture needs. He apparently finds the Lassans too passive, content to survive but not "progress" rapidly. The same perception was often expressed by Europeans concerning the tribal cultures they encountered.

The ending of the novel hints that the mutineers have changed the Lassan culture in Fletcher's term of presidency and his dealing with the "scorps," the indigenous sea life of Thalassa, when they move onto the land. The ending is ambiguous: It could be read as condemning Fletcher and the mutineers or as praising him for saving the Lassans from the scorps, which a nonviolent culture unused to self-defense could not have managed.

The extent to which the stereotype of the colonial "Other" informs the constructions of the two cultures, even with the narrator's apparent intention of showing the equality or even the superiority of Lassan culture, is clear. The attempt to reverse the stereotype does not completely succeed in this novel, especially when the gender stereotypes and ambivalent ending are taken into consideration.

8

2061: Odyssey Three
(1987)

2061: Odyssey Three is not the novel Arthur C. Clarke planned to write when he published *2010: Odyssey Two* in 1982, fourteen years after publishing *2001*. His projected third novel would have made use of the information gathered on the U.S. Galileo Mission to Jupiter. That mission was delayed after the *Challenger* tragedy, so Clarke decided to write the third Odyssey novel using Halley's comet's visit to the solar system in 2061.

Clarke has insisted from the first publication of *Odyssey Two* that the books should not be read as a linear sequence. It is possible to read each Odyssey novel as a work that stands alone. Another possibility is to consider the novels in relation to each other, which reveals that they are similar stories about humanity's attempts to learn more about the monoliths. The theme of all the books is human evolution and transcendence. A summary of all four books and a discussion of the relationship between them can be found in Chapter 6.

Odyssey Three does contain three important characters who appear in *2001* and *2010*: David Bowman, Hal, and Heywood Floyd. Bowman and Hal were transformed into a different state of existence before *2061* begins and are existing within the monolith. The book is set almost fifty years after the events related in *2010*. The human race is still dealing with the implications of the existence of an intelligent alien species whose technologies surpass humanity's. The three new worlds orbiting Lucifer (Io, Ganymede, and Callisto—formerly Jupiter's moons) are being colonized, and satellites and high-altitude balloons are being used to study

Europa. But other than that, humanity in general, and Heywood Floyd in particular, are not paying a great deal of attention to Europa, or the question of the monolith, which is presumed to still be on Europa. Instead, Halley's comet, which is beginning its regular visit, is the major focus of interest.

The novel opens with Heywood Floyd planning to join an expedition to rendezvous with Halley's comet. He is one of several celebrities invited to travel on *Universe*, a luxury space liner making its first trip into space. He agrees, and they enjoy the trip to the comet. Then the ship is suddenly recalled from the comet to undertake a rescue mission. *Galaxy*, a ship making a scientific survey of the Jovian satellite system, has been hijacked by a terrorist and forced to land on Europa, a world humans were forbidden to visit. *Universe* is the only ship available that can land and rescue the crew and scientists stranded on Europa. The monolith, the transformed Bowman, and Hal appear briefly in the closing chapters to play a vital role in the resolution of the two ships' mission, as well as revealing more information about their own mission, which has changed because of damage to the monolith. The end of the novel is set in 3001, in front of the United Nations Building in Manhattan, where a monolith is placed in the middle of the plaza. The last event of the novel describes Lucifer fading, and the monolith waking. Although the final sections of the novel hint that Lucifer will last for only a thousand years and seem to set up a possible plot for the fourth novel, Clarke chose to take *3001* in very different directions, refusing to apologize for the "transmutations" in the fourth novel (261).

This chapter examines five aspects of *2061: Odyssey Three*:

1. The plot is developed through subplots that start out as two separate series of events but finally converge in the main plot line.

2. The structure is similar to *2001* and *2010*.

3. The narrative point of view works through several major characters and an intrusive narrative voice that withholds information from readers.

4. Character development shows the potential for humans to be transformed into a state of being similar to that of the aliens.

5. The major themes.

The chapter concludes by presenting a gender reading of the novel.

PLOT DEVELOPMENT

Odyssey Three is structured around subplots that begin as two apparently separate and unrelated series of events but finally converge on Europa, the former moon of Jupiter, and reveal the main plot line. The former moon of Jupiter is home to several developing species and is the site of a new experiment for the aliens who sent the monolith to Earth millennia ago. The subplots, referred to as the *Universe* and the *Galaxy* plot lines to indicate which ship is the setting for the events, take up the majority of the narrative. The last three of the novel's sixty chapters connect the subplots to the main plot line. These chapters concern the plot line initiated by the aliens, through actions taken by the monolith, Bowman, and Hal.

The *Universe* plot describes the rendezvous with Halley's comet, undertaken by a newly commissioned luxury liner, *Universe*, which is carrying celebrities as well as scientists. Heywood Floyd is offered the chance to travel as a celebrity guest and agrees. Although he is technically over a hundred years old, his two sessions of hibernation on *Leonov* and the fact that he has been living on an orbiting space hospital since that mission have resulted in his physiological age being between sixty and seventy. He is thrilled to take another trip into space, especially under luxurious conditions. The trip to Halley occurs without any problems, but in the middle of their exploration of the comet, an emergency call comes in. Another ship owned by the same company is stranded on Europa, a world that the aliens told humans not to land on after the implosion of Jupiter.

Only *Universe* has the capability to land and take off again with the rescued crew and scientists, but it will take the ship some months to arrive at Europa. The two ships in the novel have new drives, superior to those used by *Discovery* and *Leonov* on the earlier missions. This drive is called the muon drive, and it has revolutionized space travel in the same way jet engines revolutionized air travel. The drive consists of "portable nuclear plants" that use newly developed "stable muonium-hydrogen 'compounds'" in a process of cold fusion (42). The drive still needs some fluid as a propellent, and it turns out that the best fluid to use is water.

Although the new drives make the ships much faster than the earlier ones, *Universe* must travel from Halley's comet back to the Moon, where they will refuel and drop off the celebrities before they can go to Europa. A *Universe* crew member suggests another idea. If they can tap one of the geysers on the comet for fuel, they can travel directly across the solar system, landing on Europa in a matter of weeks rather than months. The geysers are caused by the ice that makes up the comet melting as it nears the Sun. Although the Captain objects to the plan, the owner of the company authorizes it, and the attempt to tap the geyser is successful. The ship is able to cut across the solar system and reach Europa more quickly than originally planned. One evening on the trip to Europa, Heywood has an odd dream featuring a small version of the monolith entering his cabin.

The *Galaxy* plot line describes the events on the ship that was hijacked to Europa while engaging in a routine scientific survey of the former moons of Jupiter. The three other inner moons—Ganymede, Callisto, and Io—have been colonized during the fifty years since the formation of Lucifer. Despite the aliens' warning at the time of the implosion, humans have been studying Europa as closely as they can without landing on the planet. Using satellites and high-altitude balloons, they have discovered that the new world is almost continually covered with clouds caused by the boiling away of the ice and some of the original oceans. Recent radar probes have revealed that a mountain has suddenly appeared.

A geologist on Ganymede, Rolf van der Berg, is intrigued by the recent and mysterious appearance of the mountain, which has been named Mount Zeus. He begins to study it because it does not fit the profile of a volcanic formation. He finally arrives at the hypothesis that the mountain may be a diamond, although this information is not given to readers directly until well after *Galaxy* is stranded on Europa. Although he tries to keep his theory a secret, communicating only with his physicist uncle, events soon prove that the information has leaked.

When Rolf is offered the chance to travel with a scientific mission financed by an anonymous grant, he accepts. They first visit Io, then Europa. A probe is launched that should impact on Mount Zeus and analyze a core sample of its material. Within a second of impact, the probe disappears or is turned off in some way. After the failure to learn the composition of Mount Zeus, the ship is hijacked by Rosie, the steward. She is apparently a terrorist associated with a South African political group formed after a revolution that removed the white Afrikaners from power. She locks herself in with the Second Officer during the night watch and orders him to land on the coordinates for Mount Zeus.

Although the crew and most of the scientists on the ship do not understand why a terrorist would try to hijack a spaceship, Rolf believes that his theory about Mount Zeus may be the cause of it. The Second Officer cannot land safely on Mount Zeus and has to abort the landing procedure. The ship lacks sufficient fuel to reenter a stable orbit and must splash down in the ocean. Rosie realizes that the attempt was a failure and kills herself, and the crew is left to try to survive until they can be rescued.

The air and water on Europa are poisonous, but the ship's hull is still watertight. They eventually manage to beach the ship safely. While they are there, Rolf and Chris Floyd (Heywood Floyd's grandson) take a shuttle out to do several important tasks. These tasks include setting up a station to monitor Mount Zeus, delivering a wreath to *Tsien* (the Chinese spaceship that landed and was destroyed on Europa in *2010*), and visiting the monolith. While they are at the monolith, Chris has a vision of his grandfather saying good-bye to him.

The two subplots converge on Europa when *Universe* arrives to rescue the *Galaxy* crew and scientists. The successful rescue is the climax but not the end of the story. The subplot regarding Mount Zeus is soon resolved. The monitoring of Mount Zeus reveals that it is sinking into Europa. Rolf's uncle, watching the event on the media, is irritated by the commentator's assumptions about the mountain-sized diamond. He writes a letter to a scientific journal making two important points. The first point is that Mount Zeus was a fragment of Jupiter's core, which was, as described in *2010*, a solid diamond as large as Earth. This fragment was expelled during the implosion, orbited Lucifer for years, and finally landed on Europa. Other fragments are undoubtedly orbiting Lucifer and can be retrieved. The second point is that there are many industrial uses for diamond that make its use as a gemstone trivial. One of these uses would be as construction material for a space elevator, reaching from Earth to a geosynchronous satellite, which would make access to space easier and cheaper.

The main plot is left unresolved at the end of the novel. This plot line involves the monolith, Bowman, Hal, and the Europans, and, with the end of *2061*, Heywood Floyd. The questions of the potential conflict between humanity and the Europans and of what further effects will result from the alien manipulation of humans are left unanswered. The Europans have been developing under the supervision and perhaps the manipulation of the monolith. Chapter 58 repeats the information from *2010* about life on Europa before the implosion, Bowman's tour of Europa, and the changes after the implosion. Chapter 59, titled "Trinity," begins with a discussion among three unnamed characters who turn out to be Bowman, Hal, and a transformed (or copied) Heywood Floyd who is now existing as a being of pure energy with the other two inside the monolith, or perhaps inside all the monoliths. The vision created for Chris Floyd was not a temporary one, but an "immortal copy," which Bowman says is "equally real" to the first Heywood Floyd (259).

Bowman and Hal have been studying the monolith, tapping its memories and trying its powers, during the years they have spent inside it. They have brought Floyd into the monolith with them to help them act as guardians of Europa in its place. Earth is off-limits to them, but Bowman shares his experience of visiting Jupiter with Floyd, showing him the life there that was destroyed by the implosion. Floyd also learns that Europa will have only a thousand years of "summer" before Lucifer dies and winter returns. The novel ends with a final chapter, set in 3001, that begins with Lucifer starting to die.

STRUCTURE

The narrative structure of *2061* is a divided one, pursuing subplots as they develop and ultimately converge into the main plot line, which is similar to the plots of *2001* and *2010*. The monolith began the entire sequence of events that went from the beginning of man as a tool-user to the development of humanity into space travelers in *2001*. In *2010* another manipulation designed to give another species the chance to evolve occurred.

Different sections in the novel focus on covering the subplots until they converge near the end of the novel. The first section, "The Magic Mountain" (Chapters 1–14), is split fairly evenly between the two subplots. Nine of the fourteen chapters (1–5, 7, 8, 10, and 13) develop the *Universe* plot line, focussing on Heywood Floyd and on Lawrence Tsung, the multibillionaire corporate head whose company owns the two luxury liners. Five of the chapters (6, 9, 11, 12, 14) focus on Rolf van der Berg and his Uncle Paul and hint, without ever saying anything about diamonds, at their interest in Europa.

The second section, "The Valley of Black Snow" (Chapters 15–20), follows the *Universe* plot line entirely, from the rendezvous with Halley to the recall because of the news about *Galaxy* being stranded. The third section,

"Europan Roulette" (Chapters 21–31), moves back in time to describe the events that lead up to the hijacking and stranding of *Galaxy*. The order of chapters in the second and third sections does not follow the chronology of the events described in them. Readers are told about the hijacking before it is described, so the third section backtracks to fill in the story.

The fourth section, "At the Water Hole" (Chapters 32–36), shows the subplots beginning to converge as the crews on each ship work on solving technological problems. *Universe* uses a geyser to refuel and then begins its journey across the solar system. The *Galaxy* crew beaches their ship successfully. The fifth section, "Through the Asteroids" (Chapters 37–42), shifts back to focus entirely on the successful trip from Halley to Europa, going straight across the solar system, inside the orbit of Mercury. The sixth section, "Haven" (Chapters 43–48), returns to Europa and describes the exploration by Chris Floyd and Rolf, who finally confirms beyond doubt that Mount Zeus is made of diamond. The seventh section, "The Great Wall" (Chapters 49–57), shows the final convergence of the subplots. Chris and van der Berg visit *Tsien* to place a memorial wreath and the monolith where Chris sees a vision of his grandfather. *Universe* arrives, rescuing all the crew successfully. The section ends with Mount Zeus sinking and the successful return to Ganymede with all the crew and scientists.

The last two sections move away from the plot events concerning the humans to focus on events on Europa and in the monolith. The eighth section, "The Kingdom of Sulfur" (Chapters 58 and 59), repeats information about events leading to the development of intelligent life on the planet and what has happened in the monolith. The ninth section, "3001," consists of one chapter describing the awakening of the monolith when Lucifer begins to die. These final chapters connect the events in *2061* to a plot that is similar to those of *2001* and *2010* and set up a potential plot for the fourth book.

NARRATIVE POINT OF VIEW

2061 is told from the third person omniscient narrative point of view, working primarily through various characters. (See Chapter 3 for a discussion of point of view.) The major point-of-view characters are Heywood Floyd and Rolf van der Berg. Heywood Floyd is the primary point-of-view character for the events on *Universe*. The events relating to *Galaxy* are narrated through a variety of characters: Rolf, Dr. Paul Kreuger, Captain Laplace, Chris Floyd, and several minor characters on the crew. The intrusive narrator provides information about the Europans and about the characters who are existing within the monolith.

The intrusive narrative voice, as well as Rolf and Dr. Kreuger, choose to withhold certain key information from readers for a good deal of the novel. The information that is withheld concerns the details of Rolf's theory about Mount Zeus, which is introduced in the first section. There are five chapters in the first section and a chapter in the third section that relate to the theory. The information that Mount Zeus is a diamond is not openly stated until Chapter 48 when Rolf confirms his theory and informs his uncle of the information. He is willing to tell Chris what he has found but asks him not to relay the information to the ship. Rolf and his uncle try to keep the information secret from other characters within the novel, but the theory could have been stated openly from the start for the readers.

There are hints that readers might use to deduce the nature of Mount Zeus. The chapter that tells about the political groups that formed after the Afrikaners were forced from South Africa mentions the importance of diamond mines to the economy. When Dr. Kreuger is researching the scientific journals for a theory that would explain the mineralogical information, he runs across an article in *Nature*. The article referred to actually appeared in the journal, and it is cited by Clarke in the Acknowledgements of *2010* and *2061*. The narrative voice presents the information in this way:

> The editor of that eighty-year-old journal must have had a good sense of humor. A paper discussing the cores of the outer planets was not something to grab the casual reader; this one, however, had an unusually striking title. His comsec could have told him quickly enough that it had once been part of a famous song, but that of course was quite irrelevant. Anyway, Paul Kreuger had never heard of the Beatles and their psychedelic fantasies. (63–64)

The title of the article is not given, but readers familiar with one of the most famous of the Beatles' "psychedelic fantasies" might remember "Lucy in the Sky with Diamonds." Finally, if readers remember the one-sentence reference (page 219 of *2010*) to the core of Jupiter, they might guess what Mount Zeus really is. But if not, they are put in the position of all the other characters in the novel who are surprised to learn the truth near the end of the novel. Because intrusive narrators in Clarke's

novels are often more straightforward, providing the scientific information a general reader may not know, or providing information that the
characters do not know, this withholding of information is an interesting
variation, designed to create suspense and encourage readers to think
through the problem.

CHARACTER DEVELOPMENT

The main purpose of character development in *2061* is to show the
potential for humans to be transformed to the same state of being that
the aliens have achieved. There are two groups of characters in the book:
characters who are important to a subplot but who do not change over
the course of the story; and major characters who are undergoing a process of transformation.

Rolf van der Berg, Chris Floyd, Dr. Paul Kreuger, the captains and
individual crew members of both ships all serve as point-of-view characters at various points and all contribute to the events of the story. These
characters are not developed to any great extent, and they do not change
or grow over the period of the novel. In fact they are often defined as
much by their professional or cultural affiliations as anything else. Rolf
and Kreuger are Afrikaners, scientists, who are anxious to determine the
truth about Mount Zeus and publish it because they are interested in
engineering possibilities.

Chris Floyd is more important because of what he means to Heywood
than for what he achieves on his own. He is given what could be an
important role when it turns out that he was approached by unnamed
intelligence agents. He was asked to report on what happens on the ship,
but he does not solve the problem of the terrorism. He receives and sends
reports, and he flies Rolf out to Mount Zeus and around Europa, but as
an individual character, he is not developed to any great extent.

The Captain and the rest of crew are described as rather conventional
professionals. The most interesting thing about them is that the two ships
in the novel are owned by a Chinese multibillionaire, and the crew of
Galaxy at least are described as mostly Chinese. One of the crew, Rosie,
turns out to be a terrorist and hijacks the ship. Other than her skin color
(dark) and the little information given about her background in one
chapter, we know nothing about her except that she makes good coffee
and kills herself when her attempt fails. Her role in the story is dramatic

but limited, serving the plot requirement of getting a ship to Europa in spite of the ban.

Heywood Floyd is a character who has played an important role in all three novels, and he is the character who changes the most during the story. He was the original head of the *Discovery* project. When that mission failed, he felt responsible for the deaths of the crew. He chose to leave an academic job and his wife and young son to travel with the *Leonov* mission in *2010* because of guilt. In *2061* he is living alone on the Pasteur Space Hospital. He has lived in this habitat since he had a fall shortly after returning from the earlier mission. He is presented primarily as a man who is alone and still searching for something in his life.

He is happiest when exploring space. In *2061* he takes the chance to go not as a scientist but as a "celebrity" guest to visit Halley's comet. This trip is probably the last time he will be able to travel into space, given his age. He persuades the captain to allow him, and the other celebrities, to leave the ship and explore the comet. His walk on the comet is described in the chapter "The Valley of Black Snow." His companion on this walk is a famous and beautiful actress, Yva Merlin, whose work Heywood has admired for years.

This walk, and his reflections upon Yva, show that he is not that interested in her, or perhaps in women in general. She is described as the most beautiful actress of her generation, and several of her roles are considered artistic triumphs. Though Heywood admires her work, he perceives her as having no personality and little intelligence. As they walk together on the surface, all of Heywood's attention and passion are directed toward the comet. Of the two pages describing the expedition, over 90 percent of the description is devoted to the comet.

Taking a moment to pick up a handful of the hydrocarbon ice, he makes an "ebony black snowball" and has a moment of intense emotion. He remembers a childhood snowball fight and mourns that he cannot remember the people he loved; he simultaneously triumphs in standing on Halley's comet. He launches his own small comet, feeling that this moment is the ultimate moment of his life, shouting to himself in his suit, "[i]f a meteor hits me now, I won't have a single complaint" (78).

Heywood Floyd has become increasingly more important in *2010* and *2061*. He received the warning from David Bowman in *2010*, and in *2061*, when he tries to send a message to Europa, Bowman and Hal receive it. They decide to copy Heywood and bring him into the monolith. By the end of the story, there are three beings in the monolith: Heywood Floyd, a father who has lost his son; David Bowman, a son seeking a father to join him in immortality; and Hal, the ghost in the machine, a sentient computer. They have transcended the tyranny of the physical world through their transformation, and they may be starting to develop even more as a trinity.

THEMES

2061 develops the theme of the importance of aliens to the process of human spiritual and technological development. Chapter 2 has a discussion of other novels that have similar themes. But there are differences between the theme of this novel and *2010* and *2001*. In the earlier novels the aliens seemed to be omniscient and omnipotent, all-knowing and all-powerful. Their manipulation of protohumans, the scope of their technology as exhibited by the monoliths, and their implosion of Jupiter had seemed so far above human ability and powers as to be omnipotent. In contrast, *2061* presents an image of the aliens that reveals their limitations.

According to Bowman, the impact of the asteroid could not be planned for in the monolith's program. Bowman says the result of the impact is that the monolith was overturned and damaged and its programs possibly corrupted. Apparently the aliens are not able or willing to correct the problem. In *2010* Bowman was aware of the aliens; he touches their awareness at several times and communicates to some extent with them. In *2061* they seem to be absent, perhaps because the monolith has been damaged. Or perhaps there is another reason.

Bowman and Hal have been learning how to access the monolith's memories and abilities. Bowman shares this information with Heywood and also asks him to consider the ethical implications of the aliens' actions in creating Lucifer. When Jupiter was imploded, many species were completely destroyed. The reason, according to Bowman, was because they lived in a gaseous environment, which means (according to some theories) that they could not develop "real intelligence" (263). This decision to exterminate one biosphere (Jupiter) to give the Europans a chance to develop is questioned by Bowman and Hal, who have also gained access to the information that the monolith manipulated the early ancestors of humanity. Bowman, Floyd, and Hal will serve as the future guardians of the Europans. Because the aliens are absent, perhaps Bowman, Floyd, and Hal are developing to such an extent that they are becoming the equivalent of the aliens.

The three experience a different kind of immortality, a promise to humanity of future development. The question raised first in *2010* is answered. Is Bowman simply a tool of the aliens? The answer is that he is not. He sharply distinguishes between the monolith and the three of them. Bowman tells Floyd that the monolith is a tool with "vast intelligence—*but no consciousness*" (263), and Floyd, Hal, and Bowman are its superior. They are not only intelligent, they have consciousness and an awareness of ethical principles. They must become the guardians of Europa, and they must not forget the Jovians who died.

ALTERNATE READING: GENDER CRITICISM

One of the major theories drawn on by scholars in gender studies was developed by Michel Foucault, a French philosopher and writer, in *The History of Sexuality*. Foucault's arguments concern sexual identity, power and oppression, and the historical construction of sexuality. Sexual identity encompasses more than specific sexual activity, including how individuals perceive themselves in relation to their biological sex and the gender roles constructed by their culture. (See Chapter 4 for an introduction to gender theory and criticism).

Related to the cultural construction of sexual identity is the closely related issue of the cultural construction of gender identity. Sexual identity is dependent, to an extent, upon gender identity, especially in a culture that makes heterosexuality the norm and relates homosexuality to the status of deviance. The social relations that exist between people of the same gender are affected by those perceptions.

Eve Kosofsky Sedgewick argues that the various social bonds that exist between people of the same gender are related to issues of power and sexual identity. In addition, the various relationships between women can be understood as a continuum, ranging from family ties, through friendship, political activities, and mentoring. This continuum ranges from heterosexual to homosexual relationships between women, but the various relationships are understood as being related. Although it would seem likely that a similar continuum should exist for the various relationships between men, Sedgewick shows that this is not the case in contemporary Western cultures.

Some of the most important social bonding between heterosexual men requires an opposition to homosexuality so strong that Sedgewick categorizes it as homophobic. This homophobic element is not required for male dominance in a culture; the example of classical Greece, which approved of male homosexuality and also restricted women, proves that patriarchy (male-dominant cultures) can make homosexuality a condition of male bonding that excludes women (Sedgewick 2–5). Examples of all-male social groups that exclude women and are based on homophobia include many professional sports and, until recently, the military.

Critics have pointed out that much of the Golden Age science fiction reproduces the all-male, or homosocial, environment that was the social norm during the first half of the twentieth century. "Homosocial" is a term used by gender critics to describe social groups that consist of one gender. Although the term is parallel to homosexual, the two words describe different situations (Sedgewick 1). Because the earlier science fiction stories routinely described months- or years-long missions with all-male crews, some readers have speculated humorously on the sexual problems that might arise. The publishing standards and customs of the time would not allow any description of or reference to any sexual activity, heterosexual or homosexual, and even in the 1990s heated debates over graphic depictions of sexual activity in science fiction occur.

Clark's novels since the 1970s at least have openly stated that the future cultures he writes about are more open and accepting of a variety of sexual choices than contemporary cultures are. Such relationships as group marriages and multiple marriages for people working in space occur regularly. Bisexuality is offered as the healthy norm, with any individual who is exclusively homo- or heterosexual being perceived as a bit strange, and in the minority. But few of the novels develop the implications of these future social changes in any detail. As far as specific descriptions of sexual activity are concerned, Clark's works are more representative of earlier science fiction than work by some of the younger writers.

The choice to imply sweeping social changes but not describe them in detail provides an interesting area for analysis. Developing a gender reading of *2061* quickly reveals that women are so unimportant to the novel that the question must become what is the meaning of what does exist: the relationship between men. This relationship requires both the concepts of "homosocial" and "homosexual" to analyze, because there is little evidence that the relationship between the main characters—Heywood, Bowman, and Hal—is homosexual in any way. This novel is extensively homosocial, which also seems to offer space to include two gay characters briefly.

There are only a few women named in this novel: Rosie, the terrorist;

Yva Merlin, the actress; Margaret M'Bala, a novelist and feminist. The few crew members named, on either ship, are all men, which means that most of the women are on *Universe*. In any case, none of the women is particularly important to the major characters. Heywood maintains a polite social relationship with the two women celebrities, but they are not important to him. Heywood has experienced marriages and more-informal relationships with numerous women, but somehow none of them had lasted. He is not in touch with his daughters, who married men and had children. His major emotional focus is Chris, his grandson, who followed his father and grandfather into space. The two have not spent a great deal of time together, but Heywood reveals one reason for the emotional bond he feels for his grandson when he learns that Chris in on the stranded *Galaxy*. His response is that Chris is "the only person who can carry [his] name beyond the grave" (94). The sense of immortality through children exists only in the male child who will carry on the father's name, not in the female children who will marry outside the family even though, logically speaking, each child carries the father's genes.

Hal never had any ties to women. As a "child" of Dr. Chandra and as a computer, he exists in that category of nonsexual beings who are referred to by masculine generic names and pronouns. David Bowman had some ties to women in his early life, but his visit to Betty and his mother in *2010* seem to have broken the emotional ties to them. The main plot of the Odyssey series resolves itself, in terms of the personal relationships between the major characters, to the male bonding in the monolith. This relationship is compared, by means of the chapter title, to the "Trinity," which refers to the Christian perception of God in the persons of the Father, the Son, and the Holy Ghost. The emotional resonances associated with this grouping are strong, as are the connections with a more evolved or superior species who have been compared to gods. These deities are all male. Bowman describes their perspective in these terms: "[T]here are things that are greater than Love. . . . Compassion is one. Justice. Truth. And there are others" (259).

The strength of the male bonding within the monolith also seems to allow space within the novel for the only two gay, married characters that Clarke has created. Although references to same-sex love were made in earlier novels, about specific individuals, the relationships were never made an important part of the stories. In 2061 there are two intriguing characters presented briefly, in two chapters: George and Jerry. These two are Heywood's best friends in recent years. In Chapter 7 they are his guests at dinner when he tells them they are his executors. George is a conductor who has brought back classical symphonies, and Jerry is a violinist. Heywood compares their relationship to his emotional life: "Looking back on his somewhat checkered emotional career—two marriages, three formal contracts, two informal ones, three children—he often envied the long-term stability of their relationship, apparently quite unaffected by the 'nephews' from Earth or Moon who visited them from time to time" (35).

Chapter 40, which consists of a "letter" from the couple to Heywood, is nearly a commentary in itself on gender issues, both historical and contemporary. The issue of identity—related to gender, sexuality, and historical figures—is the theme of the letter. "Monsters from Earth" is a transmission from George and Jerry to Heywood on *Universe*. Because he will be away longer than planned, they briefly discuss subletting his apartment. But the major point of the letter is a discussion of "feys" (the term used in this letter to mean homosexuals). The letter contrasts their self-perception of being "gentle and kindhearted (as well as madly talented and artistic, of course)" against the military men of history who are identified as homosexual or bisexual: Hadrian, Alexander, Richard the Lion Heart, Saladin, Julius Caesar, Frederick the Great (185). The chapter is very short, and the issues are not developed in the rest of the novel.

The novel presents a future society in which two men can apparently marry and in which they can be best friends with a heterosexual man who has no problems with open expressions of that friendship such as hugging, exchanging presents, and gossiping. Though George and Jerry tend to exhibit stereotypical aspects attributed to homosexual men (artistic professions, so-called effeminate behaviors and speech patterns), their presence in the novel is unusual. The question is the extent to which this future male-bonding—either in the monolith or among men—relies on the invisible presence of women.

The Ghost from the Grand Banks
(1990)

The Ghost from the Grand Banks is based on a subject that Arthur C. Clarke cheerfully admits has haunted him all his life: the sinking of the *Titanic*. This ship was the premier engineering achievement of her time, designed and advertised to be "unsinkable." Unfortunately, she sank on her maiden voyage across the Atlantic after hitting an iceberg on April 14, 1912. So fascinated was Clarke with the *Titanic* that he has used it in his fiction for years. In the "Sources and Acknowledgements" section of *The Ghost from the Grand Banks*, he says that his first full-length science fiction story, which was never published and which he apparently destroyed, was about the collision between a spaceship (called *Titanic*) and a comet. Forty years later, in *Imperial Earth*, Clarke includes a brief description of a successful attempt to raise the *Titanic* and exhibit it in New York. *Ghost* is a novel that makes the raising of the Titanic a major plot and thematic element.

Most of this novel is set in the near future of the early years of the twenty-first century, with the exception of the first and last chapters, which are set, respectively, in 1974 and in an undated far future. The attempt to raise the *Titanic* is undertaken by both a British and a Japanese company that want to place the ship in theme parks in their respective countries. The major characters who work on raising the ship are Jason Bradley, an underseas salvage operator; Rupert Parkinson, a director of the British company; and Donald Craig, a consultant with the Japanese company. The scientific and technological elements are fairly slight extrapolations on current technologies rather than being completely speculative. Clarke uses information from the 1985 dive to the *Titanic*, which showed that the ship was broken into two pieces, recent developments in chaos theory, computer programming problems (the "Century Syndrome" described in Chapter 4), deep-sea engineering technology already in use by oil companies, and an actual 1974 CIA operation that serves as the basis for the opening chapter. He is careful to acknowledge specific sources for all these aspects of the novel, providing titles and authors for those readers who are interested in learning more about any of these things, although his CIA and KGB sources remain anonymous.

This chapter examines six aspects of *The Ghost From the Grand Banks*:

1. The plot develops from an apparent conflict between two companies to the overall conflict between humanity and nature.

2. The plot structure emphasizes planning and development rather than the successful completion of the attempt to raise the ship.

3. The narrative point of view shifts between several characters and the intrusive narrator.

4. Character development emphasizes the importance of Jason Bradley as the protagonist and personifies the *Titanic* as a female character.

5. The images of music and the Mandelbrot Set (M-Set) work both structurally and thematically.

6. The major themes.

The chapter concludes by presenting a feminist reading of the book.

PLOT DEVELOPMENT

The basic plot of *Ghost* concerns two companies' attempts to raise the ship, which lies in two parts on the sea floor, by April 2012, the one hundredth anniversary of the sinking. Each company plans to use a different technological solution. The British company plans to raise the front half of the ship by using billions of small glass spheres that can stand the four hundred atmospheres pressure on the ocean floor. A Japanese company plans to freeze water and mud around the stern of the ship and then raise the resulting "iceberg" to the surface with the ship protected inside it. Both companies plan to display their half of the ship in theme parks, making the *Titanic* into a tourist attraction.

Resistance is expressed to the planned projects by people who feel that the wreck should be respected as a grave because the bodies of the passengers who drowned were never recovered. But the greatest challenge to both companies involves technological challenges. New methods and machines must be created to do the job. The major conflict in the novel is not between human beings, although the beginning of the novel seems to focus on the conflict between the two companies, but between humans and nature. The plot involves a quest to obtain an object that is the result of human ingenuity. The difficulties that characters must conquer are primarily the physical realities of the universe, or nature. What finally halts both groups is a natural phenomenon, a seaquake in the North Atlantic, which buries the *Titanic* beyond all hope of recovery, at least by human beings.

One conflict at the beginning of the novel focusses on both company's attempts to hire Jason Bradley, an underseas salvage expert. He is considered to be the top man in the field. He finally decides to accept a high-level post with the International Seabed Authority (ISA), an international watchdog organization, instead of either company's offer. The companies then face the challenges of raising funds for their projects, promoting the projects through the media to win popular support, and complying with government and environmental regulations and agencies. Jason Bradley works closely with the men who are heading the jobs for their companies: Rupert Parkinson (with the British company) and Donald Craig (with the Japanese company). Jason and Donald become good friends during this time. In fact, during the long process, all the men involved begin to cooperate with each other rather than compete, especially on the job site itself. As the project nears completion, a major seaquake in the North Atlantic occurs. Work must stop for a time, but nobody expects any major problems, although there is the slight chance that the wreck might be buried by the underseas avalanche caused by the quake.

When an expensive robot probe fails to respond to a recall signal, Jason volunteers to go down in a submersible, a one-man submarine, to retrieve it. He succeeds in rescuing the probe but is asked to check the conductor cables that carry power used to freeze water around the wreck. They are snagged on something and must be retrieved. When the submersible is hit by a chunk of the ice that surrounds half the *Titanic*, Jason loses the flotation modules that would take him to the surface. He has one chance: Jettisoning the submersible's equipment will allow the life support sphere to float to the surface. Unfortunately the escape mechanism had never been tested under the actual conditions of four hundred atmospheres pressure because it would have been far too expensive. The escape mechanism works, but the shock waves caused by detonating the charges cause the life support sphere to implode, killing Jason before the avalanche arrives.

Jason's death is the climax but not the end of the novel. There are two events described afterwards, each in a separate chapter. One chapter describes Donald Craig's life after Jason's death. The next chapter describes a ceremony on April 15, 2012, as the Coast Guard places a final wreath to mark the fact that the *Titanic* is "lost forever to the race that had conceived and built her" (250). The epilogue then describes an event taking place in some undated future. An alien probe arrives in the solar system long after humanity has left. This probe comes in response to an earlier interstellar probe from Earth but finds little or no trace of the industrial civilization that had sent it. The only thing left is an artifact buried deep in a mountain range that is an anomaly in its shape, size, material, and complexity. The probe, known as the Seeker, decides to excavate it. Although the narrative never specifically says so, it is clear from the description that finally the "Ghost" of the *Titanic* will be retrieved—but not by human beings, who have apparently long since left the solar system to colonize other planets.

An important subplot in the novel is the story of Donald and Edith Craig's relationship. Donald Craig is in charge of the Japanese company's project to raise the *Titanic* by freezing the water around it, and he becomes a good friend of Jason Bradley. Donald and Edith are mathematical geniuses who work with computers. They meet in the course of their work, marry, and have one child, a daughter named Ada. The chapters describing the Craigs' life are the only ones that deal with the private lives of characters in the novel. Other characters are described solely in regard to their public functions, in their jobs, or interacting with other professionals.

The Craigs also bring in computer programming and mathematics (the M-Set), the theory of which complements the engineering aspects of the novel. Donald invites Jason to visit his family at their home in Ireland, and they lecture him at length on the M-Set. The personal relationship between the two men reveals differences between the theoretical sciences, understood by Donald, and the applied sciences, or technology, espoused by Jason. Both kinds of thinking are necessary to the project to raise the *Titanic*. But even though the differences in opinion held by the two men can be seen as a kind of conflict, it is in no way antagonistic or directed at each other. Instead, just as the competition between the two companies shifts in the course of the novel to cooperation, the relationship between Jason and Donald becomes a close friendship.

The relationship between Donald and Edith does not succeed. After their daughter Ada is killed in a storm, Edith suffers a breakdown. She is hospitalized and becomes obsessed with the images of the M-Set generated on the computer. Because the place where her daughter died is an artificial lake in the form of the M-Set, her obsession is understandable. When Edith finally recovers from the loss of her daughter, partially through a treatment involving computer images and the M-Set that Jason suggests to Donald, she leaves Donald. She begins a relationship with the woman who was her nurse in the hospital. Edith also plans to develop a project to reanimate a young girl whose body was preserved in a sealed room on the ship through the use of cryonics and nanotechnology.

STRUCTURE

The structure focusses more on describing all of the work that goes into planning and developing this enormous engineering project rather than showing the successful completion of the project. The novel consists of forty-four chapters organized in four sections. The first two sections (titled "Prelude" and "Preparations") contain thirty-one chapters, which introduce a number of important characters and describe the preliminary work of setting up the projects. The actual attempt to raise the ship and the resulting failure are described in the last two sections (titled "Operations" and "Finale"), which consist of six and seven chapters, respectively.

In the first two sections, the novel shifts narrative focus, following different characters and relating events that take place at different times and in different places. Public debate over the project is introduced and developed through the reproduction of different "texts," such as newspaper articles, letters, and editorials, and through the description of television interviews with the key characters. The importance of technology, but also of capitalism and public relations, is made clear. Not only does the technology need to be developed and funded, but the project needs to be sold to a sometimes hostile public. The companies that are doing the work are located in Britain and Japan, but the public concern is not limited to any one country. Funding is raised in the private sector, but pressure from environmental groups and a United Nations bureaucracy exists and affects what private companies can choose to do in the process of raising the ship. The description of the political maneuvering and eventual engineering work is interspersed with descriptions of family conflicts and other problems experienced by the characters.

The narrative in the last two sections is told from a more unified perspective, especially in "Finale" where four consecutive chapters are told from Jason Bradley's viewpoint. This section is the only place in the novel where one character is the major focus for several consecutive chapters. Jason goes down alone to rescue his agency's expensive robot probe and dies in an accident because the technology, superb as it is, does not function exactly as designed. The last chapters of the novel return to the split focus and shifts in narrative time, moving away from one man's death to an ongoing process of creation, destruction, and future exploration.

The last chapters of the novel reveal that Clarke has chosen to work with an "open-ended" structure, where the novel ends but the story is not over. The last chapter of *Ghost* describes the future after humanity has left Earth, when an alien probe comes to the planet, searches for signs of an industrial civilization, and begins to excavate the *Titanic*. Humanity's attempt to raise the *Titanic* failed, but the Ghost will be raised in this undated future. The unsuccessful attempt and Jason's death resonate powerfully, working against expectations for a happy and successful ending.

NARRATIVE POINT OF VIEW

The Ghost From the Grand Banks is told in a third person narrative voice that is omniscient and, upon occasion, intrusive and explicitly reveals events that will occur later in the novel. (See Chapter 3 for a discussion of point of view.) Each chapter in *Ghost* is told from a single point-of-view, working through a variety of point of view characters. The most important point-of-view characters are Jason Bradley and Donald Craig, as well as the intrusive narrator. Other characters provide the point of view in one or two chapters, such as Rupert Parkinson, Evelyn Merrick, Edith Craig, her doctor, and the alien Seeker. Because of the shifting narrative point of view, few events are narrated from beginning to end in a single chapter. There are always interruptions, and these interruptions work to create a sense of urgency for readers who want to know what happens next, as well as giving a multilevel view of the narrative and of the characters and society being described as well.

Jason Bradley is the most important viewpoint character, in terms of narrative time spent on him throughout the novel. Seventeen and a half of the forty-four chapters are told from Jason's point of view, far more than any other character. The sheer amount of time given Jason is an indication of his standing as a protagonist, the character who is most involved in initiating plot events and who undergoes the most changes as a result. Given Clarke's interest in both sea and space exploration, the use of the name ''Jason,'' after the Greek hero of the Argos who led the other heroes on a quest after the Golden Fleece, also indicates Jason's heroic stature.

Donald Craig also provides an important narrative perspective. Twelve chapters are told from Donald Craig's point of view, covering the project that is the main focus of the book and Donald's personal life. Donald marries and begins to raise a family, and many of his chapters describe his family life. Because his daughter Ada dies in a storm while riding in a small boat, these events also provide a reminder of the tragedy of the *Titanic*.

After Jason and Donald, the narrative point of view that is seen in most chapters is the omniscient narrator, used by Clarke in seven chapters. This narrative voice gives important background information on specific technical matters and comments specifically on the events of the narrative and what will happen to various characters. When the major characters are introduced, this intrusive narrator says whether or not they are satisfied with their lives. Other chapters include specific textual material created by Clarke to give a sense of reality to the narrative: newspaper editorials, letters, excerpts from United Nations documents, etc. This quoting of multiple texts is a convention of science fiction novels that seek to describe the culture around the characters. Placing such texts directly in the novel allows readers to experience the impact of such texts directly, rather than having characters comment on what, to them, would be a common, daily experience.

CHARACTER DEVELOPMENT

The importance of Jason Bradley to the narrative is seen not only in how many chapters are told from his point of view, but also in the extent to which Clarke develops his character. More time is spent on describing the earlier events in his life—which do not bear directly on the *Titanic* project but are similar to it—and on describing his thoughts than is spent on any other character. Important events related in the first section of the book include a secret CIA salvage mission and his encounter with a giant octopus, "Oscar." The chapters describing the earlier events repeat, structurally, the overall plot of the book. A diving operation is scheduled that requires careful planning with regard to not only technology but also the government, media, and environmental groups.

Jason's dive to dislodge the octopus, which made him internationally famous, is described in great detail. His attitude to his work, life, and death are shown by his actions, especially his encounter with Oscar. Jason is not a daredevil who lacks the imagination to fear death. He plans the details of his work with care. When faced with a huge creature, which many would view with horror, his first reaction is awe and admiration at its beauty. He makes use of his specialized knowledge to scare the octopus away, viewing it as an animal with its own responses to the environment, not as some monster from a horror film to be killed. Finally, Jason is the single major character who is consistently described as taking satisfaction in his work. Others, such as Donald and Edith Craig and Roy Emerson, have achieved fame and money but are not happy.

Clarke does present one interesting hint at the way Jason handles the stresses of his job. Evelyn Merrick, the madam of a legal brothel, who is also doing graduate work in psychology, writes up a "case description" of one of her customers. This customer is Jason, although the identification is not completely clear until near the end of the novel when Donald Craig visits the brothel on Jason's recommendation. Evelyn Merrick states in her paper that she does not give her customers' names in the case studies but is always truthful about details such as profession and preferences. The customer comes to the brothel in order to be tied up, to be completely passive. Evelyn diagnoses this customer as having a "mild case of the Saint Sebastian Complex," and as "completely heterosexual" (136). This customer has long remembered an incident where he had to see a large number of bodies left after an accident. Chapter 1 describes Jason seeing the funeral at sea of over sixty Russian sailors in 1974.

Evelyn describes a conversation in which she accuses him of having a death wish. He does not deny it but states that he is relieved of the great responsibility in his life by occasionally pretending to be completely passive. Jason is the only character in the novel whose psychology comes under scrutiny by another character within the novel. This analysis provides readers a chance to think more about the character of a man who does what Jason does. But the information is presented in a manner that creates a distance, in the form of a report written about an anonymous customer, with some of the details changed. Jason is never directly described as going to the brothel.

There are other characters in the novel whose development is important, although not described in as much detail as Jason's. These are characters who experience some changes over the course of the narrative. Donald Craig is the second most important character, both in terms of narrative time spent in his point of view and because of his relationship with Jason Bradley. At the start of the novel, the two men are competing over the *Titanic*. But they soon discover a liking for each other and spend a good deal of time with each other. Donald invites Jason to visit his family at the castle they have bought in Ireland, and Jason does so. This visit gives Jason the chance to judge the marriage and family life; he is depressed, believes that Edith dominates Donald, and that neither the marriage nor the family is happy.

The Craigs are the only characters whose family life is described. Donald and Edith are introduced before their marriage, when their work in computers brings them together on a job. They marry, have a daughter, worry that she will not be able to live up to their expectations for her in mathematics, and start to restore the castle together. The marriage is not described as particularly happy, and when Ada is killed in a storm, the relationship soon comes to an end. Edith plans to build a new life with her former psychiatric nurse and proposes a project to resurrect one of the bodies, a young girl, found on the *Titanic*, using nanotechnology and cryonics. Donald is last seen at "A House of Good Repute," the brothel that Jason had recommended to him. He goes there after Jason Bradley's death, taking his place in a way, mourning the loss of his daughter, wife, and best friend.

There is another character in the novel who is important even though no chapter is told from this character's viewpoint: the *Titanic*. This ship is the ultimate object of Jason's, Donald's, and the others' quest. From the start, Clarke personifies the ship, giving this inanimate object, the product of human technology, human characteristics such as a name and a gender. Ships are traditionally referred to as "she." The *Titanic* is the "Ghost" of the Grand Banks. Only a person with a spirit could become a ghost and haunt people after death.

The *Titanic* is also a character who stars in a large number of movies made about the disaster, several of which are mentioned in the book. One in particular, *Raise the Titanic*, provides the title and the opening section of Chapter 19. This chapter opens with a dramatic description, four paragraphs long, of a dramatic entrance. Explosive charges are set off, clouds of silt and images of the sea "boiling" are seen, and the ship rises through the waves. Only on the second page of the chapter does the narrator reveal that this description is a movie's special effects rather than the actual description of the salvage project that is the subject of the book. Clarke references the movies in his "Sources and Acknowledgements" chapter as well as the book of actual dives.

Finally, as the ultimate goal of the quest that is the main plot of the novel, the ship takes on a human dimension, all the more so when the searchers find several dead bodies sealed in a room and preserved by the extreme cold of the water and the tannic acid from chests of tea stored in the room. The description of this discovery, in Chapter 31, ends the second section of the novel. Chapter 37, "Resurrection," relates the funeral of the men found, as well as Edith's plan to reanimate the young girl (called "Colleen" but never identified) whose body is also found in the room. With the identification of Colleen with the ship, the personification is complete, although Edith moves the focus from the actual ship to the human girl.

IMAGES

Clarke makes two non-narrative images important to the novel, and they work structurally as well as thematically: the music played at the beginning and the end of the novel (Arnold Boecklin's "Isle of the Dead" and Elgar's Second Symphony), and the Mandelbrot Set (M-Set). Structurally, "Prelude" and "Finale" are musical terms that Clarke uses as section titles. These terms refer, respectively, to the opening and closing sections of a musical piece. References are made to the music being played in specific chapters within both sections. Music moves through time in a linear fashion but can be repeated later, either through technology (recordings) or through repeated performances by the same (or different) orchestras. The musical images evoke elaborate patterns of repetition and resolution, as well as specific images of death. The solemn playing of music at the funeral of the Russian sailors at the start and the laying of a wreath after the seaquake at the end show how music is linked to certain human rituals and beliefs.

The second thematic image of the novel is the Mandelbrot Set, explained both by characters in the novel and by Clarke himself in the Appendix, which includes the transcript of a lecture. Clarke spent some twenty years on the lecture circuit. He has always been concerned with educating the general public on scientific ideas, as his involvement with television programs, documentaries, and his science writing shows.

The title of his lecture and Chapter 2 are the same ("The Colors of Infinity"), and part of the lecture begins Chapter 15. The M-Set, named after its discoverer, is part of a different system of measurement, or mathematics, one that depends on irregular shapes and dimensions. When Benoit Mandelbrot was looking for a name for his new geometry, he chose a word from Latin, *fractus*, which comes from the verb *frangere*, "to break." He coined the word *fractal* as both a noun and an adjective (Gleick 98). This new approach to mathematics is used to study apparently irregular systems and processes in nature, such as weather, tides, and the human circulation system. Fractals, and the M-Set, are related to the new interdisciplinary work that has come to be called "chaos theory." This new approach—identified by some theorists as the third great revolution in the twentieth century, with the first two being relativity and quantum mechanics—first began appearing in the 1970s (Gleick 6).

The M-Set is generated by an equation that involves addition and multiplication but can only be generated by computers after the first few steps because of the size of the resulting numbers. The basic equation is: $Z = z^2 + c$. If a computer is instructed to keep plotting new points by means of a dynamic equation (where the sum of the first equation becomes the next Z), then the numbers quickly become huge. The mapped or generated image becomes complex, repeating similar patterns on different levels. Clarke notes that when he was working on the equation once, his computer quickly started approximating because it could not deal with numbers that are over thirty-eight digits long.

Clarke includes reproductions of the images generated by the M-Set in the novel at the start of each section. The images generated by the M-Set are similar to the regular irregularity of patterns that can be found in nature (clouds, leaves, etc.) that are thought to be chaotic but that reveal an underlying order of repetition. Apparently random patterns that turn out to be not so random are, as a number of theorists including Clarke have noted, a way to understanding such natural phenomenon as weather patterns. Two basic ideas of chaos theory are that there is a different kind of order, or pattern, within apparent disorder, and that very small differences at one stage of a process can have large results at a later stage. The second idea is often referred to as the "butterfly effect."

The images generated by computer mapping of the M-Set can be colored, drawing from the principles of cartography in which the color changes according to changes in elevation. The color added to M-Set is based on the speed of the calculation. Clarke makes it clear that when color is added, the image generated is one of "infinite complexity, and . . . unearthly beauty" (274). The images generated by the set are compared both to galaxies and to amoebae, to stars and to water, to space and to sea. The M-set is both mathematics and poetry, technology and treasure: "the map *is* the treasure" (274). The M-Set works as an extended metaphor for the quest for knowledge of the physical and the spiritual worlds.

The story of the *Titanic* (great technology come to grief through human error) is a narrative fractal because it is repeated several times in the novel. The repetition similar, but not exact. References to other disasters are reported in a newspaper article reproduced in Chapter 7 that notes Chernobyl, *Challenger*, *Lagrange 3*, and Experimental Fusor One. The first two are real disasters that have taken place; the second two are imagined ones. The novel also repeats the story of the *Titanic* directly in Jason Bradley's death when his ship, the submersible, is hit by an iceberg. There was an earlier seaquake in 1929 that almost buried the *Titanic*; now a later one buries the ship completely, killing Jason as well.

Being able to plot the M-Set and work with it does not mean that absolute understanding and control are possible. The M-Set is made an image in the novel in yet another way. Donald and Edith Craig make a model of the M-Set in the garden of Conroy Castle, their home in Ireland. They make ponds in the same image and plant large cypress trees around the edges to indicate the "fuzzy" areas. Their gardener objects to transplanting such large trees, but the Craigs ignore him because they want the model done in time for Benoit Mandelbrot's eightieth birthday. Later, Ada is killed in a storm while boating on Lake Mandelbrot, and Edith retreats to an obsession with the computer-generated images. She begins to recover only when Donald, following Jason's suggestion, programs into the computer an image of Ada telling her mother good-bye and that she loves her.

The images of the symphony, the M-Set and fractals, and Clarke's plot and structure reveal that despite the difference in size, the same patterns can be repeated over and over with only small variations. But also because of the difference in size, individual human beings may not be able to grasp the whole, being able only to see a small part of it at a time and understanding it in a linear fashion.

THEMES

The story of the *Titanic* and its themes are important to Clarke because of his interest in exploring the various ways that human beings have tried to materially affect the world around them through the use of technology. Chapter 2 discusses other novels that have a similar theme. In both his fiction and nonfiction, he writes about our use of technology as a major part of what makes us human beings. *Ghost from the Grand Banks* is based on a conflict between humanity and nature that is worked out through the focus on technology.

The theme is developed through plots that center on engineering projects and developing new technologies in order to learn more about the universe rather than through plots that center on conflicts between individuals. Focussing on the difficulties and triumphs of creating and building everything from bridges to spaceships, Clarke's novel presents the image of humanity working together. Problems, failures, and death are inevitable because no matter how carefully engineers plan and build, things can go wrong. But the possibility of failure does not mean that we should not dream or not attempt to make those dreams come true.

The major focus may be on technology, but Clarke's view of technology is not unqualified or naively optimistic. The theme of the novel reflects a complex view of the relationship between humanity, technology, and nature. The synergy created by this relationship is not limited to the material world but includes spiritual levels. *Ghost* is a novel that insists that the spiritual levels are important while specifying that organized religious institutions and their reliance on "superstition" are not. Spirituality is evoked through the symphonies, which create an emotional resonance for certain characters, especially Jason Bradley, and through repeated images of death that the major characters must deal with. The deaths within this novel include drowning at sea (the Russian sailors, Rupert Parkinson's lover, the dead of the *Mary Rose* and the *Titanic*, Ada, and Jason). Death and sex are connected in Jason's visits to Evelyn Merrick's brothel. The sheer unpredictability of death and humanity's inability to control for or test for all possibilities are made clear as well. The inevitability of death and unhappiness is not sufficient reason to refuse to keep developing the means to better explore the natural world, because death will come in any case.

ALTERNATE READING: FEMINIST CRITICISM

Feminist criticism over the past thirty years or so has paid a good deal of attention to science fiction. (An introduction to feminist theory and criticism can be found in Chapter 3.) One major feminist critique focusses on the ways in which women are often nearly invisible in texts or are relegated to limited roles, usually describing their sexual relationships to the males who are the major characters. Feminist critics like Joanna Russ have pointed out the ways in which science fiction does an excellent job of extrapolating and building on technological developments and a poor job of extrapolating social changes that would accompany those technological developments. One of the social changes that has occurred over the last few decades has been women's access to jobs formerly restricted to men.

Clarke's novels are interesting because he does acknowledge that there will be changes in sexual customs and values, in marriage patterns and childrearing, and in jobs and professions, especially in his later work. *The Ghost from the Grand Banks* provides some intriguing speculations about possible changes in the social and professional roles open to women in the characters of Edith Craig and Evelyn Merrick.

Edith Craig is a character who represents the professional equality open to women in the future. She is a successful and wealthy computer programmer, a field that began as one completely restricted to white men. She is introduced as one of the "small pantheon of famous women programmers that began with Byron's tragic daughter Ada, Lady Lovelace, continued through Rear Admiral Grace Hopper, and culminated with Dr. Susan Calvin. With the help of only a dozen assistants and one SuperCray, she had designed the quarter million lines of code of the DOUBLEZERO program that would prepare any well-organized financial system to face the Twenty-first Century" (21). The DOUBLEZERO program solves the problem all computer users will actually face on January 1, 2000. The computer programs we use currently date files by the last two digits of the year, for example, 94, 95, 96, etc. When the year changes to 2000, the computers will place all files ending with 00 before all the other files. Automatic figuring of bank files and others will result in chaos.

Evelyn Merrick is a character who represents the changes that will take place regarding sex and sexuality. *Ghost* is set in a future in which prostitution is a legal profession. Evelyn Merrick owns and manages an exclusive brothel and is completing her Ph.D. in psychology, using her customers as anonymous case studies. In this future, according to Edith's psychiatrist, "One good thing did come out of the AIDS epidemic—it forced people to be honest: it wiped out the last remnants of the Puritan aberration. My Hindu colleagues—with their temple prostitutes and erotic sculpture—had the right idea all the time. Too bad it took the West three thousand years of misery to catch up with them" (224). By the end of the novel, Evelyn has completed her Ph.D. and is still running the brothel.

Setting the professional equality gained by women in this future against the larger concerns of the novel shows that women are still limited compared to men. The narrative reserves the sea, the most important element of the world of the novel, for men. This exclusion is a long-standing tradition in sea novels. All the writers the narrative voice alludes to (Kipling and Hemingway especially) are male writers, and their works focus mostly if not completely on men. Perhaps the cultural associations of the sea with the feminine principles are at work here, unconsciously, or perhaps the sea is somehow seen as truly a "last frontier." In any case, not only are all the major characters and most of the viewpoint characters male, even the giant octopus and the assorted diving machines/robots are given masculine names (Oscar, Alvin, Marvin, Junior). Most of the male characters are single, or not seen with wives and families. The one exception is Donald Craig's marriage to Edith and the description of their family life in Ireland. But the family life is described from Jason's point of view, and he at least perceives Edith as a masculine and aggressive character.

When Edith leaves Donald for a lesbian relationship with her nurse, her choice supports Jason's judgment of her as a masculine, or not typically feminine, character. The accusation that "professional women" or "sexually active women" are behaving in a masculine fashion is a stereotypical insult in cultures that wish to separate and differentiate between appropriate "masculine" and "feminine" behaviors. Because there are few major female characters other than Edith and Evelyn, the narrative does not undercut that accusation. Ada's death results in Edith retreating first to the M-Set and then into a lesbian relationship with Nurse Dolores. The doctor claims at the end that her primary sexual attraction was probably always to women. Because most of the information about Evelyn is filtered through Donald's or Jason's consciousness, there is little or no sense of how she perceives the situations or of her ideas and motivations. Finally, the male characters' quests are given the major space in the narrative and tend to outweigh the narrative voice's information on the social changes involving the professional status of, and professions open to, women.

The Hammer of God
(1993)

The Hammer of God was based on a short story by Clarke that appeared in *Time* magazine in 1992. This story, the second piece of fiction ever published by the news magazine, was commissioned for a special edition devoted to what was likely to happen after the year 2000. Arthur C. Clarke seized this opportunity to write a story discussing the possibility of an asteroid hitting the Earth. He soon realized that the 4,000 word story was a "compressed novel" (232). As he makes clear in his "Sources and Acknowledgements" chapter this novel contains both fact and fiction intertwined. In *Rendezvous with Rama*, Clarke wrote about establishing an agency to map the asteroids and develop plans for dealing with any that would hit the Earth. In 1991 NASA was directed by the House Committee on Science, Space and Technology to hold a workshop to discuss the issue of asteroids. A report was then issued by the workshop, titled "The Spaceguard Survey" after the agency in *Rama*. Clarke then uses information from the report from that workshop as the basis for *Hammer*.

Clarke's foreword gives a clear indication of his purpose in writing the book: "All the events set in the past happened at the times and places stated; all those set in the future are possible. And one is certain. Sooner or later, we will meet Kali." The purpose of this novel is to educate the public about the likelihood and consequences of an asteroid hitting the Earth. An asteroid hitting Earth could cause millions of deaths and perhaps change the climate of the planet. Recent evidence has been found that an asteroid impact caused severe climate changes that resulted in the extinction of the dinosaurs.

The major events of the novel are set in 2109, although flashbacks describe earlier asteroid impacts and give background information about the characters. An asteroid is detected that seems to be on a direct course for Earth. A science ship, *Goliath*, is detailed to carry out Project Atlas to deflect the asteroid Kali. *Goliath* will transport a mass-driver out to Kali and anchor it on the asteroid. The mass-driver will deflect the asteroid sufficiently to cause it to miss Earth. The first part of the plan goes well, but sabotage by religious fanatics destroys the driver's propellent tanks.

The *Goliath* crew attach their ship to the asteroid in an attempt to deflect it. The World Council on Earth sends out a nuclear bomb as a backup plan, hoping to split the asteroid in two. The suspense builds as a cave-in on Kali ruptures the ship's tanks, resulting in a loss of its reserve propellant. The reserve would have given the ship enough fuel to return to Mars or the Moon, even if Kali strikes the Earth. Although they know that the explosion will kill them, the crew requests that the bomb be used in a final effort to deflect the asteroid. The bomb fails to go off, but the impact when it hits the asteroid is enough to break it into two fragments. One, carrying the ship, misses Earth completely; the other skims through the atmosphere, taking "a hundred thousand lives and [doing] a trillion dollars' worth of damage" in two minutes (224). The narrative voice clearly states that this result is lucky for the planet, because direct impact would have been much more devastating.

This chapter examines six aspects of *The Hammer of God*:

1. The structure creates suspense by beginning in the middle of events and then backtracking to earlier events.

2. The plot to divert the asteroid is shaped by conflict between people, shaped by beliefs in religion and in science.

3. The narrative point of view establishes Captain Robert Singh and the intrusive narrator as the two most important characters.

4. Individual character development is limited because the extreme focus on the warning makes this novel a morality tale.

5. The novel blends fact and fiction to conform to the traditional conventions of the genre of science fiction.

6. The major themes.

The chapter concludes by presenting a feminist reading of the book.

STRUCTURE

The words "story" and "narrative" are often used interchangeably, but their difference is important in understanding the way in which the structure of *Hammer* builds suspense. Even though these words can mean the same thing, a distinction often made by scholars is that a story is a sequence of events, told in a chronological fashion, whereas narrative is a conscious arranging of events in an order that may or may not be chronological but that serves the purpose of conveying a message or theme. A narrative, or plot, does not necessarily relate the events in the order in which they occurred. Sometimes a narrative begins *in medias res*, in the middle of the events, and then backtracks to tell about earlier events. This structure creates suspense and emphasizes the meaning of the earlier events as leading to and perhaps even creating the event that begins the narrative.

The structure of Hammer is a narrative that begins *in medias res*, when *Goliath* is approaching Kali, and then backtracks to describe numerous events that occurred before the rendezvous and to provide background information on the history of asteroid impacts, the life of Captain Robert Singh, and the origins and development of Chrislam. Interspersed between chapters of the novel are short sections titled "Encounters," which describe four encounters with asteroids. Three of the four encounters are historical; the fourth is the encounter with Kali. These encounters are cautionary tales designed to provide a commentary upon the narrative. The effect is to add weight to the warning to take the possibility of a major asteroid impact seriously.

The novel opens with an "Encounter" section that describes a 1972 asteroid impact in Oregon. The encounter is followed by the first chapter of the novel, which contains a leisurely and lyrical description of a father, Captain Robert Singh, spending time with his young son, Toby, outside their home in Africa. This scene is a memory, a "neural playback," or virtual reality, that Captain Singh is experiencing through his Brainman, a portable device. These devices play back memories or other stored material in such a realistic way that individuals experience the event again. In reality, Captain Singh is on *Goliath*, an hour away from the rendezvous with Kali, which is soon established to be on a direct course to Earth.

Following the first five opening chapters and the descriptions of two other encounters with asteroids are fifteen chapters that provide a history of Project Spaceguard, which is an on-going study of asteroids and how to deal with any that may impact Earth, a description of Robert Singh's past life and marriages, a history of the development of the religion of Chrislam, and a description of the Excalibur Project, which set off a bomb that produced radio waves in order to map satellites and asteroids. The purpose of many of these chapters is to provide more information on Singh and on the cultural, social, and scientific background of this future. Chapters 21 and 22 provide background on *Goliath*, and Chapter 23 resumes the story of Kali and begins to relate the attempt to divert the asteroid, called Project Atlas. The next twenty-three chapters focus on the chronological narrative of Project Atlas, the sabotage, and the use of the bomb, picking up from the events in the opening chapters.

The possibility that Kali's impact will not only destroy millions but may change the climate drastically enough to wipe out most life on Earth is made clear at the start. Then the narrative shifts to the events that took place in the past for the first half of the book. The delay in relating what is happening with Kali creates suspense. The events in the last half of the novel build that suspense by leading readers to believe that *Goliath* may be destroyed and that the asteroid may still impact Earth. The suspense is maintained until the last page of the novel, which describes the survival of *Goliath* and Earth, then ends with the warning that Asteroid Swift-Tuttle is accelerating towards its perihelion (the point in its orbit closest to the Sun). Swift-Tuttle is a real asteroid, which will intersect Earth's orbit in August 2126.

PLOT DEVELOPMENT

The major plot of *Hammer* is the attempt to deflect Kali, saving the lives of millions of people and perhaps all life on Earth from the devastation of its impact. The concept of a threat from space is not a new one for Clarke; he uses one variation or another of it in many of his novels. In many of those novels, such a threat is sufficient to make the peoples and nations of the Earth come together in the face of a shared threat to humanity. The plot in those novels is based on the conflict between humanity and the threat, often a natural event. The methods used to overcome the threat often involve technological application of scientific theories and principles.

Hammer's plot emphasizes the conflict between groups of people, rather than humanity and nature, to a greater extent than is usual in Clarke's novels. Kali, the threat at the beginning, almost disappears as the narrative backtracks to a time before her approach. She does not completely disappear as a threat, because other encounters with asteroids are described. Additionally, some of the background chapters discuss the founding of Spaceguard in the face of opposition by Senator Ledstone. But five of the seven chapters of Part II and three of the six chapters of Part III do not mention asteroids at all. Instead, the earlier life, first marriage, and career of Captain Singh are described in Part II, and the founding of Chrislam by the Prophet Fatima Magdalene is described in Part III.

These events are important to the main plot, although their relation to it is not immediately apparent. Captain Singh is the man destined to command *Goliath* on its mission to Kali, and Chrislam fanatics sabotage the Atlas mass-driver. Singh is a protagonist who is facing two antagonists. The most important antagonist is Kali, but the Chrislam fanatics are also strongly antagonistic. Their sabotage to the tanks of the mass-driver keep the story from ending in Chapter 30. The question of why any group, no matter how fanatical, would commit an act that would result in the complete destruction of Earth brings up the question of motivation.

The Chrislam group's motivation is related to events that are connected to Project Spaceguard. Chapters in Part III describe Excalibur, an earlier project related to Spaceguard. This project involved detonating a gigaton nuclear bomb opposite Earth, on the other side of the Sun but in the same orbit as Earth. The purpose of this bomb was not destructive. Instead, it emitted laser rays in all directions and allowed the complete mapping of all the "known satellites, asteroids, and asteroids . . . more than a meter in diameter inside the orbit of Jupiter" (101). Because Kali was at the far point of its orbit at that time, it was far out of range and was not mapped.

Years later, a signal is received at SETI, the Search for Extraterrestrial Intelligence. The signal is coming from the direction of Sirius and turns out to be an answer, of sorts, to Excalibur. The timing is correct for an intelligent species to have received Excalibur's signal and to have beamed back a signal at the same frequency. There is no meaning to the signal, which seems to be unmodulated noise, but it is clearly of artificial origins because of its strength, or loudness. Public opinion is split between trying to answer the signal or ignoring it, but the Reborn, a Chrislam splinter group, decide that the signal is the Voice of God. They build a radio dish and begin a dialogue with the Voice, claiming they are the only ones able to understand what God is saying.

When Kali appears, they decide that the asteroid is a messenger from God. The world will be destroyed, but the Reborn promise reincarnation through the Voice of God. They propose to record a "complete human being—all the memories of a lifetime, and the current map of the body that had experienced them" and to beam that information to Heaven, located near Sirius (108). The Reborn are a Millennial group, a group who believes that the end of the world, or the universe, is near at hand. The term for such groups is based on the fact that they tend to become more active when the end of a millennium (1000, 2000 years) occurs, believing that the number has some significance. When Project Atlas is announced, a group of Reborn fanatics, believing any attempt to interfere with Kali to be going against God's will, sabotage the mass-driver.

Captain Singh is the man in charge of *Goliath*, and the information about his earlier life comes together in his belief that he was destined to oppose Kali. The Chrislam fanatics take their religion's belief into extremism to oppose Project Atlas. The early attempts to map the asteroids and learn enough to prevent a collision with Earth actually results in a situation that supports the delusions of the Chrislam radicals. Those early attempts were intended to make saving the Earth possible. Early detection is important in responding to asteroids that will impact the planet because of their mass. Project Atlas works only if the mass-driver is attached to the asteroid before it passes Mars's orbit. The reason is that the thrust that can be applied will only move the asteroid a few centimeters, but the deflection of a few centimeters at that point will result in the asteroid missing Earth by thousands of kilometers. But Excalibur, planned to help preserve the Earth, leads to a nearly-successful attempt to destroy the planet.

The ship is fitted out with the mass-driver; the trip to Europa for refueling is successful. They rendezvous with Kali and verify that her orbit will impact Earth in the Pacific Ocean. They work on attaching the mass-driver and run a simulation to see if it will work. While they are there,

Sir Colin Draker, one of the research scientists originally assigned to *Goliath* who insisted upon accompanying them, celebrates his one hundredth birthday. As a present, Captain Singh and Fletcher take him on a tour of the asteroid. They play a prank on him by attaching a large imitation flower to the asteroid. Part of the impetus behind the joke is the constant debate between Sir Colin and another scientist about the possibility of life on asteroids. This joke serves as a moment of light relief, but the explosion of the tanks and the news about the sabotage follows almost immediately.

Just as everything seems to be falling into place for a flawless execution of the project, the sabotage is revealed by one of the group responsible, who has defected and confessed. But the information comes too late to save the project. By the time the news arrives at *Goliath*, the tanks have already blown up. Earth is doomed, but *Goliath* could return to Mars or the Moon where many of the crew have families.

The on-board computer, David, proposes using *Goliath* as a mass-driver—he is the only member of the crew who is not emotionally affected by the sabotage. They begin to work on the proposal. The World Government has also established a contingency plan by launching a rocket with a nuclear bomb on it. In theory, the bomb will split Kali, which was probably formed by the collision of two smaller asteroids, and the fragments will pass on either side of Earth. There is still a chance that one will impact Earth. The suspense builds to the end of the novel, and only through the use of both plans is Kali successfully deflected. Earth's safety is not clearly stated until the last page, and the final words of the novel are a warning that more asteroids are out there and will intersect Earth's orbit in the future.

The conflict in the novel revolves around different interpretations of a natural event. One possible interpretation is a religious one. The Chrislam sect interprets the approaching asteroid as "The Hammer of God," sent to destroy the Earth in a final judgment. In this interpretation, God is in charge of everything and is testing humanity. A second possible interpretation is scientific. Chaos theory, mentioned in Chapter 4 of the novel, is a scientific theory for analyzing complex natural systems. Though the theory states that nothing can be predicted with absolute certainty, some events can be predicted accurately, especially in the short term. These two views come into conflict over what should or should not be done with regard to Kali.

NARRATIVE POINT OF VIEW

The Hammer of God is told from a third person, omniscient narrative point of view. (See Chapter 3 for a discussion of point of view.) This point of view establishes two characters as most important: Captain Robert Singh; and the intrusive narrator, who plays a much larger role than is usual in Clarke's novels. Twenty-three of the forty-six chapters (exactly half) are told from Singh's viewpoint. These chapters describe his college experience of winning an Olympic race, his two marriages, his posting on *Goliath*, and the mission to Kali. A few other characters are point-of-view characters as well. Sir Colin Draker, the elderly scientist, and David, the computer—a "Legal Human" by virtue of the hundredth amendment—are point-of-view characters in one or two chapters. Two figures who played important roles in establishing Project Spaceguard are also the focus of several chapters: Carlos Mendoza, who argued for its establishment, and Senator Ledstone who opposed it at first.

The intrusive narrator appears in eighteen sections. Fourteen of the forty-six chapters and all four of the "Encounters" are narrated by the intrusive narrator. This voice directly addresses the reader without working through a point-of-view character. Intrusive narrators are often used in science fiction to provide a good deal of information quickly to readers. In *Hammer*, the information about asteroid impacts, Spaceguard, and the development of Chrislam is important to the main plot line. Such heavy use of the intrusive narrator can have other effects, as well. The intrusive narrator begins to be clearly the voice of the author, trying to convey a message directly and without working through fictional conventions. All fictions have a purpose, of course, or a message: the theme. But the conventions of realism and more-contemporary fictions tend to dictate less use of the intrusive narrator, compared to other literary traditions. An intrusive narrator who becomes a more developed character than the characters in the novel can often work against the author's purpose.

CHARACTER DEVELOPMENT

The importance of religion in this novel as a plot device has an interesting connection to the character development. In many ways, the novel reads more like a medieval morality play than a realistic novel. The medieval morality dramas that flourished during the fourteenth century used characters who were personified abstractions, such as Truth or Sin, rather than characters intended to represent humans. The characterization was subordinated to the message of the play. *Hammer* emphasizes the warning about asteroid impacts to such an extent that individual character development is sacrificed to the message.

Even in the flashback chapters, minimal character development occurs. Few characters are developed in any detail except for Captain Singh, and his character development is devoted to showing the path by which he arrives at command of *Goliath* in time to meet his destiny of opposing Kali. The information about his past is covered quickly: There is more detail about his Olympic race than either of his marriages, emphasizing the heroic athletic background. Within a few short chapters, he marries, fathers a child, splits up, marries again, has two more children, and achieves a certain success in his job. He prefers to see events in his life occurring randomly rather than in any predestined order, until the announcement about Kali arrives. Then, suddenly, "a sense of elation swept over him. This was what *Goliath* had been built for, decades ago. And this was his moment of destiny. . . . This was why he had been born" (125). Captain Singh is closely akin to the traditional science fiction hero, a competent man who achieves greatness through his efforts. He sees life as consisting of tests: The important ones are the Olympic race and Kali. Events in between do not seem to be as important.

Little information is given about other characters who are lost in the background and verge on being stereotypes. Sonny the steward on *Goliath* is described as having a variety of sex aids. David the computer tries to make jokes, but is not very good at it. Dr. Colin Draker is an irascible, elderly geologist. Torin Fletcher is the engineer. These characters are not meant to stand out as individuals but to represent humanity generally. Morality tales are not supposed to have fully developed characters; some critics point out that science fiction tends to rely on more generalized characters as well. The conventions of the genre work in many cases. If a reader becomes completely involved with the danger facing Earth, then the lack of characterization will not be a problem. But some readers will want more-developed characters with whom they can sympathize. This novel's character development focusses more on the generic than the individual.

GENERIC CONVENTIONS

The novel blends a good deal of science fact with fiction to conform to the traditional conventions of the genre of science fiction. The "Sources and Acknowledgements" section summarizes the factual information used in the novel. The most important fact is the paper announcing the finding of evidence that an asteroid hitting the Earth may well have been the catastrophic event that caused the extinction of the dinosaurs. This paper (by Luis Alvarez, the inventor of the radar system Clarke helped test during World War II, and his son) appeared in *Science* in 1980. The historical asteroid impacts described in three of the "Encounter" sections are all documented facts. "The Spaceguard Survey"—NASA's report on asteroid impact and suggestions for handling near-Earth asteroids—exists, and Clarke drew on it for the scientific information on asteroids used in the novel.

A letter from one of the members of the NASA Spaceguard Survey is quoted discussing the possibility of Swift-Tuttle hitting the Earth. There is a problem predicting whether or not asteroids will impact the Earth, which is related to the assumptions of chaos theory. Some asteroids contain ice mixed with minerals, and the ice begins to melt when the asteroid approaches the Sun. The melting ice geysers out and can affect the orbit of the asteroid. Swift-Tuttle is one example of this problem. Even the theory behind the Reborn group's plan to transmit human beings to Sirius is credited to an article published in *Acta Astronautica*. In addition to the scientific background, Clarke also lists the other science fiction novels that tell stories about comets hitting the Earth.

THEMES

This novel is about the use of technology for the survival of the species. Chapter 2 presents a discussion of other novels with a similar theme. In several ways, *Hammer* is similar to Clarke's earlier novels that deal with these topics: The emphasis is not so much on developing new technology, exploring space in pursuit of knowledge, or colonizing other planets. The stakes here are the survival of humanity, and perhaps the rest of life on Earth. The high stakes do not contradict the other reasons for pursuing knowledge and technological development. If anything, the idea that survival of all life may depend upon the pursuit of such knowledge is a theme in this novel. Nature, in the scientific view, does not concern herself with the survival of any individual species. The extinction of the dinosaurs is proof of that fact. That disaster allowed mammals the chance to thrive on Earth. If humanity does not take precautions, suggests this novel, it may not be long before another species is given that same chance.

Goliath, and her sister ship, are stationed on the Trojan points, two points in Jupiter's orbit that are stable. This information is conveyed in a lecture by a scientist, Carlos Mendoza, to his students before he goes to Earth to propose establishing the ships as part of the Spaceguard system. The ships here can do research while they are on permanent patrol, but they will also be available to go anywhere in the solar system, quickly, to carry out the project of deflecting an asteroid. The knowledge of these stable points comes from theoretical scientists, but practical applications can be made that could result in a better chance for humanity's survival. Clarke is returning in this novel to the more blatant propaganda of his earlier work. It is possible that recent events regarding funding for NASA and for other scientific applications may underlie this choice.

ALTERNATE READING: FEMINIST CRITICISM

Feminist criticism draws on ideas about gender and power developed by feminist theory. Feminist theory generally tries to analyze the oppression of women in order to redress the inequality of women in male-dominant cultures. (An introduction to feminist theory and criticism can be found in Chapter 3.) One major feminist critique of science fiction focusses on the ways in which women are often nearly invisible in texts, or are relegated to limited roles.

Other than the brief mention given Robert Singh's two wives and one or two lines describing the doctor on *Goliath*, there are no other women, major or minor, who appear in the novel. There are two figures who are female and who play major roles in the story. These are the Prophet Fatima Magdalene (Sergeant Ruby Goldenberg) and Kali. I refer to the two as figures because they are not characters, or in Kali's case, human. These female figures, or feminine principles, are relegated to a destructive role within the story.

All of the information about the Prophet comes from the intrusive narrator who gives information about her experiences during the Gulf War, her conversion to Islam, her development of Chrislam and the spread of Chrislam, her death and the schism, or split, that leads to the Reborn splitting off from mainstream Chrislam. As the prophet who began Chrislam, which is the first electronic religion, she is identified as the originator of the events that led to the sabotage of Atlas.

Chrislam becomes a major world religion quickly because it is spread through the new technology of the Brainman, a new approach to Virtual Reality that allows a person to experience total submersion in the created world. By releasing the three "Testaments of the Latter-Day Koran" in electronic form, with different versions scripted for different users, the Prophet, and Chrislam (which is described as "embodying the best elements of two ancient ones (with more than a touch of an even older one, Buddhism)" (95), the new religion quickly becomes a major force.

None of the point-of-view characters is a believer in Chrislam. The group who sabotage the project are a splinter group, and in fact are eventually turned over to the authorities by their own elders who do not condone their actions. Because the information about Chrislam is given only by the intrusive narrator, the religion is reduced to the figure of the Prophet, the sole female Prophet in *any* world religion, and to its most extreme believers. Chrislam extremists are nearly responsible for causing the destruction of all life on Earth.

Kali, the name of the asteroid, is the Hindu goddess of destruction. Asteroids are often given classical or mythological names. Margaret M'Bala, the writer in *2061: Odyssey Three*, produced a best-selling book about the Greek pantheon, who are the source of names for many of the planets and moons in the solar system. Kali is the consort of Siva, the major Hindu deity. She is referred to as the Goddess of Time who will oversee the destruction of the world. She has a creative aspect but is often portrayed as a figure wearing skulls and severed limbs (Brandon 388–390). As the other major feminine principle in the novel, Kali is even more potently a figure of destruction.

Hammer of God, in its emphasis on warning about the potential destruction of a planet by an asteroid, falls into the old trap of associating women with destruction. The narrative point of view, which does not present the perspective of any of the mainstream religious figures, and the lack of any believable human characters combine with the images of Kali to submerge women in overall death and destruction.

3001: The Final Odyssey
(1997)

The novel *3001: The Final Odyssey* was published in 1997, almost thirty years after the publication of *2001: A Space Odyssey* (1968). Including two other novels, *2010: Odyssey Two* (1982) and *2061: Odyssey Three* (1987), the Odyssey Quartet is probably one of the longest-running and most important phenomena in science fiction. Clarke first explored the idea of a communications device (originally a pyramid) left on the Moon by an alien civilization to notify them of mankind's move into space in the short story "The Sentinel," written in 1948, so the genesis of the series goes back almost fifty years (*3001* 257–8). Obviously, the publication of this latest novel caused great excitement among science fiction fans and critics. The novel made *The New York Times* Best Sellers List March 16, and stayed there for seven weeks, through May 18, although critical response has been mixed.

Although each Odyssey novel can be read on its own, and Clarke has insisted throughout that readers not look upon them as linear or direct sequels, there is a meta-narrative, or plot, that connects the four novels. Plot summaries of all four novels are given in Chapter 6. To some extent, the meta-plot is resolved by the final book in the Quartet (Clarke's own term for the series, as used in his "Valediction").

The meta-plot concerns the aliens, the Firstborn, who manipulated the ancestors of humanity to start them using tools and language by means of a mysterious monolith (*2001*). Four million years later, the monolith (perhaps a different one, perhaps a projection of the first) implodes Jupiter, making it into a sun (Lucifer). This new sun provides an environment which gives a native species on Europa the chance to develop intelligence. Humans are banned from visiting Europa (*2010*). For a thousand years, humans continue to colonize other planets in the Solar System, knowing of the basic existence of the monoliths and the Europans. In *3001*, the monolith apparently receives new instructions to wipe out humans by blocking the light of both "suns" (Sol and Lucifer) from any planetary body where humans live. This attempt is thwarted by a warning delivered by "Halman," the composite personality inside the monolith which incorporates "Dave" and "Hal." The warning is delivered to Frank Poole, who has been rescued and reanimated after a thousand years. Humans are able to save themselves, with the aid of Halman, by infecting the monolith with the worst computer viruses ever developed, destroying the monolith and allowing humans and Europans to meet for the first time.

This chapter looks at five aspects of *3001: The Final Odyssey*:

1. The plot development and structure resolve the meta-plot concerning the alien intervention with humanity, but the amount of narrative time given the plot resolution is equaled by the narrative time spent developing Frank Poole as a character.

2. The narrative point of view is a third person omniscient narrative voice working almost exclusively from the point of view of Poole, a character much closer to Clarke's contemporary readers than is traditional in hard science fiction novels.

3. The character development focusses primarily on Poole, the protagonist and major point-of-view character, with all other characters being presented primarily in their relationship to him.

4. The novel, to some extent, moves away from strict adherence to the conventions of hard science fiction in its method of character development and presentation of Poole's life after reanimation.

5. The major themes shift from the themes of the earlier novels.

The chapter concludes by presenting a feminist reading of the novel.

PLOT DEVELOPMENT AND STRUCTURE

The plot of *3001* is apparently the most linear and unified of the Odyssey novels, at least for the first thirty chapters or so. The Prologue of the novel describes the aliens, "The Firstborn," who created the monolith. This species has evolved, moving from "flesh and blood," into their machines, then finally into a state of being completely separated from the physical world into "pure energy" (3–4). Although the Firstborn have left physical existence far behind, they remain interested in the evolution of physical life toward the development of conscious, or sentient, intelligence. They have spent millions of years manipulating species on planets throughout many galaxies to achieve that development. The purpose of the Prologue is primarily description, repeating information about the aliens that has appeared in the earlier novels.

The action of the novel begins in the first chapter which describes the recovery of Frank Poole's frozen body from space. The recovery is made by Captain Dimitri Chandler and his crew, who are out beyond Neptune in a ship named *Goliath*, harvesting comets for use in the terraforming of Venus. The first section of the novel which consists of thirteen chapters, is set primarily in Star City, which is a "ring city" constructed by linking four towers that reach from Earth to the city which is in geostationary orbit. The narrative in this section focuses primarily upon Poole's recovery, recuperation, and attempts to fit into the culture of 3001.

No specific information is given about Poole's reanimation in terms of the specific technology or scientific principles behind it. Instead, the thirteen chapters in this section describe his physical recovery, from his first awakening through the mentoring and education he receives. Poole does not have to worry about making a living, which would be difficult because all of his former education and training is obsolete. He is apparently considered to be "a unique and priceless museum exhibit, so would never have to worry about such mundane considerations" [as paying bills]"(68). Poole is fitted with a nanochip Ident, which contains all necessary identification information, and a Braincap, an information storage and communications device. His first explorations of his new culture are exhilarating and focus on the use of technology: he learns to fly in a low-gravity environment which exists on the Tower, enjoying a holographic representation of his home in Arizona and falling briefly in love with a woman he meets there. But as time passes, he begins to develop psychological problems. He deals fairly well with the changes in technology, but finds himself increasingly mourning the loss of his family and feeling depressed because he lacks any purpose in life. He contemplates suicide.

The second and third sections (three and six chapters) describe Poole's renewed sense of purpose in life gained by his journey to Ganymede, one of the former moons of Jupiter and now a human colony. He travels on the same ship and with the same crew who rescued him from space. The fourth section (nine chapters) describes the clandestine trip that Poole makes to Europa, which has been banned to humans for a thousand years, and his communication with Halman. He is encouraged to make this trip by a philosopher who has a theory about the existence of "Dave Bowman" within the monolith, and he is helped by Dimitri Chandler to unofficially "borrow" a shuttle. Poole is allowed to land on Europa. Although he cannot establish any communication with the Europans, he is able to communicate with the entities in the monolith: Dave and Hal, or their combined personality, "Halman." Although a version of Heywood Floyd was part of this consciousness in *2061*, he (or it) is no longer present, one of the elements from the earlier novels Clarke chose to discard.

The communication with Halman results in certain information about the aliens and the monoliths being given to Poole, who passes it on. Humans had deduced some of this information, especially after discovering the monolith that changed the ancestors of humans in Africa, as described in Chapter 8 of *3001*. But Halman's action is the first time that information about the aliens and the monoliths has been communicated directly to the human characters from within the monolith. Earlier communications consisted primarily of warnings without any specific information about the aliens or the monoliths. Halman confirms that the aliens, acting by means of the monolith, which is a supercomputer, changed the ancestors of humans. Four million years later, their discovery of the lunar monolith proved humans had evolved to the level of space travel. The monolith used Bowman as a probe to gather more information on humans for its report. Halman's report confirms that the monolith has no consciousness and is a machine; moreover, this machine has been affected by time and events (such as the unpredictable collision between Europa and a fragment of Jupiter's core related in *2061*). The monolith is no longer (if it ever was) all-knowing and all-powerful. Additionally, although "Dave" and "Hal" exist as simulations within the Europan monolith, they (or the composite entity they have evolved into) do have some limited self determination and the ability to act independently without the monolith being aware of their actions. This information is relayed to humans only because of Poole's revival: Halman is aware of his presence, has monitored the media reports on him, and still bears some remote affection for him because of his former closeness with the personality's "Dave" component. In this novel, the only human Halman will communicate with is Poole. Dr. Khan has tried, and continues to try to communicate with Halman, but receives no response. In the earlier novels, of course, there was limited communication with Heywood Floyd and a few others. But this first communication between Halman and Poole, important as it may seem at first, does not seem to lead anywhere in terms of plot development. There is a large gap in time between this action and the events in the final nine chapters of the novel.

The narrative in the first four sections of the novel is related in a sequential chronological order. The events are related in the order in which they take place over what is later revealed to be about ten years; the novel covers approximately thirty years in Poole's life after reanimation. There is little effort to connect the narrated events with the expository material and transitions. But there is a change in the fifth and final section of the book (nine chapters), which opens with the information that the first communication with Halman took place twenty years earlier and that Poole has been "awake" for thirty years. The narrative focus in the last section shifts from Poole's attempts to create a new life for himself to the problem of what to do about the monolith and the resolution of the meta-plot, which has been developed in the earlier novels.

The narration does not just "skip" twenty years with no explanation: in the opening pages of the final section, a good deal of exposition is given about Poole's success in creating his new life, including his marriage and the birth of two children after his return from Europa. Finally, the major "science fiction" conflict of the book is brought forth: Halman calls Poole and asks him to activate his Braincap to receive a compressed message. The Braincap is a technological "interface" with the brain that allows transmission of information as well as recording/storage of experiences. The newest message sent to Poole by Halman provides further information on the monoliths and their controllers, information that was not available at the time of their earlier meeting.

Halman, or perhaps the Dave component, informs Poole that the monolith is part of a galactic network that reports to a central area or superior some 450 light years away. The earlier reports sent by the monolith took nearly half a century to arrive, since Clarke's aliens and their technology are limited to the speed of light. The reply to the first report has taken the same time to return, and at this point, a thousand years after the events in *2001*, Halman has become aware that the monolith is receiving new instructions and beginning to set up new programs. The exact nature of the programs is not completely clear because Halman has only limited access to the monolith's memory, but he can make an informed guess about the nature of the new programs.

This last section, approximately a quarter of the novel, also describes mankind's response to the possible threat. Poole calls a meeting of the Europa committee, and they develop a plan to deliver computer viruses through Halman to destroy the monolith's functions. The plan succeeds, and nothing else can be done for at least a thousand years: the time it would take for a message that the monolith has been destroyed to travel to the controller, and for some response to be made. At the end, a memory tablet containing the downloaded Halman (and the viruses) is stored in a safe Vault on the Moon, perhaps for future generations to "awaken." The Epilogue of the novel is a three line statement, in quotation marks, apparently the statement of the Firstborn who have the last word about the events of the novel: "Their little universe is very young, and its god is still a child. But it is too soon to judge them; when We return in the Last Days, We will consider what should be saved" (237).

The epilogue casts doubt on the idea that humans have saved themselves from the aliens, or have completely destroyed the monolith. The reference to humans' god probably refers to the monolith, which acted as a Creator in Africa. Both the monolith on Europa and the one in Africa are described as being worshipped by the developing species, and Chapter 39, which describes the destruction (or the removal) of all the monoliths (from Europa, the Moon, and Africa) is titled "Deicide." This open-ended ending, which does not describe a final destruction or removal of the aliens or the monoliths, fits with Clarke's usual narrative choice: to leave room for questions, and to imply that the human race has still further room to develop and grow. Perhaps the monoliths also have the potential for development (if they are still "children.")

By the end of the novel, it has been firmly established not only through the comments by various characters (including Indra Wallace, Poole's mentor and guide) that the twentieth century was "the very worst period in human history," and that it was "incredibly [bad] luck" that the monolith's report was sent just after it (208). Listening to the Europa Committee, the only people Poole tells about Halman's second message, Poole thinks that "the human race had undoubtedly improved," although he regrets the loss of "memorable characters" as a parallel result

(208). Perhaps progress over the thousand years that the human race has gained by means of its actions in *3001* will make a difference when the Firstborn return in the Final Days.

Considering the extent to which Clarke developed the plot concerning the aliens/monoliths in the three earlier novels, it seems odd that so little space in this novel is devoted to the resolution of that plot, and that the partial resolution comes about so easily. Given the extent to which the monoliths (and their alien masters) were described as so near omnipotence, the plot to overthrow the monolith seems to take place far too easily. Of course, the epilogue undercuts the notion that the "victory" is as impressive as humans (or readers) may think. Certain elements that were important in the first three novels, such as the presence of Heywood Floyd and the fading of Lucifer (forecast at the end of *2061*) are dropped completely. No chapters are told from Dave Bowman's or Halman's point of view. The major action of the monoliths in this novel is to try to end humanity through blocking the light of both Lucifer and the Sun. The choice of the alien-controlled monolith to end a species' life as well as to provide the "kickstart" for evolving toward intelligence is not a surprising one: the ignition of Lucifer in *2010*, after all, destroyed all the life forms Bowman observed on his visit there.

The actions of the alien-controlled monoliths are not surprising, perhaps, but the time frame in which they are narrated is short. The majority of the book is dedicated to describing Poole's attempts to adjust to his new life. Even his trip to Ganymede and Europa are not described in the kind of detail, or with the kind of scientific goals, as were the long and detailed journeys in the previous novel. Poole is important to the resolution of the alien plot because he is the only person with whom Halman will communicate. He cannot serve in any technical or specialized capacity. To the culture of the future, he is a celebrity, a museum exhibit, rather than a hero who changes the course of history.

NARRATIVE POINT OF VIEW

3001 differs from the other novels in the series in having a single point-of-view character for the majority of the novel, and in creating a point-of-view character that is much closer to Clarke's contemporary readers than has often been the case. For a discussion of the different kinds of point-of-view choices, see Chapter 3. Other than a few chapters in which other characters are point-of-view characters, or chapters which include material from the earlier novel and which reproduce events from Dave Bowman's point-of-view, Frank Poole is the point of view character in all the chapters. This choice—to move away from the split narrative point of view which is possible with a third person omniscient narrator—results in a good deal more emphasis upon Frank Poole. Readers will share his perspective on his circumstances, as well as his thoughts and responses to events, rather than seeing how a variety of point-of-view characters perceive events. Additionally, since Poole was born in the twentieth century and can remember, as a child, seeing the film *Jurassic Park* and watching *Star Trek* (at one point, he remembers meeting Patrick Stewart and Leonard Nimoy and getting their autographs), his point of view is much closer to the readers of the novel who share his time than is often the case in the other novels. His survival into the future and his awakening, by means of their more advanced technology, is a kind of time travel achieved by the unplanned cryogenic process of his death and time in space.

In some ways, Poole is well able to deal with the changes. Although the technology around him is vastly improved over that of his time, especially the technology of space travel, which no longer involves rockets taking off from Earth, much of it is simply a development of what existed in his time. This point is clearly made as he watches a media program comparing the difficulty someone living in 1001 would have had if, by some chance, he was transported to 2001 compared to the experience of someone from 2001 living in 3001. Since the technology that people living in the twentieth century take for granted was invented only in the last two centuries, the change for someone living in 1001 would be enormous, perhaps impossible to deal with.

There are other changes that Poole finds more difficult to deal with than the technology; there are on-going references to the language issue. The automatic computer systems do not always recognize his accent, and at first specialists who speak his version of English have to be brought in to communicate with him. He is unable to ever adequately learn the cultural information that will preserve him from embarrassing mistakes. The population density is vastly different (approaching one billion compared to the ten billion in Poole's time), and great changes have been made in education, especially through the advent of the Braincap. Some specific changes hinted at are the process of education, the disappearance of institutionalized sexism and racism, and the near eradication of mental illnesses (with religious belief being categorized as a mental illness).

Many of these changes are credited to the invention and widespread use of the Braincap.

What Poole eventually finds hardest to deal with is the sense of dislocation in time. He can learn a good deal about the "history" that took place between his time and 3001, and about the culture, but he is often simply out of step not only because of his ignorance, but because of the ignorance of the people around him. And he continues to mourn for the loss of his family; because of the loss of records in an earlier collision between an asteroid and Earth, he cannot find any information about any possible descendants. Lacking a purpose in life, mourning his lost life, and unable to feel at home in any meaningful sense, Poole considers suicide.

What changes his situation, and his attitude, is a visit from Captain Chandler, the captain of the ship that retrieved his body at the beginning of the novel. Chandler is visiting Earth while his ship is refitted but planning another trip to Ganymede. Poole suddenly realizes that he does have a purpose: he wants to continue his trip to Jupiter and, perhaps, make contact with Dave Bowman. After his return from Europa, he is able to successfully create a life for himself. Poole and Indra Wallace discover that they are more than friends, marry, and have two children. And, despite his physician's orders, Poole achieves one final visit to Earth although he must stay in a motorized wheelchair because of the increased gravity and finds himself uncomfortable and exhausted by just a little time spent on the surface.

At the end of the story, after he has helped defeat the monolith, Poole witnesses the placement of the memory tablet containing Halman and the viruses into controlled storage on the Moon. At this point, Poole is meditating on the events of the novel, looking at Earth, and experiences an epiphany. An epiphany, in terms of narrative structure, is an event "in which the essential nature of something—a person, a situation, an object—[is] suddenly perceived. . . . something, usually simple and commonplace, is seen in a new light" (Holman 191). Poole's epiphany includes Earth, where he will soon "cradle his first grandson in his arms," and the realization that "[w]hatever godlike powers and principalities lurked beyond the stars, Poole reminded himself, for ordinary humans only two things were important: Love and Death. His body had not yet aged a hundred years: he still had plenty of time for both" (236).

Poole is presented as being different from the kind of hero required by the conventions of hard science fiction, and is placed in the ranks of "ordinary humans." At the beginning he is an engineer and astronaut, as are many of Clarke's characters, both major and minor. In *2001* Poole is soon shunted off, literally, after his "death" and is only a minor character (since Bowman is the major point-of-view character in the journey). In *3001*, he returns as the major point-of-view character and protagonist, but with some important differences. He journeys more through time than space, and more through history and culture than across the galaxy. The situation Poole finds himself in forces him away from being an "engineer" (in the beginning, Indra tells him several times to stop being an engineer and just experience what is happening) to being something else; since the technology in which he trained is obsolete, he cannot work in his professional capacity. Instead, Poole engages in much more thought than was the case in the earlier novels (or in some of Clarke's other work). Although he does prove important in the resolution of the meta-plot concerning alien intervention, the focus of the narrative's character development is split between that aspect of the plot and Poole's experiences adjusting to his new life in the future.

CHARACTER DEVELOPMENT

The major focus of *3001* is on the character of Frank Poole, the major point-of-view character and the protagonist. Because the narrative focus is so much on his perceptions and experiences, other characters exist primarily in terms of their relationship to him. His situation as an anachronism, even a famous one, results in him feeling disconnected from most of the people he meets. The exceptions are Professor Anderson, who is the specialist in charge of his case; Dr. Indra Wallace, an historian who specializes in Poole's period, who is first Poole's mentor, then his friend, and eventually his wife; Captain Dimitri Chandler, who is Poole's friend and ally in his attempt to visit Europa; and Dr. Theodore Khan, who is a philosopher and friend of Indra's, who encourages Poole to visit Europa and try to communicate with the entities existing within the monolith. Another important relationship is described in the communications between Poole and Halman.

The secondary characters serve a specific function in the narrative: they are the people who become close to or are important to Poole. Readers do not learn much about these characters: a short description of their appearance, usually less than a sentence, is given when they are introduced. One major function for the description of secondary characters' appearances seems to be to establish directly that this future world consists of individuals who are all "multiracial." Anderson is described as "a small dapper man whose features seemed to have combined key aspects of several races—Chinese, Polynesian, Nordic" (16); Indra is described as primarily Japanese (21); and Dr. Khan is introduced as an example that Poole can no longer rely on people's names to give "a clue to [their] appearance" (131).

All of the secondary characters are flat, or static, characters, in that they do not initiate any major actions, and no major changes in their personalities or situations occur during the course of the novel. Their physical presence is reduced to a signature specific or two: Dimitri's goatee and Dr. Ted's height, for example. There is little or no information given about their pasts, nor are their points of view explored in the narrative; Chandler and Khan serve as point-of-view characters very briefly, but Anderson and Wallace are never point of view characters. An important way the characters are developed is through the series of dialogues each one has with Poole during the course of the novel. This method of characterization is an important shift away from the conventional method of characterization in the hard science fiction (which tends to focus more on action), and so a more complete discussion of the nature of the conversations can be found in the next section.

GENERIC CONVENTIONS

Although there are certain elements of *3001* that reflect the conventions of science fiction, a good deal of the way the story is told seems to move the novel away from the genre of hard science fiction. The novel retains Clarke's on-going commitment to extrapolating from known scientific principles, as his "Sources and Acknowledgements" section proves. But there is a notable absence of the lecturing/education voice (which in his other works would appear in the form of a character or in the form of an intrusive narrator) within the narrative itself. The importance of insisting upon the speed of light as a constant is revealed by its use as a plot device (in the length of time it takes a transmission to travel between the monolith and its Supervisor). The novel continues to assume that improvements in technology will result in progress and improvement in the quality of life for humans, as shown by the existence of Star City, the Braincap, and the overall presentation of the thirtieth century as a vast improvement upon the twentieth.

Much of the technology, in fact, will be familiar to a reader of Clarke's other novels: Captain Chandler and *Goliath* are part of the "comet cowboys," described as travelling beyond Neptune to "wrap" comets in a reflective material to protect them, and then aim them back at Venus to use in terraforming the planet (9–10). Large engineering feats to terraform planets are described in a number of Clarke's novels. Poole wakens and then lives in Star City, a ring city that circles the Earth by joining four geostationary towers. Star City seems very similar to the city described at the end of *The Fountains of Paradise*, a constructed habitat ringing the globe. The Braincap, like the "Brainman" described in *The Hammer of God*, is an information and storage device that interfaces directly with the human brain and can create virtual realities that are described as indistinguishable from experiencing the physical world. The likelihood of an asteroid striking Earth, the major plot element in The *Hammer of God*, is a minor event in *3001*, although its impact on Poole is fairly important (he cannot trace any possible descendants).

These science fiction elements are present in the novel, but they are not developed in great detail. The scientific principles underlying the technology are not explained by any narrative voice, character, or textual information reproduced within the novel; instead, Clarke provides brief information about the science in his "Sources and Acknowledgements" section. The science fiction plot, in general, is not developed throughout the whole novel: the first section, consisting of thirteen chapters, focusses much more on Poole's life after being reanimated. The message from Halman alerting Poole to the response from the aliens and humanity's response to the threat is described in nine chapters in the fifth section of the novel.

What does the narration cover if less time is spent on the scientific exposition of technology and space travel and on the resolution of the alien plot? A surprising amount of time is spent on reflection, conversation, and philosophy instead of on exploration. Nineteen of the forty numbered chapters focus primarily on some form of communication between Poole and others, with his primary partners in conversation being Indra Wallace, Dimitri Chandler, Ted Khan, and Halman. By saying that the chapters focus on communication rather than action, I mean that the communication between characters makes up the majority of text in a chapter (in some cases, all of the text in a chapter) in nearly half of the chapters of the book, and that some of the most significant events are reported rather than described. There are three basic ways in which the communication is described as taking place: dialogue between two characters who are in the same place (always Poole and usually one other character); transcribed recordings sent between Poole and others, often Indra, or Indra and Dimitri; and recordings of earlier events saved in the monolith's memories which are transmitted to Poole and others.

What are the characters talking about? Of course, much of the communication concerns the major events of the novel: the monolith, Halman, and the previous events concerning them. But, especially at the beginning, other kinds of conversations take place. Poole and Indra tend to spend a good deal of time discussing the differences between his time and her time; she is a scholar, an historian, who has specialized in his period, and of course these sort of discussions would be important in helping Poole to orient himself to his new time. An overview of the subjects of their conversations shows an on-going pattern of comparison between the two times, with the specific claim being made that the thirtieth century is much different and better than the twentieth century. And the changes that have come about include social as well as technological developments.

Examples of the changes discussed are the change in religious beliefs ("God" has become an inappropriate word to use in public), diet and nutrition (the idea of eating dead animals, which they call "corpsemeat," sickens both Indra and Professor Anderson), and a disavowal of the horrors of the twentieth century (genital mutilation, apocalyptic sects, computer viruses, chemical and biological weapons, and national wars).

An example of a chapter which is dedicated to a dialogue rather than to more direct physical action is Chapter 13, titled "Stranger in a Strange Time," a clear reference to Robert Heinlein's novel *Stranger in a Strange Land*, which Poole remembers reading. This chapter contains one of the more developed arguments between Poole and Indra over the horrors of the twentieth century. The argument and his memories of his earlier life which are evoked through his use of the holographic program lead to Poole's depression and consideration of suicide. Only Captain Chandler's visit, and the chance to travel to Jupiter, brings him out of his depression.

Even though he is traveling, he continues to communicate with Indra, often discussing the same issues, and part of his time on Ganymede is spent in a series of philosophical discussions about the nature of religion and religious belief with Dr. Ted Khan, a friend of Indra's. These discussions lead to Khan's proposal that Poole attempt to travel to Europa to communicate with the "Bowman" entity in the monolith. That journey results in more communication, between "Dave" and "Hal" and Poole. But this communication is not described directly; instead Poole narrates what happens in communications to Indra and Dimitri, just as later he lectures the Europa committee before allowing them to experience the recording that Halman has sent him.

This pattern of communication and interaction with other characters is a departure from the strict conventions of hard science fiction where, as David G. Hartwell notes, "the universe is external to character and the character must interact with that universe, and in so doing, achieves or validates his identity. Hard sf characters tend not to achieve validation through gaining knowledge of their own inner life but rather through action in the external environment" (34). Poole does act to save humanity, but so late and in so apparently passive or accidental a fashion that it seems apparent his characterization and his interaction with others both signal a move away from some of the conventions of hard science fiction.

THEMES

The major themes of *3001* show a shift away from the themes in the other three novels. The importance of the aliens as a cause of mystery and the spiritual evolution of humans, which was important in the other novels, is lessened. The "aliens," through their tool the Monolith, are revealed to be less than all-powerful and all-knowing, and the ethical dilemma of their choice not only to manipulate species into a specific kind of tool-using intelligence but also to destroy other species is heightened by their possible choice to destroy humanity. This attempt fails, although the conclusion of the novel leaves it open to question whether it fails because humans are successful in blocking the attempt, or because the aliens do not choose to make a real attempt to carry through with their program of genocide.

To some extent, the development of the human race that did occur over the millennium between the first and fourth novel proves that progress is possible; the open ending implies that future progress will also take place. The aliens have fulfilled that narrative function. But the importance of contact with alien life does not disappear. For the first time, contact with the culture on Europa is achieved after the monoliths are destroyed, or disappear from the Solar System.

The potential for humans to evolve into a state of pure energy is removed, or delayed. The state of consciousness achieved by the entities within the monolith is not explored further, but dropped almost completely. Poole evidently does not view "Halman" as a major step in human evolution, but as the "simulation" of humans, which can be treated exactly as computer programs: downloaded and stored. This process of storage is theoretically possible with the Braincap, one of the new technologies of the thirtieth century, which Poole is familiar with. In this respect, humans have perhaps made the first step in moving from existence in physical form to existence in some form of energy, but they are not there yet. Perhaps in another far future, that evolutionary step could take place, but *3001* does not explore that possibility.

The sense of the different theme of *3001* comes with the image at the end of the novel of Poole looking back at "the beautiful blue Earth, huddling beneath its tattered blanket of clouds for protection against the cold of space" rather than journeying to the far ends of the universe (236). He is planning to return to the planet to hold his first grandchild. There are great powers beyond the stars, but humans are still "ordinary," still tied to "Love and Death," to the physical world in which bodies of flesh die, but in which families continue to survive through time. Poole's journey is in time, and his education involves more than new sciences and technologies. The commentaries on the horrors of the century that Clarke and his contemporaneous readers inhabit are strongly directed to draw our attention to the insanity of our times as well as to our (hoped-for) eventual progress. While some of the "insanities" are an agent of salvation (the computer viruses that destroy the monolith), Poole refuses to try to draw a "moral" from that irony. Spiritual development, love, and the journey through time and space are still important themes in this latest novel of Clarke's, but perhaps the means of achieving them has changed.

A FEMINIST READING OF *3001: The Final Odyssey*

Since the development of the second wave of feminist activism in the United States over the past three or four decades, feminist literary criticism has paid a good deal of attention to science fiction. Ideas about gender and power developed by feminist theory are used by feminist literary criticism. One important aspect of feminist theory is analysis of the oppression of women in male-dominated cultures, with the goal of changing cultures to achieve social equality. An introduction to feminist theory and criticism can be found in Chapter 3. Feminist critics like Joanna Russ have pointed out that while the traditional and earlier science fiction might do a good job of extrapolating and building on technological developments, it tends to do a poor job of extrapolating the social changes which would accompany those technological developments.

As a close reading of *3001* reveals, this novel tends to pay less attention to presenting information on the technological developments and to pay more attention to discussing, literally, the social changes which have accompanied those developments. Some critics are dissatisfied with the overall novel. Richard Bernstein, in a review titled "The Decline and Fall of the Monoliths" published in the on-line version of *The New York Times Book Review*, acknowledges Clarke's imaginative ideas but claims that the "new book in this sense is full of whimsy about the world of the future. But it is so languid and unmysterious, so lacking in the elaboration of plot, character, or concept, that it reads more like a proposal for itself than like a fully realized work" (paragraph 5). Bernstein's favorite section of the book is the description of the journey Poole makes from Earth to Jupiter, but he sums up the book as, finally, lacking a "mystical soul" (paragraph 9). A review by Curt Wohleber on the on-line reviews published by Science Fiction Weekly in "Off the Shelf," criticizes the novel's "slender plot," summing it up as containing "profound ideas" and an "intriguing philosophy" but making an anticlimactic novel and end to the series (paragraph 7).

These two reviewers' comments can be set beside Clarke's comments on the novel, made while he was in the process of writing it. In an interview published before the manuscript was turned in to the publisher, Clarke says that the book is "mostly about philosophy and sex . . . and not necessarily in that order," and that he feels as if he has "discovered something that was happening in a different universe" (Kaufman). The "*3001* Homepage," created and maintained by Reinaldo A.C. Bianchi, quotes the "Del Rey Books Internet Newsletter Number 41" in which Clarke says that he's "never had so much fun writing, and the ideas are pouring out."

Critics, writers, and readers rarely agree completely about any literary work, and it is true that later works in a series often disappoint the eager fans of the earlier novels. Considering the mystique that exists around *2001*, both the novel and the movie, it would be impossible for some fans to feel that any work could live up to that initial impact. But some of the nature of that impact was connected to the time it was created as well as the personal situation of many of the fans. Clarke could never re-create the same experience. Yet he is a writer of great experience, and his excitement about the book and his sense that he was traveling in new directions cannot be ignored. His comments about the novel as well as the disappointment of two critics who review science fiction do indicate some intriguing possibilities for a feminist reading. The intriguing possibilities revolve around the "sex" that Clarke mentions; the philosophical aspects of the novel are clearly indicated and important, but the "sex" is not as clearly specified. Clarke does not seem to mean physical descriptions about sexual activity, since there is none of that in the novel. And he cannot mean only sex, in the sense of behavior, since Poole's epiphany focuses on a new knowledge of "Love and Death." But "sex" in the sense of gender, the differences between the two sexes that make up the human race is also an important aspect of love (and sexual love), and it is this aspect that leads to a possible feminist reading.

One criticism that has often been made about novels, both mainstream and science fiction, that are avowedly feminist in intention is that their plots are thin, and the story is weighted down with feminist ideas or polemics as the writers work to convince readers of the merit of feminist ideas. When a feminist reader familiar with such criticism sees words such as *languid*, *slender*, and *whimsy*, and related critical comments about the lack of plot development and the over-elaboration of ideas or philosophy, a clear sense of the connection to criticisms aimed at earlier feminist work is evoked. The summary of important elements of hard science fiction (Hartwell's listing of the importance of external action, the unimportance of the inner life or interaction with others) can read like a stereotype of what "males" are supposed to be in a patriarchal culture: all action and no reflection. As discussed in earlier chapters, much of Clarke's work and many of his male characters do not meet the stereotypical requirements of science fiction. But in this novel about "Love and Death," "philosophy and sex," he has moved even further away from some of the genre's conventions.

I am not trying to argue that this novel is necessarily "feminist." An argument could be made that, as with others of his recent novels, Clarke is focussing on character development and interaction rather than on the "science." But there are certainly clear indications of feminist ideas, and the differences in plot and characterization do shift the reader's attention more to the "personal" than the "public" (and masculinized domain) of space. Additionally, Indra's example of genital mutilation as the second of the horrors accepted in the twentieth century, which is part of her argument with Poole in Chapter 13, stands out in the list of insane behaviors that the two fight about. Indra has charged that people "calmly accepted behavior we would consider atrocious and believed in the most mind-boggled [*sic*] . . . nonsense, which surely any rational person would dismiss out of hand'' (83). When Poole asks her for examples, she gives the example of genital mutilation, which she has researched after Poole's own circumcision led to him being rejected by the woman he meets while flying: "thousands of little girls were hideously mutilated to preserve their virginity" (83). Poole does not deny it is terrible, but argues that the United States government could not have done anything to stop the practice. Indra disagrees, claiming that the government could have acted except for its reliance on oil and upon weapon sales.

This argument occurs at a pivotal place in the narrative, and is one of the events which leads Poole to feel so out of place and lost in the culture. Genital mutilation is an issue that has been brought to general attention by feminist groups in the United States and Europe. Although its mention does not take up a great deal of space, it is presented as a major issue for debate and an openly feminist declaration by a female character who is accusing the twentieth century, especially the "civilized nations," directly of failing to protect women's basic rights. This conversation and others between Poole and Indra, along with their marriage and children, their mutual agreement to separate, and Poole's knowledge at the end of the book that he will be returning to Earth to hold his first grandson, are all elements that relate to the "Love and Death" and "philosophy and sex" aspects of the novel that Clarke mentions.

More narrative time is given over to communication between characters about social changes, including the disappearance of institutionalized religion and national governments, which are two important institutions criticized for maintaining the oppression of women in patriarchal cultures. Poole's character is developed in ways that are unusual for the genre of hard science fiction. In several important respects, this novel moves away from some of the standard conventions of hard science fiction, and that move might well disappoint readers who are expecting those conventions to be adhered to in the same way some of Clarke's earlier work did. When I first read the novel, I experienced some disappointment because the story did not go in the way that I was expecting from my reading of the earlier novels. Later readings left me intrigued with the changes, and wondering about the nature of them. These later readings led me to realize that readers with other expectations might well be intrigued by the changes, and share with Clarke the sense of exploring new universes, which is still an important aspect of all kinds of science fiction.

Bibliography

WORKS BY ARTHUR C. CLARKE

Fiction

Across the Sea of Stars. New York: Harcourt, Brace & World, 1959.
Against the Fall of Night. New York: Gnome Press, 1953.
An Arthur C. Clarke Omnibus. London: Sidgwick & Jackson, 1965.
An Arthur C. Clarke Second Omnibus. London: Sidgwick & Jackson, 1968.
The Best of Arthur C. Clarke. Ed. Angus Wells. London: Sidgwick & Jackson, 1973.
Childhood's End. New York: Ballantine, 1953.
The City and the Stars. New York: Harcourt, Brace, 1956.
The Deep Range. New York: Harcourt, Brace, 1957.
Dolphin Island: A Story of the People of the Sea. New York: Holt, Rinehart, 1963.
Earthlight. New York: Ballantine, 1955.
Expedition to Earth. New York: Ballantine, 1953.
A Fall of Moondust. New York: Harcourt, Brace, 1961.
The Fountains of Paradise. London: Victor Gollancz, 1978.
Four Great SF Novels. London: Victor Gollancz, 1978.
From the Ocean, From the Stars. New York: Harcourt, Brace & World, 1962.
The Ghost from the Grand Banks. New York: 1990.
Glide Path. New York: Harcourt, Brace & World, 1963.
The Hammer of God. New York: Bantam, 1993.

Imperial Earth: A Fantasy of Love and Discord. London: Victor Gollancz, 1976.

Islands in the Sky. Philadelphia: Winston, 1952.

The Lion of Comarre and Against the Fall of Night. New York: Harcourt, Brace & World, 1968.

The Lost Worlds of 2001. New York: New American Library, 1972.

The Lost Worlds of 2001/Expedition to Earth. London: New English Library, 1980.

Master of Space. New York: Lancer, 1961.

The Nine Billion Names of God: The Best Short Stories of Arthur C. Clarke. New York: Harcourt, Brace & World, 1967.

Of Time and Stars: The Worlds of Arthur C. Clarke. London: Victor Gollancz, 1972.

The Other Side of the Sky. New York: Harcourt, Brace & World, 1958.

Prelude to Mars. New York: Harcourt, Brace & World, 1965.

Prelude to Space. New York: World Editions, 1951.

Reach for Tomorrow. New York: Ballantine, 1956.

Rendezvous with Rama. London: Victor Gollancz, 1973.

The Sands of Mars. London: Sidgwick & Jackson, 1951.

The Sands of Mars/Prelude to Space. London: New English Library, 1980.

The Sentinel: Masterworks of Science Fiction and Fantasy. New York: Berkley, 1993.

The Songs of Distant Earth: New York: Ballantine, 1986.

The Space Dreamers. New York: Lancer, 1969.

Tales from Planet Earth. New York: Bantam, 1990.

Tales from the "White Hart". New York: Ballantine, 1957.

Tales of Ten Worlds. New York: Harcourt, Brace & World, 1962.

Time Probe: The Sciences in Science Fiction. Editor. New York: Delacorte, 1966.

2001: A Space Odyssey. New York: New American Library, 1968.

2010: Odyssey Two. New York: Ballantine, 1982.

2061: Odyssey Three. New York: Ballantine, 1987.

3001: The Final Odyssey. New York: Ballantine, 1997.

The Wind from the Sun: Stories of the Space Age. New York: Harcourt Brace Jovanovich, 1972.

Collaborations

Beyond the Fall of Night. New York: Ace 1990. With Gregory Benford.

Cradle. New York: Warner, 1989. With Gentry Lee.

The Garden of Rama. New York: Bantam, 1991. With Gentry Lee.

Rama II. New York: New York: Bantam, 1989. With Gentry Lee.

Rama Revealed. New York: Bantam, 1994. With Gentry Lee.

Richter 10. New York: Bantam, 1996. With Mike McQuay.

Non-Fiction

Astounding Days: A Science Fictional Autobiography. London: Victor Gollancz, 1989.

Beyond Jupiter: The Worlds of Tomorrow. Boston: Little, Brown, 1973. With Chesley Bonestell.

Boy beneath the Sea. New York: Harper, 1958. With Mike Wilson.

The Challenge of the Sea. New York: Holt, Rinehart, Winston, 1960.

The Challenge of the Spaceship: Previews of Tomorrow's World. New York: Harper, 1959.

The Coast of Coral. New York: Harper & Row, 1956. With Mike Wilson.

The Exploration of Space. London: Temple, 1951.

The Exploration of the Moon. London: Frederick Muller, 1954. With R. A. Smith.

The First Five Fathoms: A Guide to Underwater Adventure. New York: Harper, 1960. With Mike Wilson.

Front Line of Discovery: Science on the Brink of Tomorrow. National Geographic, 1994.

Going into Space. New York: Harper, 1954.

Indian Ocean Adventure. New York: Harper, 1961. With Mike Wilson.

Indian Ocean Treasure. New York: Harper, 1964. With Mike Wilson.

Interplanetary Flight: An Introduction to Astronautics. London: Temple, 1950.

Into Space: A Young Person's Guide to Space. New York: Harper & Row, 1971. With Robert Silverberg.

The Lost Worlds of 2001. New York: New American Library, 1972.

The Making of a Moon. New York: Harper & Brothers, 1957.

Man and Space. New York: Time, 1964. With the editors of *Life*.

The Odyssey File. New York: New American Library, 1985.

Profiles of the Future: An Enquiry into the Limits of the Possible. London: Victor Gollancz, 1962.

The Promise of Space. New York: Harper & Row, 1968.

The Reefs of Taprobane: Underwater Adventures around Ceylon. New York: Harper & Brothers, 1957. With Mike Wilson.

Report on Planet Three and Other Speculations. New York: Harper & Row, 1972.

The Scottie Book of Space Travel. London: Transworld Publishers, 1957.

The Snows of Olympus: A Garden on Mars. New York: Norton, 1995.

Space, the Unconquerable. Colombo, Sri Lanka: Lake House Investments, 1970.

Spring, 1984: A Choice of Futures. New York: Fawcett, 1984.

Technology and the Frontiers of Knowledge. Garden City, N.Y.: Doubleday, 1975.

The Telephone's First Century and Beyond. New York: Thomas Y. Crowell, 1977.

The Treasure of the Great Reef. London: Arthur Barker, 1964.

The View from Serendip. New York: Random House, 1977.

Voice across the Sea. New York: Harper, 1958.
Voices from the Sky: Previews of the Coming Space Age. New York: Harper & Row, 1965.
The Young Traveler in Space. London: Phoenix House, 1954.

WORKS ABOUT ARTHUR C. CLARKE

General Information

Beraducci, Michele C. "A Content Analysis of the Science Fiction Writing of Arthur C. Clarke, Lester del Rey, and Isaac Asimov." Master's thesis, Long Island University, 1971.

Clareson, Thomas D. "The Early Novels" (in symposium, "Arthur C. Clarke: Man and Writer"). *Algol* [fanzine] 12 (November 1974): 7–10.

———.The Cosmic Loneliness of Arthur C. Clarke." Olander 52–71.

Clarke, Fred. "Arthur C. Clarke: The Early Days." *Foundation: The Review of Science Fiction* 41 (Winter 1987): 9–15.

Edward, James. "The Future Viewed from Mid-Century Britain: Clarke, Hampson and the Festival of Britain." *Foundation: The Review of Science Fiction* 41 (Winter 1987): 42–51.

Erlich, Richard D. "Ursula K. Le Guin and Arthur C. Clarke on Immanence, Transcendence, and Massacres." *Extrapolation: A Journal of Science Fiction and Fantasy* 28.2 (Summer 1987): 105–129.

Harfst, Betsy. "Of Myths and Polyominoes: Mythological Content in Clarke's Fiction." Olander 87–120.

Hollow, John. *Against the Night, the Stars: The Science Fiction of Arthur C. Clarke*. San Diego: Harcourt, 1983.

Malmgren, Carl D. "Self and Other in SF: Alien Encounters." *Science Fiction Studies* 20.1 (March 1993): 15–33.

Nicholls, Peter. "Clarke, Arthur C." *The Encyclopedia of Science Fiction*. 2nd ed. Ed. John Clute and Peter Nicholls. New York: St. Martin's, 1993.

———."Science Fiction and the Mainstream, Part 2: The Great Tradition of Proto Science Fiction." *Foundation: The Review of Science Fiction*, 5 (January 1974).

Olander, Joseph D., and Martin Harry Greenberg, eds. *Arthur C. Clarke*. New York: Taplinger Publishing Company, 1977.

Priest, Christopher. "British Science Fiction." *Science Fiction: A Critical Guide*. Ed. Patrick Parrinder. London and New York: Longman, 1979. 196+.

Rabkin, Eric S. *Arthur C. Clarke*. West Linn, Ore.: Starmont House, 1979.

Samuelson, David N. "Arthur C. Clarke, 1917–." *Science Fiction Writers: Critical Studies of the Major Authors from the Early Nineteenth Century to the Present Day*. Ed. Everett Franklin Bleiler. New York: Scribner's, 1982.

Sless, David. "Arthur C. Clarke." *The Stellar Gauge: Essays on Science Fiction Writ-*

ers. Ed. Michael J. Tolley and Kirpal Singh. Carlton, Victoria, Australia: Norstrilia Press, 1980. 91–107.

Slusser, George Edgar. *The Space Odysseys of Arthur C. Clarke.* San Bernardino, California: Borgo Press, 1978.

Spector, Judith A. "Science Fiction and the Sex War: A Womb of One's Own." *Literature and Psychology* 31.1 (1981): 21–32.

Thron, E. Michael. "The Outsider from Inside: Clarke's Aliens." Olander 72–86.

Weinkauf, Mary S. "The Escape from the Garden." *Texas Quarterly* 16 (Autumn 1973): 66–72.

Wolfe, Gary K. "The Short Fiction of Arthur C. Clarke." *Survey of Science Fiction Literature.* Vol 4. Ed. Frank N. Magill. Englewood Cliffs, N.J.: Salem Press, 1980. 1926–1929.

Biographical Information

Bernstein, Jeremy. "Profiles: Out of the Ego Chamber." *New Yorker* 45 (9 August 1969): 40–65.

McAleer, Neil. *Arthur C. Clarke: The Authorized Biography.* New York: Contemporary Books, 1992.

Moskowitz, Sam. "Arthur C. Clarke." *Amazing Stories Fact and Science Fiction* 37 (February 1969): 67–77.

REVIEWS AND CRITICISM

Rendezvous with Rama

Harrison, Harry. "Machine as Hero." *Encyclopedia of Science Fiction.* 1st ed. Ed. Robert Holdstock. London: Octopus, 1978. 86–103.

Labar, Martin. "Arthur C. Clarke: Humanism in Science Fiction." *Christianity Today* 22 (2 June 1978): 27.

Molyneux, Robert. Rev. of *Rendezvous with Rama. Library Journal* (August 1973): 2339.

Parrinder, Patrick. *Science Fiction: Its Criticism and Teaching.* London and New York: Methuen, 1980. 108–110.

Ruddick, Nicholas. "The World Turned Inside Out: Decoding Clarke's *Rendezvous with Rama.*" *Science Fiction Studies* 12.1 (March 1985): 4–50.

Sheppard, R. "Celestial Pit Stop." *Time* (24 September 1973): 125–126.

Starr, Carol. Rev. of *Rendezvous with Rama. Library Journal* (15 November 1973): 3474.

Sturgeon, Theodore. Rev. of *Rendezvous with Rama. New York Times Book Review* (23 September 1973): sec. 7; 38.

Imperial Earth

Jonas, Gerald. Rev. of *Imperial Earth*. *New York Times Book Review* (18 January 1976): sec. 7; 20–21.

Lawler, Donald L. "*Imperial Earth*." *Survey of Science Fiction Literature*. Vol. 3. Ed. Frank N. Magill. Englewood Cliffs, N.J.: Salem Press, 1979. 1019–1025.

Molyneux, Robert. Rev. of *Imperial Earth*. *Library Journal* (15 January 1976): 362.

Ownbey, Steve. Rev. of *Imperial Earth*. *National Review* (14 May 1976): 519.

Rose, Mark. Rev. of *Imperial Earth*. *New Republic* (20 March 1976): 29.

The Fountains of Paradise

Bryfonski, Dedria, ed. *Contemporary Literary Criticism: Excerpts from Criticism of Today's Novelists, Poets, Playwrights, and other Creative Writers*. Vol. 14. Detroit: Gale Research, 1980. 148–156.

Budrys, Algis. Rev. of *The Fountains of Paradise*. *The Magazine of Fantasy and Science Fiction*(September 1979): 25–26.

Herbert, Rosemary. Rev. of *The Fountains of Paradise*. *Library Journal* (15 January 1979): 212.

Jonas, Gerald. Rev. of *The Fountains of Paradise*. *New York Times Book Review* (18 March 1979): sec. 7; 13+.

Myers, Tim. Rev. of *The Fountains of Paradise*. *New Republic* (24 Mar. 1979): 40.

Sheffield, Charles. Letter to the editor. *SFWA Bulletin* 4 (Summer 1979): 47.

2010: Odyssey Two

Burns, Mary Ellen. Rev. of *2010: Odyssey Two*. *The Nation* (5 March 1983): 281–282.

Deweese, Gene. Rev. of *2010: Odyssey Two*. *Science Fiction Review* (February 1983): 15.

Easton, Tom. Rev. of *2010: Odyssey Two*. *Analog: Science Fiction, Science Fact* (May 1983): 164–165.

Jonas, Gerald. Rev. of *2010: Odyssey Two*. *New York Times Book Review* (23 January 1983): sec. 7, 24.

Nickerson, Susan L. Rev. of *2010: Odyssey Two*. *Library Journal* (15 November 1982): 2191.

Richard A. J. and Philip M. Tucker. "The Alchemical Art of Arthur C. Clarke."
     Foundation: The Review of Science Fiction 41 (Winter 1987): 30–41.
Stoler, Peter. Rev. of *2010: Odyssey Two. Time* (15 November 1982): 91.

The Songs of Distant Earth

Cassada, Jackie. Rev. of *The Songs of Distant Earth. Library Journal* (15 April 1986):
     97.
Charters, Lawrence I. *The Songs of Distant Earth. Fantasy Review* (April 1986): 21.
Easton, Tom. Rev. of *The Songs of Distant Earth. Analog: Science Fiction, Science
     Fact* (January 1987): 178–179.
Jonas, Gerald. Rev. of *The Songs of Distant Earth. New York Times Book Review* (11
     May 1986): sec. 7; 23.

2061: Odyssey Three

Cassada, Jackie. Rev. of *2061: Odyssey Three. Library Journal* (December 1987): 131.
Easton, Tom. Rev. of *2061: Odyssey Three. Analog: Science Fiction, Science Fact* (September 1988): 183.
Jonas, Gerald. Rev. of *2061: Odyssey Three. New York Times Book Review* (20 December 1987): sec. 7; 16.
Rev. of *2061: Odyssey Three. Science Fiction Chronicle: The Monthly SF and Fantasy
     Magazine* (February 1988): 42.
Rev. of *2061: Odyssey Three. Time* (11 January 1988): 76.

The Ghost from the Grand Banks

Easton, Tom. Rev. of *The Ghost from the Grand Banks. Analog: Science Fiction, Science Fact* (May 1991): 181.
Jonas, Gerald. Rev. of *The Ghost from the Grand Banks. New York Times Book Review*
     (3 February 1991): sec. 7; 33.
Rev. of *The Ghost from the Grand Banks. Science Fiction Chronicle: The Monthly SF
     and Fantasy Magazine* (February 1991): 44.

The Hammer of God

Bryant, Edward. Rev. of *The Hammer of God. Locus* (May 1993): 23.
Jonas, Gerald. Rev. of *The Hammer of God. New York Times Book Review* (13 June
     1993): sec. 7: 22.

3001: The Final Odyssey

Bernstein, Richard. "The Decline and Fall of the Monoliths." *The New York Times Book Review* (1997): 9 pars. Available: http://search.nytimes.com/books/sea. (26 March 1997).

Bianchi, Reinaldo A. C. "*3001* Homepage." June 10, 1996. Available: www.si.usp.br/~rbianchi/clarke/3001.html. (4 April 1997).

Wohleber, Curt. Rev. of *3001. Science Fiction Weekly*, Issue 37 (1997): 7 pars. Available: www.scifi.com/sfw/issue37/books.html. (9 April 1997).

OTHER SECONDARY SOURCES

Aldiss, Brian W. *Trillion Year Spree: The History of Science Fiction*. New York: Atheneum, 1986.

Barr, Marleen. *Alien to Feminity: Speculative Fiction and Feminist Theory*. Contributions to the Study of Science Fiction and Fantasy 27. New York: Greenwood Press, 1987.

———. ed. *Future Females; A Critical Anthology*. Bowling Green: Bowling Green State U Popular P, 1981.

Barry, Peter. *Beginning Theory: An Introduction to Literary and Cultural Theory*. Manchester, England: Manchester U P, 1995.

Benford, Gregory. "Real Science, Imaginary Worlds." Hartwell 15–23.

Books in Print, 1995–1996. New Providence, N.J.; Bowker, 1996.

Brandon, S.G.F. *A Dictionary of Comparative Religion*. London: Weidenfield & Nicholson, 1970.

Brigg, Peter. "Three Styles of Arthur C. Clarke: The Projector, the Wit, and the Mystic." Olander 15–51.

Cramer, Kathryn. "On Science and Science Fiction." Hartwell 24–29.

Clute, John, and Peter Nicholls. *The Encyclopedia of Science Fiction*. New York: St. Martin's, 1993.

Cornillion, Susan Koppelman. *Images of Women in Fiction: Feminist Perspectives*. Bowling Green: Bowling Green U Popular P, 1972.

Del Rey, Lester. *The World of Science Fiction, 1926–1976*. New York: Garland, 1980.

Foucault, Michel. *The History of Sexuality: An Introduction*. Trans. Robert Hurley. New York: Pantheon, 1978. Vol. 1 of *The History of Sexuality*. 3 vols. 1978–1986.

Friedan, Betty. *The Feminine Mystique*. New York: Dell, 1983.

Gleick, James. *Chaos: Making a New Science*. New York: Penguin, 1987.

Greenblatt, Stephen, and Giles Gunn. *Redrawing the Boundaries: The Transformation of English and American Literary Studies*. New York: MLA, 1992.

Harmon, William, and C. Hugh Holman. *A Handbook to Literature*. 7th ed. Upper
    Saddle River, N.J.: Prentice Hall, 1996.
Hartwell, David G. "Hard Science Fiction." Hartwell 30–40.
Hartwell, David G., and Kathryn Cramer, eds. *The Ascent of Wonder: The Evolution
    of Hard SF*. New York: Tom Doherty, 1994.
Kaufman, Marc. "At 79, Five Years from 2001, Arthur Clarke Writes '3001'"
    Seattle Times, Arts Alive (21 July 1996): M-3.
Lefanu, Sarah. *In the Chinks of the World Machine: Feminism and Science Fiction*.
    London: The Women's Press Ltd., 1988.
Lerner, Frederick Andrew. *Modern Science Fiction and the American Literary Com-
    munity*, Metuchen, N.J.: The Scarecrow Press, 1985.
Millett, Kate. *Sexual Politics* Garden City, N.Y.: Doubleday, 1970.
Olander, Joseph D., and Martin Harry Greenberg, eds. *Arthur C. Clarke*. New
    York: Taplinger Publishing Company, 1977.
Phadnis, Urmila. *Religion and Politics in Sri Lanka*. Columbia, Mo.: South Asia
    Books, 1976.
Riley, Dick, ed. *Critical Encounters: Writers and Themes in Science Fiction*. New
    York: Frederick Ungar Publishing Co., 1979.
Rohrlich, Ruby, and Elaine Hoffman Baruch, ed. *Women in Search of Utopia: Mav-
    ericks and Mythmakers*. New York: Schocken, 1984.
Russ, Joanna. "The Image of Women in Science Fiction." Cornillion 79–94.
———. "Recent Feminist Utopias." Barr *Future Females* 71–85.
———. "What Can a Heroine Do? or Why Women Can't Write." Cornillion 3–
    20.
Said, Edward. *Orientalism*. New York: Pantheon, 1978.
Samuelson, David N. *Arthur C. Clarke: A Primary and Secondary Bibliography*. Bos-
    ton: G.K. Hall, 1984.
Searles, Baird, Martin Last, Beth Meacham, and Michael Franklin. *A Reader's
    Guide to Science Fiction*. New York: Avon, 1979.
Sedgewick, Eve Kosofsky. *Between Men: English Literature and Male Homosocial
    Desire*. New York: Columbia U P, 1985.
Tarbert, Gary. *Book Review Index*. Detroit: Gail Research Company, 1973-June
    1996.
Weedman, Jane B., ed. *Women Workdwalkers: New Dimensions of Science Fiction and
    Fantasy*. Lubbock: Texas Tech, 1985.

Index

About the Author

ROBIN ANNE REID is Assistant Professor of Literature and Languages at Texas A&M University–Commerce, Commerce, Texas. She began reading science fiction at the age of seven, under the influence of her father, who is a geologist. Her scholarly interests also include feminist and multicultural theory, and detective fiction. She enjoys writing poetry and fiction, as well as literary criticism.